conservation fallout

CONSERVATION FALLOUT

NUCLEAR PROTEST AT DIABLO CANYON

JOHN WILLS

UNIVERSITY OF NEVADA PRESS

RENO ⋰ LAS VEGAS

University of Nevada Press, Reno, Nevada 89557 USA
Copyright © 2006 by University of Nevada Press
All rights reserved
Manufactured in the United States of America
Design by Kathleen Szawiola

LIBRARY OF CONGRESS CATALOGING-IN-PUBLICATION DATA
Wills, John, 1971–
Conservation fallout : nuclear protest at Diablo Canyon / John Wills.
       p.   cm.
    Includes bibliographical references and index.
    ISBN-13: 978-0-87417-680-3 (hardcover : alk. paper)
    ISBN-10: 0-87417-680-8 (hardcover : alk. paper)
       1. Antinuclear movement—California—Diablo Canyon.
2. Nuclear power plants—Environmental aspects—California—Diablo Canyon.
3. Environmental policy—California—Diablo Canyon—Citizen participation.
4. Diablo Canyon Nuclear Powerplant (Calif.)   I. Title.
HD9698.U53D539 2006
333.792'40979478—dc22   2006012049

The paper used in this book meets the requirements of American
National Standard for Information Sciences—Permanence of Paper
for Printed Library Materials, ANSI Z.48-1984. Binding
materials were selected for strength and durability.

FIRST PRINTING
12   11   10   09   08   07   06

5   4   3   2   1

contents

list of illustrations

Map of Region, xvi

(following page 80)

Diablo Canyon nuclear power plant, 1997,
   aerial view

Front cover design for *Sierra Club Bulletin*
   (February 1967)

Mothers for Peace pamphlet

"A License to Kill," Abalone Alliance flyer, 1979
   The 1981 blockade, *It's About Times*
   (October–November 1981)

"Transform Diablo," Abalone Alliance flyer, 1978

The Mutant Sponges, *It's About Times*
   (September 1980)

"Reagan's Arms Control Plan,"
   It's About Times (May–June 1982)

"Peacekeeper on Earth," *It's About Times*
   (December–January 1983)

"What's Wrong with This Picture?"
   Abalone Alliance poster

Diablo Canyon nuclear power plant

preface

Sitting on the porch of his California home back in 1997, gazing down at the forested valley below, veteran Sierra Club activist Martin Litton had offered me a trip to see Diablo Canyon firsthand. Given that Diablo, a nuclear site owned by Pacific Gas and Electric on the central California coast, was strictly off-limits to the public, not to mention some 250 miles away, I puzzled as to how exactly Martin could promise such a thing. The answer was simple. We would meet at Palo Alto airport and travel to Diablo by plane.

As Martin started the propeller turning on his 1951 Cessna 195, its gleaming silver body flaunting its vintage age, I pondered what this journey would mean to him. In some ways, the white-bearded conservationist, eighty years in age, was revisiting his distant past. Although Litton flew toward Los Angeles on business trips, Diablo Canyon was unlikely to have figured in his usual journeys south. I wondered when he last seen the headland. Was it as far back as the 1960s, when he had shown Diablo to David Brower and other Sierra Club directors, attempting to rally support for protecting the coastline from development? Perhaps our excursion would remind Litton of his solitary wandering in the region: a time when, accompanied only by his camera, he had first noticed the pristine coastline, a time when the place had little meaning to anyone.

Turning away from the Central Valley and toward the coast, we flew over Morro Bay en route to Diablo Canyon. Morro Bay was a strange landscape, preparing us for the even stranger one ahead. The ancient volcanic peak of Morro Rock rose up from the shore—its softened contours the result of quarrying activity—a local attraction shaped by the forces of industrial capitalism. In the same glance, we spotted the scenic partner to the Morro, its surrogate twin: a gas-fired power plant, smoke stacks rising into the sky.

Closing in on Diablo, the plane entered thick coastal fog. It enraptured us, blanketed us, a sense of expectation grew. Through the clouds I first spied Diablo Canyon. Remnant white clouds parted to reveal the white froth of the power plant's discharge into the Pacific Ocean. The dark brown hue of the huge turbine building resembled a giant earth mound, a modern-day burial site. Land adjoining the plant was cordoned off, protected for its archaeological significance—Chumash Indians buried their dead just where the plant now lay. The reactor domes seemed dull and old. Radiation was once perceived as futuristic and exciting, a cure for all, with the atom imbued with great promise—cheap electricity for everyone. Instead, Diablo presented the nuclear age as an epoch past, a concrete relic, something near retirement.

The domes and the turbines were what I expected to dominate the landscape. But from the air I noticed the number of roads, outbuildings, the unreal blue glow of two cooling ponds that looked too good to swim in, and electricity cables everywhere. On this Sunday afternoon, there did not appear to be any activity. Diablo seemed silent and peaceful, almost otherworldly.

Martin was also silent as we circled the plant from the air. He was fairly busy swinging the plane around on tight loops, but I wondered what he was thinking. I recognized that this trip was different from the ones he had offered club members in the 1960s. Here, today, he was taking me to witness the disfigurement of Diablo, the impact of the nuclear age, or—perhaps more personal to him—a material landscape that embodied some of the failings of his dear Sierra Club.

As we entered California's fog once more, heading toward San Luis Obispo airport, it was striking how quickly Diablo faded out of focus. We had returned to civilization—the town of San Luis, its airport, the middle-class hubbub below. A few days earlier, Martin had bemoaned how few knew of the place. It was now much easier to realize the true significance of such a comment.

◼ ◼ ◼ ◼

I REMEMBER the poignancy of the phrase "The place no one knew." That was the line used by the Sierra Club in the 1960s when lamenting the loss of Glen Canyon, a remote and spectacular spot along the Colorado River. The club acquiesced to a hydropower project at Glen Canyon in order to save nearby Dinosaur National Monument in Utah from damming. The worth of the region ignored, Glen was flooded in 1963, with Lake Powell reservoir the result. Glen was lost to water politics and energy development, the true forces of change in the American West. A few years later, a similar kind of debate emerged over Diablo Canyon. Caught up in the controversy, the Sierra Club almost split over the atom. Diablo was also sacrificed to the energy needs of the modern West. That Diablo appeared, like Glen, a place no one knew, a landscape obscured from view, made it special to some, and instantly forgettable to others. In the mid-1970s, the Disney Corporation filmed part of the live animation musical *Pete's Dragon* on the coastline precisely because a hidden landscape represented an ideal location for a huge dragon called Elliot to hang out. Disney constructed a fake lighthouse on the northernmost tip of the headland, with the U.S. Coast Guard alerted when the light went on. At all other times, Diablo seemed shadowy and isolated.

All this changed in the late 1970s and early 1980s with an explosion of nuclear protest. Suddenly, Diablo became the place everyone knew, a subject of television and press interest. Mass demonstrations against the energy project ensued. Singer-songwriter Jackson Browne was arrested on-site. News reporters swarmed the region. Marvel Comics produced a comic book based at Diablo that featured She-Hulk and The Thing. Alongside Three Mile Island, Diablo Canyon served as the American ground zero of nuclear power. What happened on the coastline really mattered to people.

And yet, there is no historical record of what occurred on the headland. No timely understanding of atomic matters. This book attempts to fill that void. It maps out "the place no one knew." It explores the secret coastal wilderness of Diablo past and the atomic landscape of present. It captures the antinuclear and pronuclear visions and probes the immense power of atomic imagery over corporations and conservationists alike. It also sheds new light on California's energy woes and on the resurrection of nuclear power as a national energy source. Through this book, more people will know of Diablo and come to realize what the nuclear age means.

acknowledgments

You should always visit a place that you hope to write about. For the chance to explore the Diablo lands, I thank Sally Krenn and Sue Benech, biologists on contract to Pacific Gas and Electric Company in the late 1990s. Sue kindly provided me with a tour of the coastline, stopping off to watch sea otters, brown pelicans, and a wily coyote. Dedicated conservationist Martin Litton of the Sierra Club flew me in his 1951 Cessna airplane from Palo Alto to San Luis Obispo and back, circling the Pecho Coast several times. I also walked the Pecho Coast Trail—thanks to Mike Heler and Paul Provence for some company—and attended a "Sunset Tour" of the Diablo plant and its environs one balmy California evening in 1997.

During my stay in California I relied on the hospitality of a number of people while researching this book. For making their home my own, I thank Marge Lasky in Berkeley; Sandy Silver, president of the Women's International League for Peace and Freedom, in Santa Cruz; Liz and the late Hank Apfelberg in Arroyo Grande; Rochelle and Tom Becker in Grover Beach; and Bill Denneen in Nipomo (who provided me with a memorable horse-and-cart ride of the region). At his home in the Berkeley Hills, the late David Brower provided conservation stories and pointed out an impressive spider's web on his porch. He will be sadly missed by the U.S. environmental movement. In Nipomo, Kathy Goddard-Jones, a wonderful local conservationist, took me on a stroll of the Nipomo Dunes and offered me tea at her house. She passed away in 2001; the dunes have lost their savior.

Many people involved in the history of Diablo gladly took the time to talk with me. In the San Francisco region, the list includes Lauren Alden, Jackie Cabasso of the Western States Legal Foundation in Oakland, Charlotte Davis, David Hartsough, the film director Judy Irving, Barbara Levy, and Brook and Phoebe from the Reclaiming Collective. In San Luis Obispo County, salutations to Raye Fleming, Dick Krejsa, Pam Metcalf, William Miller, Willard Osibin, June Von Ruden, and Bob Wolf. Thanks also to Chris Gray, Mary Moore, Chumash representative Pilulaw Kush, photographer Jay Swanson, spiritual writer Starhawk, and Ward Young. The Abalone Alliance Clearinghouse in San Francisco, presided over by Roger Herried and Don Eichelberger, was a gold mine of information concerning antinuclear issues. Staff of the San Francisco office of the American Friends Service Committee opened their files and plied me with fine coffee. I also used archives at the Bancroft Library, University of California, Berkeley, and various collections at California Polytechnic State University, San Luis Obispo. Janet Linthicum and Brian Walton at the Predatory Bird Research Group in Santa Cruz were very obliging. Marcy Darnovsky, ex-Abalone, now associate executive director at the Center for Genetics and Society in Oakland, has been of great support in getting this book published.

Back in England, I thank William Beinart at Oxford University and Peter Coates of the University of Bristol for introducing me to environmental history in the first place. At the University of Essex, best wishes to Jeremy Krikler, Colin Samson, Mary-Ellen Curtin, and Lisa West, and at the University of Kent, warm regards to Tim Bowman, Lesley Brown, Mark Connelly, Angela Crolla, Charlotte Sleigh, Joe Street, and Jackie Waller. I thank Margaret F. Dalrymple, my editor at the University of Nevada Press, for her dedication to this project, and Gerry Anders for his skillful and sympathetic copyediting. I should point out that my work on Diablo was often a shared experience. My soul mate, Karen Jones, a fellow Americanist, traveled with me to the Diablo "wilds" and along the streets of "Berzerkley" and San Francisco, and never failed to enliven each journey.

conservation fallout

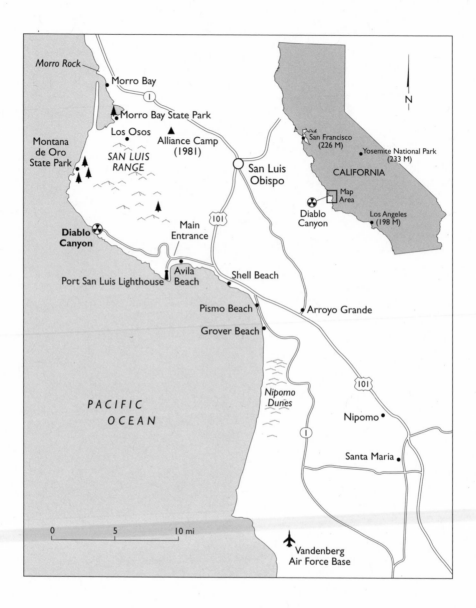

Morro Rock

Morro Bay

Morro Bay State Park

Los Osos

Montana
de Oro
State Park

SAN LUIS
RANGE

Alliance Camp
(1981)

San Luis
Obispo

Diablo
Canyon

Main
Entrance

Port San Luis Lighthouse

Avila
Beach

Shell Beach

Pismo Beach

Arroyo Grande

Grover Beach

PACIFIC
OCEAN

Nipomo
Dunes

Nipomo

Santa Maria

0   5   10 mi

Vandenberg
Air Force Base

San Francisco
(226 M)

Yosemite National Park
(233 M)

CALIFORNIA

Map
Area

Diablo
Canyon

Los Angeles
(198 M)

N

Introduction

From its beginnings at Leggett, 190 miles north of San Francisco, California Highway 1 follows the contours of the coast so closely that, at times, it nearly falls into chilly Pacific waters. On automobile maps, a red line denoting highway and a blue trace indicating shoreline together mark the limits of westerly travel on continental American soil—or, more accurately, asphalt. Tourists treat California's premier scenic highway as a drive-by nature theater, while Hollywood appropriates it for celluloid images of tight curves, crashing waves, and careening cars, best captured in Clint Eastwood's movie *Play Misty for Me* (1971). Winding south, the road cuts through redwood forests, Point Reyes National Seashore, the San Francisco Presidio, and Big Sur. Then, at Morro Bay, 200 miles south of San Francisco, Highway 1 turns inland. A range of hills abruptly rises to block the accustomed coastal view. Hidden behind them is Diablo Canyon.

Diablo lies on the Pecho Coast, a fifteen-mile stretch of land that juts out into the Pacific Ocean. The San Luis Range, undulating hills formed by the San Andreas Fault over thousands of years, separates Diablo Canyon from the rest of California. The inward turn of the freeway illustrates the extent to which civilization once bypassed the headland. Until the 1960s, geological forces helped insulate the Pecho promontory from industrial and commercial encroachment. A geographical barrier thwarted the kind of development that was occurring elsewhere across the state. Despite being situated on the Central

Coast, exactly midway between the metropolises of San Francisco and Los Angeles, and within easy driving distance of Vandenberg Air Force Base and the popular tourist staples of Hearst Castle and the Madonna Inn, Diablo seemed detached from the broader forces shaping California life. Diablo existed merely as a backwater.

In the 1960s the backwater was discovered and given purpose by two groups holding very different visions of California. Local conservationists recognized in the rugged cliffs and grassy knolls of Pecho an alluring preserve of classic, preindustrial coastline, similar to the eye candy found on Highway 1, minus the concrete coating and gasoline redolence. In 1965 the northern edge of the headland, along with the spectacular sandspit of Morro Bay, were set aside as Montana de Oro State Park. The state park offered a refuge from statewide development, a protected enclave of "old" California untouched by Hollywood, condos, or industrial and technological revolutions—in short, modernity. During the same period, Pacific Gas and Electric Company (PG&E), a major utility and California's biggest energy provider, identified Diablo Canyon, on the southern stretch of the headland, as an appropriate site for a nuclear power plant. PG&E envisaged Diablo as a base, or ground zero, for a new age of energy production. A generous array of nuclear reactors on the coastal site would help power California's technological and economic ascendancy over other states, if not the globe. The remote and undeveloped qualities of Diablo thus attracted two competing visions. The north side encapsulated an old frontier of wilderness, while the southern tip evinced a new frontier of technological abundance.

While the northern bluffs passed smoothly into state park ownership, the fate of Diablo Canyon on the southern Pecho Coast remained contested for several decades. In the late 1960s the Sierra Club, a leading national conservation organization with solid roots in California, struck a land deal with Pacific Gas. Club directors condoned the nuclear project at Diablo as a means to free up corporate-owned land farther south along the coastline for state park purchase. The controversial "sacrifice" of Diablo Canyon almost split the club. Divisions in the local community took longer to emerge. With Diablo promising cheap electricity and lucrative tax revenue, residents of San Luis Obispo County initially welcomed their new atomic neighbor. The peaceful atom touted great things in the 1950s and 1960s, and county politicians wore with pride atomic pins handed to them by PG&E representatives. However, stories of radiation dangers and flawed reactor designs in the early 1970s led the American public to question the need for a national landscape marked by atomic artifacts. When a fault line was discovered within three miles of Diablo Canyon, doubts grew over the appropriateness of a nuclear plant on the headland. Fresh from protesting American involvement in Vietnam, the Mothers for Peace, a local women's group, initiated a legal campaign against the atomic project. In 1977, antinuclear activists from across the state formed the Abalone Alliance, a nonviolent direct action organization, with the intention of stopping the plant from going on-line. Two years later, an Alliance rally in San Francisco attracted 25,000 Californians, while 40,000 gathered in San Luis Obispo. During a two-week blockade of the Diablo plant in September 1981, 1,900 activists were jailed, including, most famously, singer-songwriter Jackson Browne. It was the largest arrest in the history of American nuclear protest. The controversy continued into 1984. That May, the Democratic Party's soon-to-be presidential candidate, Walter Mondale, visited San Luis Obispo, informing prospective voters that in their own backyard, "the shadow of a devil—a Diablo—hangs over you."[1]

▪   ▪   ▪   ▪

TWO DECADES ON, the story of Diablo has yet to be told. Six years spent researching and writing this book have convinced me that such a story not only matters, it has something to say to all of us. When I first started this study, I pondered how one tiny stretch of California coastline could possibly enlarge our understanding of environmental protest, the nuclear age, what it means to be a Californian, or the clash between natural and cultural (read technological) landscapes. Researching in the late 1990s, with the cold war over, I recognized that atomic issues (in both peacetime and wartime guises) no longer pervaded the American psyche like they had done in prior decades. Most Americans rarely considered the safety and security of nuclear sites. Blissfully ignorant of security issues, I myself took an airplane ride that circled directly above the Diablo plant in the summer of 1997. Energy deregulation had kicked in across California in the mid-1990s, but only a few Californians expressed strong reservations. Looking back, a sense of complacency reigned in many arenas of American life, including that of environmental protest, where mass mailings requesting donations constituted the standard offense of the formerly "radical" movement.

Upon finishing this title, I could not help but realize that greater fallout was happening about me in the form of 9/11. As a nation struggled to comprehend the unthinkable, nuclear terminology suddenly resurfaced—reemployed by journalists and critics alike to offer some sort of scale to the terrorist event before them. The burning embers of the World Trade Center towers served as the new ground zero for the twenty-first century, replacing hitherto popular images of Hiroshima, Nagasaki, and the Nevada Test Site. Using the phrase *ground zero* intimated that the flames and horrors of that day bespoke the worst of human imaginings and attested to an inhumane capacity for destruction. As an analogy, only nuclear holocaust came close. As part of President George W. Bush's subsequent "war against terrorism," rumors of weapons of mass destruction (including nuclear weaponry) justified military action against Iraq in spring 2003. News stories as well as popular television dramas (take the myriad terrorist-inspired nuclear and biological threats portrayed in such shows as *The Agency, Alias,* and *24*) played on resurfacing nuclear fears. Atomic issues were important again.

Other crises occupied the American psyche. The energy crisis in California was brought home literally for the first time in enforced brownouts and "rolling blackouts" across the state in early 2001. On the eastern seaboard, energy supply problems were implicated in the sudden power outages across several states, including New York, in August 2003. Initial fears of terrorist attacks proved bogus but clearly reflected lingering 9/11 anxieties. Growing sense of a nationwide energy crisis provoked the Bush administration to put forward schemes for increasing domestic capacity, including a new nuclear energy plan. Back in California, the implacability of energy woes contributed to a popular vote to recall Governor Gray Davis in October 2003 and bring in problem-Terminator Arnold Schwarzenegger as a replacement.

Arguably, environmental protest is also in flux. While established organizations such as Greenpeace and the Sierra Club appear healthy, the thorny issue of not doing enough to offset rising U.S. pollution levels remains. Environmental issues continue to take second billing to economic and political headlines. The environment regularly drops off the radar of what is really important to everyday Americans.

In its own way, the story of Diablo provides useful context to all these narratives. It shows how popular anxieties spread in the community, how a general fear of catastrophe, of doomsday, takes hold. It informs on the practical making of the energy crisis in California, the ardent clash between conservationists and energy boosters over California's development, and the costly nature of the route taken. And it highlights the changing fortunes and tactics of the U.S. environmental movement in the post-1945 period, and the merits and follies of pursuing a more confrontational protest strategy.

▪ ▪ ▪ ▪

DESPITE CASTING a long shadow over middle California, Diablo has garnered little attention from scholars and is long overdue its first history. Chapter 1 provides a brief overview of life on the headland before the onset of the nuclear age, taking us through Native American, Spanish, and early statehood times. The chapter is compromised by a few notable gaps in the historical record (including questions over Diablo's naming), and it is easy to imagine a blanket of coastal fog periodically settling on the headland, shrouding it in mystery. Those looking for a monograph recounting Diablo's nuclear politics will perhaps question my decision to explore the region's hazy prenuclear history. But the first chapter in Diablo's history is crucial to our understanding of the forces at play in the region. It shows that, across a vast span of time, the California landscape has been utilized by a variety of communities. The construction of a nuclear plant amounts to just one phase in the region's history. Furthermore, in recognizing several thousand years of land use, we gain a comprehension of the transitory nature of nuclear energy production. By looking at Native American and Californio attempts to obtain food, water, and whale oil on the headland and even harness small-scale hydropower, we find that Diablo served as an "energy landscape" (in a broad sense) well before the advent of atomic technology. This intriguing idea of a sustained energy landscape will be explored later in the book.

Chapter 2 turns to Diablo in the 1960s. For historians of the Sierra Club, Diablo is best understood as a divisive episode in club history, reminiscent of the controversy in the 1910s over damming the Tuolomne River in Hetch Hetchy Valley, north of Yosemite Valley (in Yosemite National Park). Diablo emerges not so much as a physical realm, but more as a dispute over conservation philosophy and the club's "historical mission," a gaudy example of the organization's "battles within." The social scientist Susan Schrepfer situates the Diablo power plant wrangle as central to the club's move "from a traditional, wilderness conservation agenda toward a comprehensive environmental perspective." Diablo, she argues, forced directors to confront "complex new problems" and reconsider the dangers of atomic power. Whereas conservationists had previously welcomed nuclear plants as an alternative to damming wild rivers for electricity generation, nascent concerns over nuclear waste, radiation, and thermal pollution shattered confidence in the atom. Along with the question of what Diablo meant for the Sierra Club, I additionally explore what Sierran debates meant for Diablo.[2]

Little has been written on the two antinuclear organizations that arrived at Diablo in the 1970s. Scholars have consistently overlooked the activities of the Mothers for Peace, an omission rectified by my third chapter. Here I offer the first academic treatment of this organization notable for its community base, legislative focus, and gendered politics. Chapter 4 turns to the period 1977–84, the heyday of the Abalone Alliance. In *Political Protest and Cultural Revolution* (1991), a text surveying the rise of nonviolent direct action in the 1970s and 1980s, Barbara Epstein highlighted the contributions of the Alliance to new ways of grassroots organizing in the Golden State. In chapter 4 I emphasize how environmental and "pronature" sentiments played a key role in determining Abalone conduct and radical action. In fact, one of my main contentions is that protesters were motivated by a strong sense of atomic energy as a fundamental threat to the integrity of natural (or ecological) systems. Significantly, Alliance protest was shaped by the environmental age as much as, if not more than, by the civil rights era.[3]

In chapters 5 and 6, I tackle the period from 1985 to 2000, focusing specifically on issues of land stewardship and nuclear safety at PG&E's plant. These chapters shift the lens away from environmental protest and, in a similar vein to chapter 1, highlight broader interactions between people and landscape. Despite the high performance levels attained by the Diablo plant, criticism of Pacific Gas is all too easy to find during this period. Diablo continued to symbolize the incompetence and irresponsibility of corporate America. The *San Francisco Bay Guardian* consistently presented the giant utility as the archenemy of public interest, a capitalist ogre and social miscreant. The propensity for Californians to criticize Pacific Gas was evidenced by the popularity of a Hollywood movie depicting corporate malpractice at Hinkley, San Bernardino County. *Erin Brockovich* (2000) related the discovery of a contaminated local water supply by a legal assistant, and her battle to expose PG&E as the guilty party. Chapters 5 and 6 indicate that the situation at Diablo may be more complex than such celluloid narratives of good versus evil suggest.

A few notes on my own approach and rationale are useful here. First, I place the Diablo landscape at the forefront, rather than on the periphery, of events. Existing scholarship on environmental protest groups has often underplayed the role of the landscape itself in proceedings. In this title, the Pecho coastline joins the Sierra Club boardrooms and Abalone house-meets as a shaper of policy. Such an approach sheds valuable light on the interactions between environmentalists and the lands they seek to protect.[4]

We also gain a sense of how the material landscape changes. Along with archaeological reports, oral interviews, newspaper cuttings, and scientific studies, there is much to learn from Diablo itself. A quick glance at Pecho topography reveals a coastline party to human interest for thousands of years. Native American artifacts and bones relate the ancient presence of California Indians at Diablo Canyon. A modern inventory of flora elucidates the material impacts of Spanish rule on the region, exotic wild oats and ripgut demonstrating the lasting invasiveness of ecological imperialism. That bovines munch on Diablo's foliage indicates the spread of domesticated cattle across the Golden State in the early nineteenth century. A decaying wooden cabin conveys the story of American pioneers settling the coast in the latter half of the 1800s. Peregrine falcons nesting at Diablo Rock suffer the lingering maledictions of DDT, an insecticide used widely in crop spraying during the 1950s and 1960s. Poison oak, a native shrub that causes skin rashes, lurks in the canyons, while alongside it rests an exotic nuclear plant with its own health issues. Only by noticing the material landscape can we ponder the broader implications of human interference in ecological systems.[5]

Second, on top of this material-minded groundwork, I document shifts in social and environmental outlooks. How does environmental protest change over time, how do we socially construct nature, and how does the nuclear age impact the American psyche? The book deals with human sensibilities and belief systems. It is not a bureaucratic or political treatise. Scholars of legal history may lament my fragmentary comments on Nuclear Regulatory Commission documents and judicial matters. The Diablo nuclear plant was the subject of courtroom quarrels for over a decade, and the U.S. Congress investigated the conduct of PG&E with regard to its construction record on the Pecho headland. The cursory attention paid to the legal arena in this study reflects more my cultural-environmental mandate than any concrete decision to deprioritize the role of regulatory issues. Rather than relate the whole political record regarding Diablo's licensing, I instead concentrate on Diablo's significant ties with atomic culture, popular protest, and environmental consciousness. This is also not a book about PG&E. The complex relationship between Pacific Gas, propaganda, and nuclear power is explored to some extent. But any definitive assessment of PG&E's nuclear strategy is made difficult by corporate reservations over public access to business records. While mapping out two competing visions of California and America, one broadly tagged as "environmentalist," the other held by the "nuclear industry," this book delves deepest into the mind of the protester.[6]

Third, in my coverage of Diablo Canyon I deliberately situate the nuclear age as a period driven by difficult human-nature relations rather than superpower rivalries. Despite its association with otherworldly properties and the iconography of uniqueness, the atomic era represents just another stage in human relations with the natural world based around energy supply and demand. In common with the mineral booms of the nineteenth century and drives for biotechnology and genetic engineering in the early twenty-first century, atomic energy manifested a timeless sapient quest to tinker with natural systems on an elemental level. The atomic reactor, like the nodding wellhead pump in the oil field or the combine harvester on the wheat-planted prairie, was a machine deemed capable of servicing dreams of energy abundance and individual prosperity, a testament to our power over nature and our willingness to innovate and transform. As part of a historic dialogue between people and place, atomic machinations fit within a complex and continually evolving environmental discourse of human-nature relations. Links abound between individual atomic projects and wider land practices, of nuclear fears coinciding with shifting ecological perspectives. At Diablo Canyon, the nuclear institution conventionally thought of as pivotal and unique actually related to enduring antipathies and amities toward place and ecology. This book deconstructs the dominant nuclear image to see what lies beneath.

And what of this nuclear image? There can be no doubt that atomic controversy made Diablo special. "It wasn't until September 1966 that Diablo Canyon started to become a household word in San Luis Obispo County," explained a writer for the local newspaper, the *Telegram-Tribune*. PG&E's plans became a topic of conversation in bars, offices, and homes across the Golden State. In the chapters that follow, we discover how Californians connected Diablo with a much broader nuclear landscape, associating the coastline with glossy pictures of futuristic, clean atomic plant sites or with less-promising footage of bombed-out, irradiated test sites. Citizens smothered Diablo with a patchwork quilt of atomic images, using documentary films, press reports, and Hollywood movies for inspiration. Diablo Canyon became part of the nuclear age, a monument to atomic history, years before Pacific Gas actually brought nuclear fuel on-site. The mechanisms by which Diablo performs as a microcosm of U.S. atomic culture are of interest throughout.[7]

Nuclear landscapes have often been treated as wastelands or "sacrifice zones," places devoid of nature due to their destructive mandate. The *Atlas of the New West* (1997) even furnished a map of "A Nuked Landscape" in a chapter fittingly dubbed "The Ugly West." The relationship between the nuclear age and ecology is assumed to be wholly negative. However, the underlying issues in the "clash" of nuclear technology and ecological balance are often ignored. Few have paused to consider how attitudes toward the natural world intersect with the controversial deployment of nuclear missiles and power plants, or how nuclear developers' hopes of improving nature's lot contrast with protesters' moans about Planet Earth under attack. This book argues that the nuclear age has been fundamentally influenced by popular concepts of nature, dominant environmental belief systems, and our troubled relationship with the land. The story of Diablo strongly suggests that the nuclear age is about human ties with nature as much as about cold war competition or technological inventiveness. Conventional interpretations of the nuclear age have concentrated on issues of politics, science, and technology, reflecting the social store put in cold war rhetoric and superpower saber rattling. When faced with the quintessential atomic icon, the mushroom cloud rising above the desert, eyes have focused on the man-made, technological, artificial expression. The ground below seems just a backdrop, a landscape rendered insignificant in a greater, unfurling story of human progress. This work follows a different approach to ground zero, and returns with different findings. In *Nature's Economy*, Donald Worster noted how "the age of ecology opened on the New Mexico desert, near the town of Alamogordo, on July 16, 1945, with a dazzling fireball of light and a swelling mushroom cloud of radioactive gases." The nuclear age is about the directions we choose to take toward nature and ecology, with Diablo Canyon one of the many trail signs.[8]

■ ■ ■ ■

Throughout this work, three core ideas gain prominence. I mention them at the outset so that they might serve as a useful guide to the main text.

■ THE SOCIAL CONSTRUCTION ■
OF NATURE AT DIABLO CANYON

Cultural theorist Raymond Williams once called *nature* the most complex word in the English language. Nature can mean anything from a statement of human character or an inherent guiding force to a description of the organic world. At Diablo the latter form, the biological realm, is of interest here. However, even what we understand by material nature is eminently negotiable and frequently controversial. We imagine the landscape as we wish to find it. At Diablo, the same terrain received widely divergent descriptions in the post-1945 period. A vocal contingent of conservationists and corporate officials in the 1960s struggled to present an accurate image of the California headland. Some saw Diablo as barren and worthless, while others declared it fertile and spectacular. The intrinsic character, the *nature* of the California landscape, remained deeply contested. Ultimately, at Diablo and elsewhere, what "nature" we choose to emphasize is socially agreed and reflects a combination of cultural, temporal, and geographic factors. But what happens when an image cannot be agreed on, when no common ground exists? This quandary underlies the history of Diablo and is something that I return to at the end of book.[9]

■ CALIFORNIA AS AN ESCALATING ENERGY LANDSCAPE ■

Issues of landscape perception do not take place in a social or political vacuum. Political agendas on local, state, and national levels influence and are influenced by prevailing notions of nature. The exchange between dominant images and dominant politics produces a specific set of environmental regulations, building projects, and park protection schemes. Not only ecology (as in the material world) but also *images* of ecology intersect with culture and politics. One of the prevalent images of California's intrinsic worth, its intrinsic nature, is that of an energy landscape.

The image of an energy landscape dates back to Native American conceptions of California as a bounteous land able to provide them with food, clothing, shelter, and spiritual direction. While the universality of this image was weakened by Spanish and Mexican inroads in the eighteenth and early nineteenth centuries, whereby cattle came to browse the land and Christianity situated salvation in a heavenly plane above the earth, the biggest revision came with the California gold rush of 1849. Suddenly California was defined by its mineral worth alone. Human energies focused on the mass retrieval of nuggets of gold. The natural energy reserves of the Golden State engendered demographic expansion, ethnic strife, and overnight statehood. Mineral wealth and the hazards it encompassed, an overriding boom-and-bust mentality, indelibly shaped the California landscape. The Golden State has arguably never escaped its gold rush roots. It remains trapped in the vision of energy-impregnated land, with consummate riches on tap for all and sundry. In the twentieth century, Central Valley agricultural schemes further situated energy in the land. Fertile soil (with added pesticides) furnished produce and profit. Water projects—liquid energy—in turn laid the foundation of grand cities such as Los Angeles that would never have existed without this massive infusion. Technological invention aided in forging a national picture of California as a place in continual motion, a place of inexplicable dynamism, movement, and energy. The growth of Silicon Valley in the 1970s charted new forms of energy hidden in computer chips. California today remains on the edge of the frontier, a presage of where the rest of the country is heading, its landscape imbued with expectations of creativity and endless possibility. California represents a multidimensional energy landscape in the twenty-first century.

However, not every newfangled scheme that promised to add to California's energy output, or its energy reserves, has met with success. Within this greater story, PG&E's plans for Diablo Canyon in the 1960s constituted one attempt to fuel statewide expansion and meet rising energy demands that fell on thorny ground. The Diablo plant was meant to usher in a new age of energy abundance for the Golden State. California seemed destined to become a fertile energy landscape based around nuclear power thanks to the Diablo project. Instead, the Pecho Coast served as a battleground between environmentalists and corporations, energy users and conservers, radicals and conservatives. In light of current energy woes in California today, the story of Diablo helps explain the unfolding state crisis, and how the Golden State ultimately lost its way.

▪ ENVIRONMENTAL PROTEST, DIABLO CANYON, ▪ AND "CONSERVATION FALLOUT"

Until the 1960s conservation was an eminently respectable and courteous affair. The Sierra Club operated as a gentrified outdoor-pursuits club, with an elite membership of mostly white and wealthy Californians. In the decades that followed, environmental protest underwent meteoric change. By the 1980s members of Earth First! spiked trees to stop logging practices, while grassroots environmental justice groups highlighted the exploitation of people of color in urban environments. Along with Earth Day, the Santa Barbara oil spill, Chernobyl, and Love Canal, Diablo Canyon contributed to the fundamental shift in conservation practices and philosophy in the latter half of the twentieth century.

Going into the Diablo dispute, the Sierra Club, at least on the outside, maintained its credentials for quiet diplomacy and a willingness to work with corporations. Most San Luis Obispo conservationists thought little of PG&E's nuclear plans. Diablo Canyon overnight became a metaphorical nuclear bomb that, on detonation, blew conservation in the Golden State sky high. In the immediate chaos, the Sierra Club lay splintered and close to collapse. Executive director David Brower was shunned for his part in the explosion, and set about forming a new lobby, the Friends of the Earth. The gigantic plume that rose into the sky in the late 1960s carried with it not just conservation rhetoric but other contemporary ideas associated with the civil rights era. As the radioactive dust settled, new splinter cells emerged from the debris with radical environmental agendas based around social justice, nonviolent protest, and dissenting voices. The story of Diablo Canyon exemplifies this. It is, put simply, the story of America's conservation fallout.

ONE _Diablo Canyon Wilds_

"I f you like to hike and want to experience the diversity of landscape and life that characterize this spectacular area, join docents for a seven-mile round-trip along the Pecho Coast Trail," invited a 1990s trail leaflet distributed by PG&E volunteers. By calling 805/541-TREK, visitors could reserve their space on a guided walk across the south side of the Pecho headland— their chance to discover firsthand the intertwining history of nature and humanity on Diablo lands.[1]

Along the trail, ramblers took advantage of lofty hillside vantage points, pausing to peer down on the piers, boats, and bathers of Avila Beach. Guides told stories of industry on the headland, of whaling, shipping, and lighthouse beacons. Weaving amongst the dense bush and oak woods, hikers immersed themselves in the grand scenery of the Pecho Coast. As living monuments of age-old geological forces, the coastal bluffs and rugged cliffs testified to the dynamic power of nature in the region. Ocean swells and waves crashing against Diablo rocks echoed a distant past when water traveled more freely eastward, the sparkling expanse of the Pacific Ocean reminiscent of the scene 25 million years earlier when shallow seas covered much of western California. Ancient relatives of today's abalone, clams, and whales prospered in a then-submerged San Luis Obispo County. Meanwhile, the crumpled appearance of the Pecho crags and hillsides related the volatile birth of the region between two and five million years ago, courtesy of plate tectonics. Grinding against its North American counterpart (at the San Andreas Fault), the Pacific Plate lifted and folded, raising terraces and forging hills. Sedimentary rocks formerly buried in ocean waters rose up to form the distinctive California coastal range. The local series of volcanoes known as the Morros also surfaced during the Pliocene period, forced above the waterline by plate faulting and retreating seas. Pacific storms then buffeted the exposed Diablo rocks, gradually refining the coastal canvas.

The shaping of the headland by elemental natural forces lent it an alluring, primeval quality. As the Pecho Coast Trail leaflet proudly recounted, "Volcanic flows, earthquake movements and ocean sculpting formed this land." Recasting volcanoes and earthquakes as creative tools rather than havoc-wreakers, the handout portrayed Diablo as an impressive piece of organic architecture. A series of grand, histrionic displays of natural phenomena had forged an appropriately "dramatic stretch of coastline," capable of supporting "a wealth of life" from bobcats to surf birds to lizards.[2]

The trail offered few discernible clues as to early human use of the region. Gazing down at Avila, walkers were reminded of the port's bustling late nineteenth-century heyday, while a visit to the restored Point San Luis Lighthouse nearby offered a rare peek at the shining "Victorian Lady." At best, the Pecho Coast trail seemed a journey back in time of a mere hundred years. Although Native Americans had walked the same coast thousands of years earlier, trailside signs of ancient human presence remained shrouded, footprints from antiquity washed away by Pacific storms and covered by sprouting spring grasses.

■ ■ ■ ■

THE FIRST HUMANS to frequent the Pecho Coast probably followed a nomadic or semisedentary lifestyle. The search for food and shelter led them across wild and flourishing environments. Archaeologist Roberta Greenwood surveyed the coastal region in 1968–69, identifying the earliest residents of Diablo as likely descendants of the Early Playa–Flake peoples residing in the American interior. Greenwood found relics at Diablo dating back to 7370 B.C. The coastal terrain provided a rich and diverse larder, a consummate energy landscape. During the first millennium of occupation Diablo residents learned to grind seeds using handstones. The evolution of an Early Milling Stone culture on the headland possibly related to contact and trade with other inland groups or reflected a new recognition of fertile and edible plant life on the bluffs. Inhabitants continued to hunt on the Pecho lands, gradually honing their skills through new technology. By 3000 B.C., hunters used lunate knives, fish spears, and projectile points to down their prey. The proliferation of bone items discovered at Diablo burial sites enshrined the Hunting Period on the Pecho Coast.

Between A.D. 500 and 1000, Diablo residents developed more intricate crafting methods. Vestiges of the hunting culture converged with a sophisticated "Canalino" lifestyle that valued trade and handicrafts. Greenwood discovered artifacts endemic to the Hunting Period, such as flaked stone vessels, alongside Canalino-associated J-shaped fishing hooks and Olivella (small shell) disk beads. Native Americans frequenting Pecho shores gradually built on their cultural heritage and, by A.D. 1000, had forged a way of life at Diablo Canyon clearly recognizable as historic Chumash.[3]

In 1891 John Wesley Powell of the Bureau of American Ethnology referred to the Native Americans of central California as Chumashan. Powell grouped together various tribes—many with their own vernacular and cultural traits—under one common banner. The label Chumash came from the native word *Michumash,* used by mainland villagers to describe Santa Cruz Island, or "place of the islanders," and its inhabitants, "those who make shell bead money." Chumash territory historically spanned seven thousand square miles of coastal terrain, stretching from the Santa Monica Mountains to San Simeon. Greenwood speculated that the Pecho Coast may have served as one of the "early localities" responsible for seeding tribal expansion, with Diablo possibly "the major focus of settlement and social organization" along the immediate coastline. Residents of Diablo possibly forged settlements at nearby Avila, Morro Bay, and Pismo Beach. In the search for new food supplies and trade opportunities, native groups from Pecho and other early communities gradually dispersed across coastal California. Villages boasted several hundred residents. Shisholop (today's Ventura) probably supported four hundred people, living in a few dozen round thatched dwellings. Elaborate social networks developed with the expansion of communities, chiefs (*wots*), shaman-doctors, messengers (*ksens*), and craft guild members exerting considerable influence over village life.[4]

Pecho denizens followed a simpler, earlier form of Chumash culture to that found in villages such as Shisholop. Through her work at Diablo, Greenwood identified a "long span of occupation with only slight change and evolution of artifacts through time" with "no drastic shifts in subsistence pattern." An absence of canoes or fishing nets possibly reflected the community's lack of knowledge of new technology. Well-honed traditional skills secured ample foodstuffs without resorting to ocean travel. Out-migration also eased pressures on the Pecho environment, leaving villagers with little need to adopt innovative means of gathering food. Although some trade artifacts were found at the Diablo site, the coastal settlement remained some distance from popular Chumash trading routes with the Salinan to the north and Yokuts and Mohave to the east. The nearest known route, along the Santa Maria–Cuyama River drainage, lay some ninety miles inland, a week's trek away.[5]

Diablo Indians wandered the bluffs and canyons, hunting, fishing, and gathering seeds. Intimate knowledge of the surroundings fueled an overriding sense of place and belonging. The Pecho Coast signified the focal point of everyday existence for the community of Indians who resided there. Meanwhile, shared stories, travel, and exchange fashioned images of the larger California landscape. As predominantly coastal dwellers, the Chumash felt comfortable with the notion of their world as an island afloat a great expanse of water. María Solares, of Chumash and Yokuts ancestry, related: "Here where we live is the center of our world—it is the biggest island." This world (*'itiašup*)[6] relied on two giant snakes (the *masaqsiq'itašup*) to support it. When the serpents tired, they wriggled about, causing earthquakes above their heads. The movement of the reptiles provided the Chumash people with an understandable, naturalistic explanation for sudden tears and ripples in the land. Local Chumash probably subscribed to legends of two other worlds operating above and below the Pecho Coast. Beneath the snakes lurked *c'oyinašup*, "the other world," inhabited by malevolent creatures known as the *nunašiš*, while a third world, *'alapay*, prevailed above California skies. Resting on the wings of the great *slo'w* (or eagle), *'alapay* sustained supernatural beings such as Sun and Coyote of the Sky. Occasionally the great *slo'w* stretched his wings, which, according to Solares, inaugurated the phases of the moon.[7]

Native Californians depended on their immediate environment for clothing, subsistence, shelter, and ceremonial items. Greenwood describes Diablo as "a viable economic unit from which the Indians derived their food, water, lithic and other resources." The Pecho Coast thus represented a prime energy landscape, a place that sustained Native American communities by virtue of its abundant natural resources and by its ability to consistently meet the material demands of an active hunter-gatherer society. Pecho creeks provided local Indians with drinking water. Tangled oak groves and dense woodland hid acorns, berries, and seeds. Mule deer, coyotes, and badgers frequented the numerous wooded canyons. Along the waterside, Native Americans collected clams, abalone, and other shellfish from tide pools and inlets. Chumash employed tiny shell hooks to catch fish, while larger marine shells served as trading currency. Seals and sea lions resting on Pecho rocks presented tempting targets to trap, club, and spear. Greenwood discovered a panpipe forged from pelican bone at one Diablo burial site. Native Americans tapped the ecological vigor of the headland for their own lifestyle succession.[8]

Chumash Indians living at or close to Diablo saw themselves as a natural, intrinsic part of the environment and viewed other creatures wandering the Pecho bluffs as kindred spirits. Chumash Fernando Librado recounted how his grandfather "told him that all animals are related." Librado believed that "we are all brothers, and our mother is one: this mother earth." Chumash stories and religious beliefs fleshed out the lives of fellow fauna beyond their corporeal existences. Centipedes, eagles, swordfish, and rattlesnakes took on shamanic identities, all contributing to the spiritual energy of the coastal landscape. One of the many Coyote stories told by the Chumash recalled the good times shared by roaming animal spirits, Coyote and Bat "always hunting and doing things together" prior to Bat's becoming "misshapen" during a sweat-lodge endurance contest.[9]

Chumash stories inferred a relatively ambiguous or nondeterminist role for humans in nature. Compared with Judeo-Christian writings that instructed humans to "rule over the fish of the sea and the birds of the air, over the livestock, over all the earth" (Genesis 1:27), Native American parables rarely encouraged people to explicitly take control of "their" environment. Arguably the Chumash Indian conceived him/herself as little different from the other residents of the natural world. In the Chumash story "The Making of Man," animal spirits of the upper world molded some "new people," with the shape of the human hand decided by a sly move from Lizard. Native Americans appeared the chance product of 'alapay dialogue, even trickery, in contrast to biblical tales of "chosen people." Organic forces operated in the landscape beyond the control of Native Americans. A good harvest arrived as manna from the spirits of the upper world. Chumash interpreted beached whales as a fortuitous gift from supernatural swordfish that, with their swords as hands, played games with sea mammals, occasionally throwing them ashore.[10]

Archaeologists discovered an ancient Native American cemetery at Diablo Canyon in 1968. A partial excavation uncovered fifty-four bodies and a collection of ceremonial offerings, including bone whistles, shell beads, and knives. Chumash traditionally marked their burial grounds with whalebones or stone tablets, and in June 1969, slabs of rock were duly discovered at the Pecho site. The Diablo cemetery reflected Chumash fascination with the coastal environment, as well as their firm understanding of the Pecho Coast as a place of spiritual energy.

As described in "The Soul's Journey to Šimilaqša," the Chumash believed in a land of dead souls, a place they called "Šimilaqša," reachable only by traversing a great expanse of water, equivalent to the Pacific Ocean. According to the story, the Native American soul faced a number of trials before crossing the sea, including a deep ravine with clashing rocks and an attack by two "gigantic qaq" (ravens) that pecked out the eyes of the traveler. On finally entering Šimilaqša, the Chumash soul received a special reward of blue abalone eyes to compensate for the ravens' abuse. Šimilaqša itself served as an abundant land for resting spirits. Reinvigorated after a twelve-year stay, some souls then returned to California shores in reincarnated form. Point Conception, south of present-day Vandenberg, provided a spiritual gate for Chumash souls embarking on their ethereal voyage across ocean waters. However, in the late 1990s anthropologists Brian Haley and Larry Wilcoxon argued that regional differences inherent within Chumash culture led individual tribes to establish their own gateways to Šimilaqša rather than using a common "Western Gate" at Point Conception. Haley and Wilcoxon noted how Obispeño Chumash (those living in the region correspondingly roughly to present-day San Luis Obispo County) never mentioned the Point in conversations with anthropologist John Peabody Harrington in the early twentieth century. The Diablo headland, with its abalone coves, rocky ravines, and ocean views, may have provided local Chumash with their own unique causeway westward, the headland allowing the transition from one form of energy to another, from physical matter to celestial energy.[11]

From practical sustenance to spiritual uplift, Diablo proved itself an important energy landscape to Native Americans on myriad levels. However, it may be wrong to conceptualize the first users of Diablo Canyon as perfect and benevolent ecological agents. A number of arguments demonstrate the need for caution.

First, modern research into indigenous land practices shows how tribes manipulated ecological systems to their advantage—exploiting the natural resources on offer. California Indians used their intimate knowledge of the natural world to encourage the growth of edible plants and attract wildlife to hunting grounds. Chumash hunters near the Pecho Coast quite possibly lit fires in attempts to herd animals into traps or cleared woodland in order to kill prey more easily. Native Americans intentionally burned vegetation on grasslands and savanna to accelerate fresh growth and increase seasonal food supplies. They expended physical energy on the land in order to guarantee tribal subsistence. Indigenous communities consciously spread their favorite plants across territorial landscapes, in the process creating valuable food reserves. Ethnobiologist Jan Timbrook suggested Chumash Indians even imported tobacco to Santa Cruz Island. Families local to Diablo most likely engaged in such agricultural endeavors to assure their survival and growth. Native Americans fundamentally altered natural environments.[12]

Reflecting fresh research into native land practices, scholars now label California Indians expert "native gardeners." Was such gardening automatically benign? On one level, gardening represented a natural activity. Chumash locals were not the only ones to alter the landscape. At Diablo the seasons saw coyotes feeding on rodents, bears digging up tasty roots, sea otters toying with shellfish. The Chumash learned *from* nature how to *change* nature. Prior to European discovery the Pecho Coast was always a fluid and energetic place rather than a static, timeless picture. Historian William Preston argues that indigenous tribes improved, even maximized, the biodiversity of California. Californian Indians made ecological systems work for them, turning an already productive coastline into a greater energy-giving landscape. The natural abundance of the Golden State that European explorers judged the fine work of a Christian God was in fact the result of the supposedly "idle savage." Landscapes such as Diablo elucidated the first energy landscapes crafted by Americans.[13]

But did the Chumash take their activities too far, exploiting the land past the point of ecological sustainability? Was Diablo, as an early energy landscape, often depleted? The fact that Greenwood found a long span of occupation at Diablo Canyon suggests some ecological sensitivity, indicating that Native Americans sustained the energy resources on offer there. Native American stories themselves give some indication of attempts to regulate use, to temper the amounts of energy expended on and taken from the landscape. Spiritual traditions reined in nascent desires to overexploit the natural environment, preventing an understood right to live and hunt on the Pecho Coast from escalating into an ethos of dominion. However, the historic Diablo landscape offers only a limited vessel for understanding thousands of years of Indian occupancy. Chumash Indians could have exploited the natural resources of Diablo then left the area for short periods, only to return when biotic recovery kicked in. Low long-term impacts might relate more to chance, limited technology, and modest demographic numbers than to a conscious attempt at environmental sustainability. Those more cynical of idealizing indigene ways of life might see in Diablo historic signs of exploitation rather than horticultural improvement. Moreover, the reason that the Chumash effected only subtle changes to the coastal landscape might reflect the sheer abundance of resources in the region instead of rigorous social restraints. The taking of plants and animals for food, the tapping of Diablo's energy, might even be taken as evidence of the first commodification of the headland.

The key point here is to recognize that the early use of Diablo for energy purposes involved direct contact with natural resources, but that such contact was neither crudely simple nor unconditionally benign. Despite signs of long-term energy sustainability, the complexities, or even ambiguities, of Native land traditions preclude any singular statement of perfect environmental stewardship out on the Diablo coast. The landscape changed, albeit not at a pace comparable with twentieth-century industrial forces. Native oral traditions point to a multilayered treatment of energy resources by Chumash Indians. A Chumash story of the *matavenado* or Jerusalem cricket that decides to limit human population by instigating a process of death is instructive in this regard. On the one hand, the story explains mortality in terms of wider ecological balance. After all, the *matavenado* fears that "the earth will get too full of people and there will be no room to stand," if men rejuvenate rather than die. On the other hand, after hearing the story, many Ventureño Chumash vowed to kill any *matavenado* they met. Such a tale adeptly illuminates the strengths, the weaknesses, and most of all, the complexities of Indian environmental stewardship on the California coastline.[14]

■ EUROPEAN DISCOVERY ■

During the sixteenth and seventeenth centuries European cartographers often depicted California as an island. *The North Part of America* (1625), drawn by Henry Briggs, marked a substantial channel between "the large and goodly island of California" (including Baja California) and "America Septentrionalis." Early explorers hoped the channel would provide a link between the Pacific and Atlantic oceans.[15]

In June 1542 Juan Rodríguez Cabrillo set out to discover this "Northwest Passage," or Strait of Anian, his ships navigating seas off the Baja peninsula. At present-day San Diego, Cabrillo officially claimed the mysterious lands north of Mexico for the Spanish flag, naming the territory Alta (Upper) California. Local Native Americans "gave signs of great fear" when approached by the Spanish, an appropriate response given that Cabrillo had just unceremoniously snatched their homeland. Storms and strong winds buffeted the ships during their slow progress northward. Cabrillo may have passed close to the Pecho Coast during November 1542. In 1587 the Basque seafarer Pedro de Unamuno, a pilot on the Manila trade route and servant of the Spanish Crown, anchored his galleon somewhere between Morro Bay and Avila Beach, and thus close to Diablo Canyon. In common with other European explorers, Unamuno treated the California landscape as an untapped resource, a bounteous place. The local coastline provided his crew with "an unlimited quantity of fish of different kinds," as well as timber for shipbuilding and fuel. Right from the start, Spanish California operated as an energy-giving landscape, a provider. Eight years later Sebastian Rodríguez Cermeño, captain of the *San Agostin,* spotted Native Americans on rocky outcrops near Diablo Canyon. The Chumash cried "Christinos" and "Mexico" in response to the passing Spanish galleon, phrases presumably acquired during Unamuno's visit.[16]

Ideas of colonizing the Golden State gained precedence some 150 years later. In 1769 Captain Gaspar de Portolá and Franciscan Father Juan Crespi, accompanied by sixty-three soldiers and Indian helpers, followed an overland route north along the California coastline. The Portolá expedition hardly compared in size or stature with the forays of Lewis and Clark in 1804–1806, but Crespi's diary provided one of the first detailed descriptions of the American Far West by a European observer. The Franciscan father chronicled early Spanish contact with the flora, fauna, and indigenous peoples of coastal California. On August 30, 1769, the expedition crossed the Santa Maria River into territory known today as San Luis Obispo County. On September 4 the Spanish visited a Chumash settlement near Price Canyon, a few miles south of the Pecho Coast. Crespi described how the "chief of that village has a large goitre which hangs from his neck. On account of this the soldiers named him El Buchon, which name he and the village retained." The Franciscan priest meanwhile heard the bells of future missionary churches ringing in his ears, alternatively christening "the place San Ladisloa, so that this saint may be its patron and protector for its conversion." Crespi portrayed the villagers as hapless inferiors akin to wild animals, "poor creatures" that urgently needed godly direction to lead them toward civilized humanity.[17]

The expedition turned inland, skirting the edges of the San Luis Range and bypassing the Pecho Coast. Portolá's cartographer, Miguel Constansó, described the hills as Sierra de Buchon in a map of the coastline. An investigation of Diablo appeared too much of a detour. In a nearby valley, the party encountered "troops of bears." Crespi noted that the bears "kept the ground plowed up and full of holes which they make searching for roots which constitute their food." He also documented the environmental practices of local Chumash ("the heathen") who utilized the same plants, "which have a very good flavor and taste." Portolá's soldiers named the region La Canada de los Osos, the Valley of the Bears, and eagerly met the resident fauna with a hail of bullets. In the ensuing gunfire, the Spanish showed their desire to control the California wilderness by technological dominance, spiritual proviso, and physical prowess. On June 3, 1770, the survivors of the expedition founded the second Spanish California mission and presidio at Monterey, celebrating the occasion with High Mass, musket firing, flag planting, and the "tearing up and scattering of grass and earth." The heady mixture of Catholicism, guns, nationalism, and ecological disturbance symbolized the beginnings of the European colonization of California.[18]

Armed with the Bible and the musket, an eminently persuasive combination, the Spanish began to convert local Native Americans to Christianity.

By 1784, 616 local Chumash had been baptized at San Luis Obispo Mission. Elsewhere along the California coast, from San Diego to San Francisco, Indian nations found themselves similarly co-opted into colonial and religious servitude. Franciscan fathers referred to their Indian slaves as neophytes, or newly planted seeds. These newly planted seeds represented one crop in a broader conversion project. The Spanish hoped to transform the wild, unfamiliar terra firma of California into something more palatable to European taste buds. Imperial idealists sought to create an Old World pastoral landscape on New World shores, envisioning a country of regimented agriculture, animal husbandry, and unmistakably sapient promise—a conventional energy landscape founded on European design. Dispassionate colonists viewed the native terrain as akin to its indigenous human residents, as raw material—raw energy—to be molded into a civilized form. The richly textured California landscape denoted a blank canvas. Fray Francisco Palóu, a Spaniard who gained some intimacy with coastal California by traveling between San Diego and San Francisco in 1774, regularly couched his commentary on local nature in terms of resource potential. Passing through the San Luis region, Palóu, in utilitarian fashion, noted that the mission site had "the advantage of much good arable land, timber, firewood and water," with fine prospects of irrigation by tapping "an arroyo with a little running water" just "a gunshot away." Nature represented organic capital to be transformed into provident agricultural land. The Franciscan explorer also mentioned Chumash activity close to the mission, whereby "heathen of the neighboring villages harvest an abundance of very savory and nutritious wild seeds, have game, such as deer and rabbits; and the beach Indians catch large quantities of fish." Palóu feared that "it will not be so easy to induce them to live at the mission" with such a rich environment on hand, and that energy might be better spent elsewhere.[19]

Intrigued by the new culture available to them, the promises of spiritual salvation, and material offerings of beads, clothing, and food, some Chumash freely chose to join the missions of central California. Franciscan fathers appointed male Native Americans as alcaldes—mission Indian officials with authority over their fellow converts. However, for the majority of Native Americans, missionary life entailed strict rules, manual labor, curtailed freedom, and regular lashings. The Spanish priests took seriously their divine quest to craft an Eden-like paradise from raw California wilderness and fashion local Indians into good Christians. In the mid-1780s the French visitor Jean-François de La Pérouse noted the "extreme patience" needed to change the Indians. In 1785 Fermin Lasuen replaced Father Junípero Serra as *presidente* of California missions. Lasuen sought to "denaturalize" the natives: "To make them realize that they are men." Wary fathers feared the return of the converted Indians to a life of savagery, lured by ancestral pagan religion and dark forces lurking in the wilderness.[20]

Chumash expert Bruce Miller notes how many Central Coast Indians died inside the missions "of European enlightenment—hard work, diseases, and an unaccustomed diet." However, the harshness of Spanish servitude, coupled with surviving Native traditions, provided ample inspiration for resistance. Signs of unrest manifested themselves on church floors, bored members of the congregation turning to graffiti rather than God. Neophytes regularly fled Spanish settlements to seek refuge in familiar woods and groves or join up with sympathetic groups. The "heathen" (probably Yokuts rather than Chumash) burned the San Luis Obispo Mission in November 1776, possibly to distract the Spanish while stealing their horses. Chumash Indians deliberately torched the Santa Ynez Mission and adjacent soldiers' quarters during February 1824 in a revolt sparked by the flogging of a resident neophyte.[21]

California missions and presidios along the Camino Real (a trade route linking Spanish enclaves from San Diego to San Francisco) represented epicenters of ecological as well as cultural disruption, with the outward movement of airborne spores and grazing bovines akin to shock waves rippling across the country. Ships off-loaded cattle, sheep, goats, and pigs onto California shores, creatures that immediately delighted in the unfamiliar taste of native grasses. Settlers cleared spaces for European crops, plants, and even gardens, expending vast amounts of energy on reshaping ecology. Unintended ecological consequences followed. Supply ships unknowingly transported insects and less-favored plants ("weeds") to the new land. Ripgut, mustard, and wild oats uprooted native grasses, while foraging cattle overgrazed fragile flora to reveal barren earth. European practices altered the ecological fabric of California, shifting the energy of the land. The Spanish, without realizing, removed the keystone species of the California ecosystem, the Native American. While a few species, such as the grizzly and deer, temporarily prospered from the drop in Indian hunters, a stable environmental system fell under a new process of transformation.[22]

Within ten miles of San Luis Obispo Mission, the Pecho Coast was close enough to experience ecological changes based on fresh cultural paradigms. Seeds of mustard, wild oat, and filaree may have traveled westward to find fertile soil on Pecho bluffs. Determined cattle perhaps worked their way through the winding canyons, receiving a tasty reward of native foliage on reaching the Diablo grasslands. Spaniards probably walked the Pecho Coast as part of territorial exploration or searched the woodlands during efforts to root out fugitive neophytes. However, the infrequent nature of colonial incursions tempered the impact of Spanish rule on the coastal environment. Settlers preferred to fashion land immediately surrounding missions and presidios into colonial gardens and fields, leaving more distant territories for later transformation. Diablo remained a pariah landscape. In essence, a line had been drawn between two worlds. While Spanish colonists drew comfort from their familiar environs, manufactured islands of empire floating above a sea of wilderness, outlying regions such as the Pecho Coast, deemed unsuitable for settlement by their distance from trading trails and tilled fields, became icons of the untamed wild. The undulating hills of the San Luis Range embodied the divide between civilization and isolation, safety and danger. Compared with the regimented lands of Franciscan missions, the Diablo region was chaotic and disorderly. While early explorers had once hoisted wild California as a divine "garden of Eden," the reality of the Pecho Coast suggested a more tangled web of nature. The naming of Diablo Canyon itself (intonating a place of evil and malfeasance) reflected broader Euro-American views of wild nature as a malevolent property.

▪ NINETEENTH-CENTURY RANCH LANDS ▪

On April 27, 1843, a Mexican land grant declared "Rancho Pecho y Islay" the property of Francisco Bodilla (Padillo) on the authority of Governor Micheltorena. The grant encompassed 10,300 acres of land stretching along the Pecho Coast from Pecho Creek (near the southerly tip of the promontory) to Islay Creek (on the northern slope). *Pecho*, Spanish for "breast," sometimes connoted courage but, in the case of the Diablo lands, more likely offered commentary on the shape of the headland. *Islay*, meanwhile, derived from *slay*, the Salinian Indian term for wild cherry. The name of the land grant paid homage to both Native American and Spanish eras of California history. It also inaugurated a new stage in the land-use history of the Diablo lands: private property.

Francisco Bodilla had shuffled into central California as a convict in chains during 1825. On release from prison he decided to stay in the region. Described as "a shady figure often at odds with the law," he nonetheless mounted a successful legal claim to Pecho shores. After securing a land grant, Bodilla took up residence in a cabin on the south rim of Pecho Canyon. Two years later he sold Pecho y Islay to Captain John (Juan) Wilson and James (Diego) Scott for $1,500. They also purchased the adjacent "Canada Los Osos" land grant. Wilson and Scott then successfully petitioned Governor Pio Pico to recognize the combined plot of 32,430 acres, or "Canada de Los Osos y Pecho y Islay," as legally theirs.[23]

Born in Dundee, Scotland, in 1798, seafarer John Wilson captained an English ship reputed to be "the fastest vessel of the coast." Wilson spent several years sailing along the California coast trading hides, tallow, and otter and seal skins. He married into the Mexican aristocracy in 1836. By the time the United States took control of California in 1848, Wilson had established himself as "far and away the wealthiest man in San Luis County." With its crashing ocean waves and weathered feel, the Pecho Coast seemed an ideal location for a sailor to set up home. However, the Wilson family generally resided farther inland, at a two-story house next to the San Luis Obispo Mission (Wilson, Scott, and James McKinley purchased the mission for $510 in December 1845). Living on mission land in the center of San Luis Obispo reflected the high social standing of the Wilson clan. In comparison, the remote, unknown shores of Diablo Canyon threatened to isolate the family from county affairs, and Pecho soil lacked prestige. By 1850 Wilson had accumulated 53,434 acres of ranch and farmland, along with sizable property holdings in San Luis Obispo town. His tax bill totaled $639.20, the highest in the county. For taxation purposes, county supervisors rated top-quality land at $1.25 an acre, yet the Diablo lands came in at just 28 cents per acre. This unusually low valuation reflected the degree of worthlessness attached to the Diablo coastline.[24]

During the 1850s Wilson invested in ranching, acquiring 6,300 head of cattle. In 1851 the captain registered his "Pecho y Islay" breed, allegedly "the

first brand recorded in San Luis Obispo County after American statehood."
Quality cattle roamed the Pecho Coast, although only a small percentage of
the terrain offered them quality feed. Diablo proved marginal land in terms
of its capital return. While the coastal terraces provided bovines with fine pasture, the steeper slopes of the Irish Hills and dense, wooded valleys afforded
limited grazing opportunities. Productive for Native American hunter-gatherers, the coastal environment was not ideally suited for wandering cattle, and
ranchers expended much energy retrieving their stock from Pecho ravines.
The "Diablo" name itself possibly refers to the "devil of a time" spent herd-
ing branded cattle out of the tight and twisting canyon.[25]

The situation changed in 1849 when the California gold rush fueled a sudden demand for beef. The new mines and cities of the Far West needed meaty
sustenance to keep dreams of mineral wealth and prosperity alive. Across the
state, ranchers filled their lands with bovine herds, hoping to trade steers for
bullion. Even the remote and isolated Pecho Coast possibly felt the effect of gold
rush fever, with the Pecho y Islay brand an unlikely hallmark of the mining era
(Captain Wilson's interest in ranching no doubt stemmed from the tasty lure
of the quick buck as much as a fondness for fine cattle). Environmental repercussions were scarcely considered in the keen pursuit of profit. The excesses
of the 1850s cattle era exacerbated problems of land management endemic to
prior decades of colonization. Spanish and Mexican ranchers had paid scant
regard to the deterioration of California rangelands. Typical ranchero practices between the 1830s and 1860s left cattle herds to fend for themselves and
wander roughshod over delicate native grasses. Resource sustainability was
not on the colonial radar. As the historian Hazel Pulling pointed out, "Spanish
and Mexican Rancheros, and indeed the early American range-cattle owners,
were not in the least disturbed by any impending damage to range forage.
The range was grazed for decade after decade, and if the flora changed at all
during the time, little attention was paid to it." Indeed, the native flora usually did change, usurped by Old World plants and consumed by hungry herds.
At Diablo Canyon, Wilson's cattle munched across acres of native grasses on
the Pecho bluffs. The local ecology changed in consequence. An 1858 map
of Rancho "Canada de Los Osos" and "Pecho y Islay" by the U.S. surveyor
general bore the unexpected description of land immediately north of Diablo Canyon as a "Beautiful Plain covered with wildoats." The beautiful, and

exotic, wild oats had flourished in the place of indigenous grasses, the biotic energy of the land transformed by colonial infractions.[26]

Maritime explorers and traders viewed the Pecho Coast from a different perspective than those onshore. Land dwellers approached the coastal bluffs through the Irish Hills and dense, winding canyons, their views framed by the contours of the terrain as well as spiritual and economic dictates. Sailors instead witnessed the broad coastal expanse from passing ships. While colonists focused on acreage and cattle carrying capacity, ocean explorers defined land by its points, length, and oceanographic position. In November 1793 George Vancouver, captain of the HMS *Discovery*, sailed past the Diablo lands during a survey of the California coastline. He described the Pecho Coast (identified by the mark of Buchon) as a "conspicuous promontory," noting its length and "rounding direction about s.36E."[27]

Seafarers nonetheless evinced similar valuations of nature as their land-lubber counterparts, viewing the landscape in terms of profit, power, and resource exploitation. During the early nineteenth century, marine mammals in the waters off Diablo Canyon faced a growing contingent of fishing vessels. The aquatic environment was tapped for its energies in common with terrestrial biota. Russian, Spanish, Mexican, and English sailors, along with Native American hunters, targeted sea otters for their skins and whales for their bone, oil, and blubber. Whaling ships arrived from New Bedford to scout Pacific waters. Moving from one fur-bearer to another, veteran beaver hunters crossed from their traditional killing grounds in the Rockies to the otter territories of California. Equivalent to land-based pursuits where market hunters proudly accumulated piles of bison and wolf skins, marine hunters amassed otter pelts on ship decks and lined their fur-trimmed pockets. Apprehending nature as an abundant storehouse, western exploiters of the aquatic frontier shared the same acquisitiveness and wastefulness of the forty-niners. Faced with an international force of seasoned killers, whales and sea otters relinquished their time-honored coastal routes to patrolling sea vessels. Numbers of marine mammals dwindled accordingly. In 1832 Captain John Rogers Cooper lamented the scarcity of otters: "Whereas there was taken 700 a few years ago, I took but 32 from San Francisco to Monterey and

I do not think we shall get 600 skins on all the coast." Demand for hide and tallow soared during the 1830s, offering coastal vessels a fresh cargo. Veteran sailors farmed the waters of the Pecho Coast, tapping the marine energies of the Pacific to satiate the growing demands of industrial and civic society.[28]

The publication of *Moby-Dick* in 1851 coincided with clear signs of whaling excess in California waters. A fifty-year assault had rendered right and sperm whales as rare and elusive as the mythic white whale hunted down by Captain Ahab. The mysticism and adventure that had marked Pacific waters was no more, leaving deep waters perennially overpopulated with whaling vessels and underpopulated with large marine mammals. In response to declining whale numbers, the industry shifted its attention closer to land. From the 1850s, smaller boats, operating just offshore, homed in on abundant (but less commercially valuable) California grays and humpbacks migrating up and down the coast. San Luis fishermen used Point San Luis, the southerly tip of the Pecho Coast, as a base for whaling operations. The tiny shore and rocks offered a sheltered hauling site ideal for carcass trimming. Locals referred to the landing place as Whaler's Point. Close by lay a small rocky mound just above the waterline, nicknamed "Whaler's Island."

While local hunters no longer committed themselves to long voyages across ocean waters, killing whales close to home still entailed considerable risk. Charles Scammon, who hunted gray whales at lagoons in Baja California during the nineteenth century, explained the popular "devil-fish" tag as "significant of the danger incurred in the pursuit of the animal." Scammon's "devil-fish" migrated along the coast, passing close to Diablo, or Devil's, Canyon. There the species met fishermen from Whaler's Point, armed with sharpened harpoons. However, California's shore-whaling industry proved far from sustainable. The enterprise collapsed during the 1870s in the face of decimated herds and declining prices for whale oil due to new petroleum products. Cheaper and easier-to-procure fuels rendered Diablo's whaling industry moribund.[29]

■ FROM UNEXPECTED DROUGHT ■
TO ENTREPRENEURIAL OPTIMISM

A severe drought between 1862 and 1864 that claimed up to 300,000 cattle and 100,000 sheep brought an end to the California cattle boom. Local historian Annie Morrison blamed the ranchers for the calamity, noting that they traditionally made no preparations for such an emergency: "No hay was raised, no attempt whatever was made to provide food for the cattle, if Nature failed to do it." The industry did not operate by environmental limits. The scenes of turmoil reminded Morrison of the bloody conflict between Union and Confederate armies in the early 1860s: "While in the East men were fighting the awful battles of the Civil War and meeting death, here on the great ranges hundreds of thousands of cattle were fighting a losing battle with Nature." After years of fine pasture and easy pickings, the severe conditions came as a shock to many ranchers. Both Francisco Bodilla and John Wilson died during the period. Amongst an array of titles, Wilson bequeathed Rancho Los Osos to his son, John Wilson, and Pecho y Islay to his daughter, Ramona Hilliard.[30]

Luigi Marre arrived in California in 1854 from Borzonasca, Genoa, aged fourteen. During the 1860s and 1870s Marre traded in cattle, often driving herds from the Mexican border to be sold in San Francisco or Nevada. In 1879 he leased 3,800 acres of land on the southern Pecho Coast from Ramona Hilliard. Following two decades of indifferent land management, the arrival of Marre signaled a renewed interest in molding the Pecho Coast to human design, of tapping its energies in a concentrated manner. Treading a similar path to the late John Wilson, Marre envisaged the land about him as fine cattle country. According to Morrison, Marre quickly emerged as not only "one of the largest stockmen of central California as well as the wealthiest man in San Luis Obispo County," but also "the cattle king of the central coast section." Along with stocking the southern Pecho Coast with domestic animals, he also attempted agriculture. The sloping coastal terraces south of Diablo Canyon provided a degree of fertility and accessibility, and over several decades of ownership the Marre family planted grain, beans, peas, and sugar beets. Marre lived for a time at an adobe on the headland. However, following his purchase of the Rancho San Miguelito land title in 1882, his interest gravitated southward, past Diablo and toward Avila Beach. As a fledgling port and tourist town, the resource potential of Avila far outshone that of nearby Diablo Canyon. Marre acquired the Ocean Hotel as part of the land deal. During the 1880s he entertained the first tourists to frequent San Luis Obispo Bay.[31]

In 1892 San Francisco liveryman Alden Spooner II took out a lease on 6,500 acres of coastline north of Diablo Canyon, the portion of the Pecho y Islay lands unoccupied by Luigi Marre. In 1905 he extended his property northward by purchasing the Bernard Coll ranch. Spooner named his venture El Pecho Ranch after the original Pecho y Islay grant. He built a simple cabin on the bluffs next to Buchon Landing (now Spooner's Cove), north of Buchon Point, with fine ocean views. He quarried rock near the landing point to provide materials for a breakwater at Avila (then Port Harford). The subsequent tunnel (or "glory hole") through the cliff side provided Spooner with a loading chute for transporting goods such as wheat and barley onto docked vessels. Diablo became a center of local trade. The *San Luis Obispo Morning Tribune* remarked upon this "new shipping point . . . of much importance to this neighborhood" in October 1892. Enthused by the possibilities of trade and export, Spooner expanded his output of dairy products. He dammed Islay Creek, using an elaborate scheme of trenches, pulleys, and a waterwheel to power his milk house and increase butter production. Diablo was diversifying its role as an energy provider, taking on small-scale hydropower technology alongside traditional agricultural and ranching operations. It was becoming a dedicated enterprise landscape. Spooner even tried his hand at grain production. The *Morning Tribune* declared the first year of planting "a brilliant success . . . The crop averaged 2500 punds [sic] to the acre." He also kept around five hundred cattle and a number of well-bred horses on the ranch. Spooner built his personal success on the Pecho Coast, taking full advantage of its coastal access, fine pastures, and winding streams. Displaying considerable entrepreneurial verve, he fully exploited Diablo's energy resources and adeptly linked the remote Pecho lands to the wider forces sweeping California at the turn of the century. The basic three-room cabin on the bluffs became a ten-room ranch house, a residential testament to his growing enterprise.[32]

Both Spooner and Marre eagerly stamped their authority on the land, transforming portions of the coast into fields, pasture, even pigpens, according to the rubrics of Western civilization and economic progress. In contrast to former Chumash residents of the Pecho Coast, late-nineteenth-century settlers exercised little restraint when managing local habitat. The ethics of acquisition cast nature as a simple raw material for conversion into profit.

Technological innovations and accessible trade markets broadened the scale of change. Having imported the first Holt Caterpillar tractor to the county by way of his landing cove, Alden Spooner worked the landscape with bold, abrasive strokes. Steel machinery replaced Chumash stone tools. Both Spooner and a man named Hazard, who owned a ranch on the northern edge of the Pecho Coast, planted Australian eucalyptus trees on their properties, a species that took root at the expense of other flora. Monocultural groves replaced complex ecosystems. Californians planted eucalyptus for quick timber, as a cash crop, but the wood fell short of expectations. Several decades passed before horticulturists realized the long-term environmental repercussions. From the first bovine hooves and alien seeds to modern tractors and exotic plantings, the momentum of change had gathered speed on the Pecho Coast. The headland still remained on the periphery of development, but by the turn of the century Diablo no longer appeared the wild land of precolonial times. Rickety fences amongst overgrown bushes and cattle wandering Pecho bluffs indicated a pastoral, or ranchero, landscape. The noise of farm machinery heralded further energy transformations.

In the 1890s San Luis Obispo County financed a breakwater extending southward from Whaler's Point to protect vessels docked at Port Harford (now Port San Luis/Avila Beach) from adverse Pacific weather. Following the loss of the ocean steamer *Queen of the Pacific* in 1888, Congress meanwhile provided $50,000 for a lighthouse at Point San Luis. The development of the coast augmented the hopes and ambitions of local business magnates. Marre fancied the Central Coast as a California trade center. In February 1892 he wrote a letter to the *Morning Tribune* imploring citizens not to hold back development of a county-funded rail service linking the port with a main statewide line, likening California to "a strong man lying with his feet in the bay, his head pillowed on the Sierra Nevadas, his arms stretched out with Los Angeles sitting on one hand and San Francisco on the other, and the Southern Pacific railroad running across his breast." Marre exaggerated Port Harford's significance to the rest of California, and the future of the region lay in oil, not steam.[33]

A "PIECE OF ROUGH COUNTRY"

In 1911 English émigré J. Smeaton Chase rode along the coastline on horseback, hoping to take one last look at California before "the hurrying stream of Progress" swept "the older manner of life in the land" away. Entertained at Avila Beach with California stories, Shakespeare, cigars, and locally caught rabbit, Chase considered his contour map which "showed an interesting piece of rough country lying near the coast, which would be missed if I took the direct road." This "piece of rough country" was the Pecho Coast.

On the hills by Diablo, Chase discovered a burned forest of knob-cone pine. Chase noted how "most of the old trees [knob-cone pine] were dead," yet "around them flourishing squads of pinelings were growing. They were already bearing cones, as if Nature had hurried to forestall another fire, which, if it had come before the young trees bore their fruit, would have ended the succession." Chase construed the recovery of the pines as "a vivid illustration of St. Paul's eloquent argument for the resurrection." Biotic succession on the edges of the Pecho Coast proved to Chase the productivity of California's native ecology, albeit courtesy of divine handiwork.

At the same time, Chase seemed threatened by the lingering wildness and remoteness of the region. His horse, Chino, nearly lost his footing on the hill ridges. Chase stayed overnight at a cabin that "was deserted and had fallen into the quick decay that overtakes man's abandoned outposts in the wilderness." The following day he encountered a rattlesnake in Diablo Creek: "We had a lively engagement for a minute or two, but as I was not wearing my revolver and he was too discreet to come into the open, I had the mortification of seeing him slip into a cranny where neither shot, stick, nor stone could reach him." Chase usually killed any rattlesnake he came across, and regretted missing the "evil-doer" at Diablo.

Despite expressing distaste for development along the California coast, Chase brought a little of the pioneer spirit with him on his travels, the explorer's discomfort in the Diablo wilds and excuses for killing being reminiscent of a typical settler mentality. After a "debate" with his horse over the arduousness of the journey and the accuracy of "Uncle Sam's map," Chase eventually found an exit from Diablo Creek and headed northward to Morro Bay.[34]

■ TWENTIETH-CENTURY SIRENS OF CHANGE ■

The First World War offered farmers across the United States the opportunity to make a profit on their agricultural commodities. Prices soared on the dried navy bean, an ideal emergency food with no need for refrigeration. Crops brought in as much as $10,000 to $15,000 per harvest. The "bean boom" hit San Luis Obispo County, with local farmers temporarily abandoning their traditional harvests in preference for the money-spinning crop. Spooner and the Marre family duly began planting barley and pink beans on their Pecho ranches. In response to wartime prices, the two men increased their crop beyond fertile coastal terraces onto land unfit for sustained agriculture. Harold Miossi, writing in 1973, described how "beans were farmed even on the steeper hillsides where the plow lines are still visible." Fleeting prosperity left its mark on the Diablo lands, the exhaustion of the local environment testifying to the primacy of profit over ecological stewardship.[35]

Meanwhile, concerns grew over the vulnerability of Port San Luis to wartime attack. U.S. infantry units defended the valuable oil supplies and shipment operations at Avila. Coast Artillery units occupied Diablo lands, transforming the headland into a strategic military point. Military officials considered the Pecho Coast vulnerable to enemy landings. Soldiers conjured images of Axis invaders wreaking havoc at Diablo, a foreign foe far more formidable than the native rattler encountered by Chase. Despite its distance from military conflict, the Pecho Coast was temporarily enlisted in America's global war machine, a vital strategic outpost. Generals plotting total war transformed even the remotest, wildest, and least significant places into hypothetical battlefields, sometimes war zones.

During the 1900s and 1910s Alden Spooner remained eminently in command of his ranching business. Spooner not only sported "some of the finest Holstein cattle to be seen in the county," but a ranch that was "modern in equipment," with "the machinery operated by steam power." Spooner had turned a wild plot into a dairy, cattle ranch, and agricultural endeavor, utilizing new technology to craft a successful energy landscape. The Diablo lands bespoke hard work, progress, and capitalist vigor. His enthusiasm for working the soil paid homage to the Jeffersonian pastoral ideal, and such land toils rewarded Spooner with financial gain and local esteem. Yet behind the success lay a coastline of diverted streams, quarried rocks, cut timber, and overgrazed grasses. The transformed, humanized state of Diablo relayed a transfer of power in the natural landscape from biotic agency to human engineering. Dominant cultural values had locked land resources into a process of harvesting, coastal forces harnessed for the production of everyday consumables. The ecological legacy of Spooner's achievements nonetheless passed unnoticed. He died in 1920, leaving the ranch to his three sons.[36]

During the conservative 1920s national prohibition reached as far as California. The outlawing of the sale, manufacture, and transportation of alcohol forced drinking under the table, and procuring liquor became a clandestine act. Smuggling came to the Pecho Coast. The remote coves attracted shady importers of Canadian alcohol during the 1920s and early 1930s. Pecho smugglers disguised their contraband by stashing it in "camouflaged produce trucks piled high with hampers of peas, and then routed to metropolitan markets." The Great Depression stretched county resources and tested the resolve of struggling Obispans. Poor Portuguese families living in the Irish Hills behind Diablo relied on a local grocer for provisions, who in turn required a loan from the mayor to keep his shop running. Both the Spooner and Marre ranches survived the depression, although scant information remains concerning how Pecho residents endured such difficulties. With the high prices of the "bean boom" a distant memory, Japanese tenant farmers working at the Spooner ranch eked out an existence cultivating peas on coastal terraces.[37]

The surprise attack on Pearl Harbor in December 1941 spawned a backlash against Japanese Americans across America. "Free shaves for Japs," advertised one barbershop in California, with the small print accepting no responsibility for "accidents." Removed by the government to a War Relocation Camp, the Japanese farmers at Diablo quickly became victims of wartime prejudice. Elliot Curry, in an article on wartime San Luis Obispo, described the "general fear and suspicion that the Japanese might have saboteurs or spies along the coast, ready to direct an attack on California." The Pecho Coast apparently represented "one of the most likely spots for an enemy hideout" in the county, and six hundred cavalrymen searched the Diablo lands for lurking foes. Such sentiments perhaps reflected lingering Euro-American antipathy toward untamed spaces. At the very least, the military encountered substantial problems navigating the coastal landscape. While the undulating terrain supposedly offered ideal protection for invaders, Curry related how "neither riders nor horses were ready for the oak and chaparral covered mountains and deep cut canyons." The two cavalry units used at Diablo were mechanized soon after.[38]

In 1942 the Spooners sold their 9,000-acre ranch to Oscar and Ruby Field for $250,000. The Fields settled down on the Pecho Coast, establishing a ranch near Point Buchon. In 1954 they sold the northernmost half of their land (4,500 acres) to Irene Starkey McAllister. She named her new entitlement Montana de Oro, or Mountain of Gold. The Marre Land and Cattle Company meanwhile continued to run the southern Pecho Coast. During the Second World War the Coast Artillery, along with cavalry units, returned to Diablo. Between ninety and three hundred troops reinforced the Coast Guard at Point San Luis Lighthouse following Pearl Harbor. San Luis Obispo County resembled one large military camp during World War II, with 436,000 men receiving combat training at Camp Roberts in the far north. An Army Air Corps field at Paso Robles, naval station at Morro Bay, and Camp Cook (later Vandenberg Air Force Base) added to the martial contingent. The evident military presence alerted locals to the changing shape and fortunes of their county. Since the 1880s the "sleepy little Spanish town" had gradually been incorporated into mainstream California, awakened by the sound of road and rail traffic to the developmental opportunities of the Golden State. While still retaining a semblance of its isolation and wildness, Diablo had not escaped these pressures. Priorities of economic production and military security ensured a developing interest in the headland. A siren on top of San Luis Obispo's city hall announced the end of World War II "with a mighty series of blasts," echoing the success of American atomic bombs dropped on Japan. The "all-purpose" siren sounded an American victory tied to the dawning nuclear age. The howl of the siren proved prescient. In subsequent years a sanguine group of atomic industrialists would focus their attentions on Diablo Canyon. As Elliot Curry observed, "it was plain to see that San Luis Obispo would never be the same again."[39]

TWO From Cattle Ranch to
Atomic Homestead

In the immediate years following World War II, Diablo remained a landscape of anonymity. Traditional small-time ranching and agricultural pursuits continued on the coastline. A slow pace of change, together with Diablo's geographical isolation, meant that few citizens had reason to pay heed to events on the headland. In the 1960s control of Diablo passed from one pioneer to another. The meaning of Diablo shifted dramatically. As one California newspaper noted, for "many years" the Marre family had been "pioneers in San Luis Obispo County." In 1966 the Marres leased six hundred acres of their land to Pacific Gas and Electric. Once a combination of "rough-and-ready pioneer gas and electric companies" dating back to 1852, PG&E could claim a frontier past of its own. By the 1960s the company had grown massively to become the state's main energy provider—and a nuclear trailblazer. Diablo Canyon appeared an ideal place to venture further into atomic power and to buttress California's energy empire. In June 1967 the promotional magazine *PG&E Life* explained to its readers that an isolated stretch of coastline, "an area of private ranchland, where hardy Mexican cattle graze on the short native grasses," had been secured for the construction of an "essential power plant." This remote and rural headland, a picture of California past, would be transformed by PG&E into one of California's newest energy landscapes.[1]

▪ ▪ ▪ ▪

IN 1953 President Dwight Eisenhower had offered the nuclear dream not just to California but to the whole world in his "Atoms for Peace" speech to the United Nations. One year later the U.S. Atomic Energy Act allowed private utilities to develop "peaceful atoms" for electricity generation. In 1957 Eisenhower started up the first American commercial nuclear power plant, at Shippingport, Pennsylvania, using a magic wand prop for visual impact. During the same year government subsidies helped entice Pacific Gas to join the atomic era. Together with General Electric, PG&E constructed what it dubbed a "pioneer plant," an experimental reactor called Vallecitos, in Livermore Valley, California, not far from the nuclear weapons research being conducted at Lawrence Livermore National Laboratory.[2]

A wave of popular optimism, led by both science and government, surrounded atomic energy in the 1950s and early 1960s. The atom was commonly connected with a fresh technological culture, an advanced civilization that would guarantee American success at home and abroad. Atomic power spelled cheap electricity for all. The more kilowatts available, the more an automated society could establish itself, and the more free time everyday Americans would have. President Lyndon Johnson expressed a widely held opinion: "By learning the secret of the atom, we have given mankind—for the first time in history—all the energy that mankind can possibly use." By the late 1960s reactor vendor General Electric faced a rush of orders from utilities across the country.[3]

PG&E eagerly boarded the atomic bandwagon. Recognizing huge technological advances ahead, PG&E promised a new era for California energy provision through developing the "fuel of the future." The company bought heavily into nuclear engineering and encouraged its investors to do likewise. Uranium replaced gold as the new ore of optimism for California. Energy corporations had found a mineral capable of powering postwar development in the Golden State. A welcome period of energy abundance seemed just around the corner.[4]

PG&E advertised for investors to "Join the Second Gold Rush." The "rush" was to supply enough atomic "gold" to fuel California's post-1945 boom in residential and economic development. Realistic predictions that demand could soon outstrip supply, that the "appetite for energy in home, factory and field has grown even faster than the population," brought a sense of urgency to energy planning. Noting the rise in state residents from 9,452,000 in 1945 to 19,469,000 in 1966, the corporation highlighted a pressing need for new energy resources. Fossil fuels could not be relied upon to keep up with California's meteoric growth. Nuclear power could plug any shortfall. As one PG&E document explained, "Happily, atomic energy assures mankind a source of energy that will last long after other fuels are used up." PG&E's conviction that a "growing California has growing needs" propelled plans to double the company's electrical capacity every ten years. The company responded with a "mammoth-scale state wide PG&E expansion program" that promoted the use of nuclear power. The atom seemed ideal for a state with boundless possibilities but restricted energy resources. As Californians were taking to futuristic new kitchens and power-hungry appliances, introducing an innovative energy source to match domestic changes appeared only natural in the forward-looking Golden State. Only the question of suitable land remained.[5]

Unfortunately, in its search for undeveloped real estate PG&E regularly acquired sites of natural beauty for power plant construction. In such cases California's development seemed to clash directly with California's conservation. The utility's list included Morro Bay, next to a volcanic peak, and Moss Landing, an attractive coastal spot. PG&E invested approximately $4 million between 1958 and 1964 in a scheme for a nuclear reactor at Bodega Head, fifty miles north of San Francisco. At the same time that Alfred Hitchcock filmed *The Birds* (1963) at Bodega, some residents expressed concern over a nuclear rather than a "natural" threat materializing on the promontory. Birds swooping down to peck to death innocent locals signified one disaster fantasy for Bodega; another concerned an earthquake-induced atomic incident. A determined campaign, under the leadership of Berkeley resident David Pesonen, was launched against PG&E. The outcome of the controversy seemed uncertain until a geologist, Pierre Saint-Amand, discovered that an auxiliary line from the San Andreas Fault ran through the site of the proposed reactor. PG&E sensibly withdrew its project.

In 1963 the utility purchased from Union Oil the Nipomo Dunes, representing 1,100 acres of coastal land south of San Luis Obispo. PG&E's acquisition was based upon the idea of constructing a line of nuclear power plants to serve the south coastal area. The local newspaper, the *San Luis Obispo County Telegram-Tribune,* interpreted five reactors as a lucky number: "When the five projects are completed, San Luis Obispo County will be number one 'power county' in the state." However, Nipomo had other admirers who preferred a recreational purpose for the sand dunes. Local conservationists campaigned for the picturesque site to become a state park rather than a nuclear park. Encouraged by local members, the Sierra Club, renowned for its conservation battles, took an interest in the plight of the dunes, and club officials recommended the preservation of Nipomo in June 1963.[6]

Just as the situation over Nipomo seemed to be heading toward what the local press thought would be "a long hard battle" or "another Bodega Head," confrontation was averted by a diplomatic offensive. PG&E wisely began a dialogue with conservationists. The company met with Kathy Jackson, a local Sierran; club directors Richard Leonard and Will Siri; and Leonard's wife, Doris, who represented Conservation Associates, a small foundation that mediated between industrialists and conservationists. Both sides courted each other. When Jackson took PG&E staff on a nature trail across the dunes to win them over, Pacific Gas returned the favor by giving her a nuclear power plant tour. Jackson in particular was dedicated to saving Nipomo Dunes and felt a special affinity with the place. "The Dunes offer tranquility for the human spirit," she later related.[7]

To the great relief of Jackson and her peers, the corporation agreed to consider other options to construction at Nipomo. In a corporate document discussing alternative sites, Diablo Canyon emerged as a likely substitute for Nipomo. Along with topography, rights of way, and transportation issues, PG&E considered public reaction an important factor in the placement of its nuclear project. The company rated Diablo "OK" in terms of community acceptance, with the judgment being that "Resources Agency, conservation groups, County, and many local organizations approve." By comparison, sites surveyed at Point Sierra Nevada, Morro Bay, and Point Sal appeared complicated by residential development and park use. The utility settled on Diablo Canyon as the preferred location for its new reactors. In May 1966 the Sierra Club board of directors recommended that the club consider Diablo Canyon "a satisfactory alternative site" to the Nipomo Dunes in order for PG&E to release the latter property for state park purchase. PG&E emerged as a veritable ally of conservation and duly pledged to transfer the dunes to state park lands.[8]

In San Luis Obispo County most residents welcomed plans for a nuclear plant at Diablo Canyon. In Walt Disney's promotional cartoon *Our Friend the Atom* (1956), a fisherman discovered an atomic vessel with its own magical genie. The nuclear genie granted humanity "power" (in the form of nuclear energy), "food and health" (courtesy of radioisotopes and research), and "peace." The Diablo plant promised the more tangible gifts of tax revenue, jobs, and new schools for the San Luis Obispo community. Pacific Gas promoted atomic energy as unrivaled in terms of economics, environmental protection, human safety, and aesthetics. The company's predictions of a $150 million price tag and "electricity at a lower cost than any post-war steam or hydro plant on the PG&E system" went unchallenged, as experts knew no different. "Environment is our concern," PG&E further declared, illustrating the point by photographs contrasting a clean-looking Vallecitos with the smoke and smog of traditional factories and power plants. Nuclear power came with none of the pollution problems associated with fossil fuels. The atomic project at Diablo appeared such a boon to California that few people considered it necessary to delve too deeply into any negative effects associated with nuclear power. The utility justifiably claimed "widespread" support for its nuclear project across the county and state. *PG&E Progress* magazine noted that the new plant was "expected to be another landmark in the economical generation of electric energy."[9]

■ THE SIERRA CLUB DEBATE: ■
SEEDS OF DOUBT AND DISSENSION

While PG&E moved forward with its plans for Diablo, all was not well in the Sierra Club. Club directors had initially accepted the sacrifice of Diablo Canyon as a means to protect the Nipomo Dunes. With immediate attention focused on the plight of the dunes, few concerned themselves with the fate of the canyon. Diablo was simply presumed to be of little interest to conservationists. In their desire to rush through a deal with PG&E, Sierra directors labeled Diablo worthless. Those who vouched for the region's having "no special merit" included Kathy Jackson, who cherished Nipomo above all other landscapes. Only two directors, at the most, even knew of Diablo, while none had experienced that section of coastline for any length of time. However, there were signs of doubt and dissension at the crucial board meeting. Director Frederick Eissler disagreed with the negative assessment of the region, while executive director David Brower expressed reservations over reaching a decision too quickly.[10]

Director Martin Litton, who missed the May meeting, was angered to find on his return to California that a land deal had been struck. Litton had seen the Pecho Coast firsthand, and he immediately set about challenging the board's decision. He sent a letter to the president of PG&E, Shermer Sibley, claiming that the club vote had been "fraudulently obtained" (referring to descriptions at the meeting of Diablo as a "treeless slot"), and indicated that the issue was far from over. He also requested of Sibley: "I hope you will not consider this matter settled until you have personally watched the wonderful pageantry of marine wildlife below the low bluffs of the proposed site and have walked into and through the exquisite woodland of Diablo Canyon itself." With the aid of his prodigious camera skills and vociferous campaigning, Litton set about transforming Diablo from an unknown place into one valued for its natural worth. He declared: "If the people of all the United States had an opportunity to walk through this canyon I wonder what they would say about this plant." Diablo Canyon was about to be thrust into the public limelight. Its remote, uninhabited, and untouched qualities made it an ideal site not just for a nuclear plant, but also for a nature park. Diablo had attracted both nuclearists and naturalists.[11]

By early 1967 two sides had emerged within the Sierra Club. Leonard, Siri, and the acclaimed nature photographer Ansel Adams represented the key proponents of the deal, while Brower, Litton, and Eissler became its leading challengers. The save-Diablo lobby wanted both Nipomo and Diablo protected from development and offered the southern Pecho Coast as "the kind of remote, unspoiled, essentially natural terrain that the club has normally tried hard to preserve for the enjoyment of future generations." Pro-dealers responded by lauding the unique splendors of Nipomo over the "typical" canyons of the Pecho Coast. One Sierran reminded his colleagues: "The importance of saving the dunes was and is uppermost. Diablo Canyon is not unique to the point that no substitutions can be had." Newsletters and articles during 1966 and 1967 usually described the dunes as "rare" and "exceptional," while Diablo's nature was derided as "common" and "barren." It was all too easy to envisage Nipomo as a nature park and Diablo as the nuclear construction site.[12]

At a board meeting in January 1967 the save-Diablo group brought forward a petition for the club's members to vote on the issue, with opposing arguments to be presented in the February edition of the *Sierra Club Bulletin*. The wording of the petition and the proposed contents of the *Bulletin* were fiercely debated. In the final version of the *Bulletin* Siri and Adams asserted that "Diablo Canyon was prophetically named. It grew as a contentious issue out of the moving sands and rare flora of the Nipomo Dunes to sow doubt and dissension." Diablo Canyon was cast as the serpent in the Garden (or Dunes) of Eden, a malignant force luring conservationists from their true task. In the April referendum, members were presented with the choice to reaffirm or reject board policy concerning Nipomo Dunes and Diablo Canyon.[13]

■ SAVING CALIFORNIA'S COASTLINE ■

In order to compete with the natural charms of Nipomo, the save-Diablo lobby constructed the Pecho Coast as an equally alluring landscape. Diablo, with its tall trees, rugged formations, sheer cliffs, and waterfalls, fast became a place of monumental scenery. Eissler promoted Diablo Canyon as "the region's geographical and scenic climax" with "the embayment at Diablo Canyon . . . the largest most impressive along this Point Buchon coast." Litton claimed that the coastal live oaks came close to world-record size, with one specimen's lower branches spreading out 123 feet, another roughly 129 feet. He wrote to Stewart Udall, U.S. secretary of the interior, over the potential loss of Diablo and its record-breaking trees. Photographs of the Canyon focused on complex spiderwebs of oak branches winding around each other in intricate patterns. The pictures relayed an alternative form of natural beauty to that of Nipomo's stark sand shapes. Diablo's oaks were all the more impressive given the opposition's contention of a "treeless slot" at the original board meeting. Thomas Jukes, a Berkeley biochemist, attempted to undermine Diablo's newfound dendron icon (and those members in the Sierra Club's Atlantic Chapter who believed in it) by insisting, "Hills far away look green; from New York, 3,000 miles away, the vision of a coast live oak in Diablo Canyon assumes the proportions of a giant redwood." Pro-dealers claimed that the trees were in fact dying.[14]

Reflecting the club's preference for natural areas unspoiled by development, Diablo was duly offered as a pristine wild landscape. One member suggested: "The Diablo Canyon area is of finer value than the Nipomo Dunes area since it is *roadless* and not near other municipal areas and industrial plants." While Diablo featured a single dirt track and was surrounded by wild land, Nipomo suffered a highway close by and an oil refinery in full view, already amounting to an ugly energy landscape. The *Pasadena Star-News* related how conservationists wanted to save Diablo "because the area is unspoiled. The sea life, the animal life, the plant life are untouched." Eissler in particular idealized Diablo, offering it as a "landscape made by the forces of nature, by the Creator. It is not landscape altered or created by man with his buildings and highways and his artificially designed and controlled plantings. . . . Here at Diablo is Californian landscape virtually the way it was originally created. In a real sense it is God's country."[15]

Pro-dealers vehemently argued against moves to portray Diablo Canyon as virgin wilderness. They drew attention to the region's lengthy ranching history. Doris Leonard pointed out "places badly eroded from overgrazing" in the canyon itself. Jackson resiliently argued that "Diablo Canyon has not been wilderness since 1832. It is an overgrazed oak woodland and chaparral canyon." As for claims of a roadless sanctuary, Diablo may not have had Highway 1, but "little mention is made of the good dirt road which runs the 3-mile length of this obviously overgrazed 'wilderness' canyon; and no listing of the buildings existing at the end of this road: a substantial padlocked tool shed and a privy." To pro-dealers, Diablo had already been spoiled, and it did not matter if a tool shed and a privy were to be soon replaced by two nuclear reactors and a turbine building.[16]

Defenders of Diablo disagreed and stubbornly continued to offer the Pecho Coast as a geographic capsule untouched by state development of any kind. By the 1960s the California coast commonly served as a symbol of the state's recreational spirit, a vision that also accorded a premier position to the automobile. California's scenic coastal drive, several hundred miles long, marked most of the coastline. The Pecho Coast was noteworthy for avoiding such recreation-spawned development. Highway planners had chosen a route behind the San

Luis Range, the hills providing Pecho with a natural defense from the highway. Diablo's defenders proved keen to promote the canyon as the only place in coastal California south of Humboldt County untouched by roads. Given the ubiquity of the freeway in American culture, the southern Pecho Coast seemed especially remote and wild. The Diablo area was allegedly "the only extensive coastland still unmarred by highway or railroad rights of way in 600 miles of shoreline between the Mexican border and Humboldt County." A draft Sierra Club resolution suggested: "The area is indeed of scenic importance to the state and, in view of rapid encroachment of development of seacoast, to the nation as a whole." Diablo's importance was being defined by the loss of similar coast to human activity, industrial, residential, and recreational.[17]

The quarterly conservation journal *Cry California* showed the kind of concern vented over Diablo Canyon to be in line with a growing sense of unease among state conservationists over coastal development. Throughout the 1960s the journal carried articles detailing the myriad threats to local coastal environments. In "Life and Death along the California Coast," Vladimir and Nada Kovalik contrasted an elegant photograph of the Nipomo Dunes as "the living coast" with a picture of Huntington Beach, its "nodding donkey" (of the oil-pump variety) and ugly telegraph poles symbolizing "the dead coast." The tangible effects of environmental ignorance could be found all along the California coastline, from southern oil refining to northern logging. To conservationists, California was fast becoming a dirtied energy landscape. Martin Litton drew attention to Raymond Dasmann's warning in *The Destruction of California* (1966), and used Diablo as a case study: "In The Destruction of California, Ray Dasmann says the way to stop 'growth' is not to prepare for it. It is a sad mistake to believe that PG&E's ambition must be accommodated by the Sierra Club, when in our hearts we know that it can only result in the destruction of what we hold dear." To Litton, the largest live oaks' giving way to a nuclear switchyard appeared just one example of greed outweighing conscience.[18]

The canyon represented the once-typical California coastline that by the 1960s had mostly been transformed by industry and capital. Diablo's defenders suggested that its representative character deserved protection just as much as the unique dunes of Nipomo. Representative landscape was arguably as important as monumental scenery. Diablo symbolized a last chance to save a quintessential slice of wild California shoreline. Litton and Eissler's 1967 *Bulletin* piece appropriately went by the title "The Diablo Canyon Area: California's Last Unspoiled Pastoral Coastline." Diablo also served as an uncomfortable reminder of the club's failure to protect more of the California coast. At the February 1967 board meeting, members linked Diablo with a broader policy goal, noting that "preservation of the scenic coastlands that are left in California should be one of our highest conservation concerns of a priority at least equal in importance with the redwoods and Grand Canyon issues."[19]

Sierra Club directors were not alone in their fears for California's wildness. Prominent local conservationists such as Ian McMillan and Harold Miossi lambasted the Diablo plant for its effects upon the county. Living the life of a "rural homesteader" as a wheat and cattle rancher near Shandon (thirty miles northeast of San Luis Obispo), McMillan resented industrial intrusions. Diablo's appeal for him lay in its isolation from twentieth-century forces and its small-scale ranching heritage. The Pecho Coast was part of "cow country," the landscape of San Luis Obispo County he had grown up with and come to cherish. But while McMillan and other local conservationists tried desperately to hold on to their traditional ranching and agricultural lifestyle, PG&E offered the region a new atomic age that promised to turn "swords into plowshares" and "spears into pruning hooks." Nuclear power symbolized fertility, the breeder reactor as atom farmer, the taming of the atom compared to plowing and harvesting fields. A nuclear plant both symbolized and encouraged development in the region. The majority of San Luis residents welcomed the atomic boom in revenue, incomes, and jobs. Meanwhile, the likes of Miossi and McMillan believed they were losing a larger landscape than just the 585 acres that would be directly consumed by the plant at Diablo. Rural, peaceful, and endearing San Luis Obispo seemed also at stake. PG&E represented an uninvited nuclear pioneer, with a wagon train of other unwelcome developers sure to be following its electricity cables and bulldozer tracks.[20]

▪ **THE PARK QUESTION** ▪

When Diablo Canyon was first raised as an alternative plant site in 1966, a lot of work had already been done to secure park status for Nipomo Dunes.

Trips had been led through the shifting sand hills. Many believed that the area was overdue for protection. By contrast, preserving Diablo for parkland signified a new idea and lacked a groundswell of support. Whereas a 1965 statement of Sierra Club policy described the dunes region as one with "unique grandeur of distinguished park value," initial discussions of Diablo noted that "the site has no special merit as a scenic or natural area such as other parts of the coast possess." Critics argued that Diablo amounted to a lost cause in recreational terms—even if PG&E officials were defeated, the canyon would likely serve as a residential area rather than a wildlife refuge. Pro-dealers further drew attention to the state park acquisition list that failed to grant Diablo priority status. Sierra Club member Mrs. Harold C. Bradley wrote to the *San Francisco Chronicle* asking why, if Diablo was so important, nobody had taken steps to secure the area before the nuclear controversy began.[21]

Frederick Eissler proved vociferous in his defense of Diablo Canyon. Visiting the area convinced him that "the whole territory is of superb park quality." Eissler pointed out at the Sierra Club's 1966 board meeting that the Pacific Coast Recreational Area Survey (1959) had rated the Point Buchon region as equal to the Santa Maria Dunes. The National Park Service, which carried out the survey, asserted that this "large, unspoiled area possesses excellent seashore values and should be acquired for public recreation and conservation of its natural resources." A save-Diablo draft resolution for the club in 1967 carried forward this idea but met with little success.[22]

The establishment of Montana de Oro State Park a few miles north of Diablo Canyon only complicated the situation. In 1965 the state of California purchased 4,481 acres of coastal land between Morro Bay and Point Buchon. Supporters of the new park were tempted by ideas of expansion southward, especially given the alternative fate of the Pecho region. Eissler hoped that Montana could be enlarged to include the Diablo lands, a promising idea given their ecological similarity and shared historical past. He extended the praise of the California Department of Parks and Recreation for Montana to the surrounding area, suggesting that "the high rating received by Montana de Oro" applied "with similar cogency to the Diablo region." Local conservationists also pointed to plans already in existence that incorporated Diablo lands into the state park. A 1965 General Development Study by the Division of Parks and Beaches for Montana de Oro referred to the whole area's "outstanding resource potential." The Division of Parks and Beaches had its own development plans for Diablo: the installation of recreational infrastructure and facilities. Proposed development of the region included various campgrounds, car parks, a golf course complete with clubhouse, and a "marine development" close to where Pacific Gas planned to construct its nuclear reactors. Transforming Diablo into a state park implied significant changes, albeit not on the same scale as PG&E's nuclear plans. Financial considerations compromised securing the region for recreational use. Meanwhile, pro-dealers claimed the "representative coast" was represented enough in Montana de Oro, without the need to secure any more shoreline.[23]

▪ LOOKING TO SCIENCE TO SOLVE THE DEBATE ▪

Looking back on the Diablo-Nipomo controversy, Richard Leonard suggested that the issue pivoted on "the relative natural values of the two locations." However, in practice the Sierra Club struggled to compare the two places without conceding to personal bias. A clear opportunity existed for science to offer a much-needed sense of objectivity in the disagreements over Diablo's worth. Scientific reports of various kinds circulated through the club's offices during 1966 and 1967. Unfortunately, they revealed not so much indisputable facts as a highly subjective debate, not far removed from the board's altercations. One botanical report by Clare Hardham rightly identified Diablo as having "become a symbol of the destruction of our environment by the population explosion" and argued that a thorough investigation seemed vital. However, Hardham's work was compromised by political comment on the club ("I am sure that a conservationist who refuses to consider alternative solutions to a problem will end by destroying more than he saves") and unconvincing statements on Diablo ("The only reason to mention these oaks is to demonstrate that those who admire them do so emotionally rather than with any real appreciation of their nature or significance"). By contrast, botanist Carl Sharsmith lauded Diablo as "an unchanged natural area" and a "fine place to linger!" where the visitor "is reminded of certain passages of Muir's writings concerning other places and times."[24]

Neither Hardham's nor Sharsmith's reports indicated the clinical detachment associated with modern science and its assumed advantages. Both experts proved partisan in their contentions. The local *Telegram-Tribune* carried a story entitled "Botanists Battle on Diablo's Value" detailing the key players in the "undeclared war" over "uniqueness and value." Hardham reported not only to the Sierra Club but also to PG&E. She explained to Pacific Gas that the "average Conservationist, you must realize, is governed more by sentiment than reason or knowledge and the biologically educated conservationists curse them just as much as you must." As she saw it, on one side stood the objective science of "real" biologists, PG&E, and a few Sierra Clubbers, while on the other side were arrayed those who wanted to save Diablo, who "know the jargon of biology, especially ecology, though they do not, in my opinion, know what it is really about."[25]

In January 1967 the board commissioned a committee to investigate the ecology of Diablo Canyon. At the February meeting the committee presented its findings: that "the Diablo Canyon region was remarkably worthy of preservation." Nonetheless, new scientific comment failed to reverse the majority view on Diablo's sacrifice. Eissler's appeal for the findings to be honored, that the "club's greatest strength . . . is its appeal to the nation's conservation conscience on the basis of firmly-grounded facts," went ignored.[26]

■ UNCERTAIN HAZARDS ■

Sierra Club arguments over Diablo were also confused by the uncertain impact of a nuclear power plant on a coastal landscape. Pro-dealers argued that Diablo Canyon would effectively hide PG&E's nuclear plant from the county. Jackson suggested that people would be able to walk the Pecho Coast "and yet *could* be unaware of power plants nested in nearby Diablo Canyon." A nuclear plant was essentially treated as a development issue— little different from a suburban subdivision or a shopping mall. The club's Mother Lode Chapter commented: "Many people feel that nuclear power plants contemplated for construction along the California coast are no more aesthetically damaging to the beauty of the coast than the multitude of industrial and tract housing developments which continue to proliferate without significant opposition from conservation groups." Mother Lode wanted to know why so much time had been wasted on Diablo when other construction schemes passed unchallenged.[27]

By contrast, defenders of Diablo Canyon portrayed a nuclear plant as a total devourer of nature. On first hearing of the Diablo deal, Litton was shocked by the club's "endorsing a PG&E site only eleven miles from PG&E's present monster steam plant at Morro Bay." Once PG&E began to bulldoze and clear parts of Diablo, Litton chose to highlight the visual changes to show how the landscape was being "lost." He homed in on the earthmoving and trenches, showing an area of vehicle tracks and mud seemingly devoid of nature through the presence of machinery. The natural beauty of remaining land surrounding the construction activity was highlighted in the contrast. Here was a landscape clearly under immediate threat, conjuring images of redwood clear-cutting farther up the coast. Such pictures produced a vision of complete landscape loss, the idea that the bulldozers would just keep going—hence dramatizing the save-Diablo cause. Some members may have been touched by images of decimated terrain, and hence converted to Litton's side. But to others the photographs embodied visual proof of a lost cause. Meanwhile, the dominance of aesthetics on both sides reflected a club used to debating the impact of humans on nature in scenic terms, but not in ecological or atomic dimensions.[28]

Frederick Eissler was the only director outspoken in his fears specifically of an *atomic* plant at Diablo. Eissler expected the whole ecology of Diablo Cove to be disturbed by nuclear operations, and he expressed reservations over relying too much on an as yet unproven energy source. In the antinuclear climate of the 1970s, Eissler's fears would have seemed cautious and probably identified him as a "conservative" Sierra Clubber, yet in the 1960s he was labeled as unscientific, radical, and obsessive. For the save-Diablo group as a whole, there did appear some underlying recognition that a *nuclear* power plant at Diablo threatened the local environment, but without sufficient evidence (or a sympathetic public) members proved wary of speaking out. As Martin Litton remonstrated in a letter to PG&E, "If we had wanted to raise the real bogey, it would have been the danger of radioactive contamination, which was omitted completely from the list of conservationists fears because we ourselves could not have produced positive evidence to suggest it. Yet it is there." More conventional anxieties over thermal pollution seemed difficult to prove without taking on the issue of radiation. Ultimately the burden of proof fell on linking pollution with nuclear power. Some indications of problems would arrive in the late 1970s, too late for the Sierra Club but perhaps not too late for other environmentalists to stop nuclear power and "save" Diablo's land.[29]

During the run-up to the club referendum, personal accusations appeared not only in members' private letters, but in San Francisco newspapers as well. A public airing of the club's dirty laundry occurred. One member protested, "The Sierra Club is no place for the kind of dirty pool that is being played at present by Siri and his group." Another sent in a telegram requesting "that directors discuss how to stop rumors and innuendoes that are perverting philosophy of club." The advice went ignored.[30]

One of the biggest controversies surrounded the publication of the *Sierra Club Bulletin* on Diablo Canyon, due for print in February 1967. It was meant to offer a chance for the two sides to state their cases so that the membership had an opportunity to register an informed vote. The *Bulletin* instead served as a battleground between the two factions. Siri and Adams delayed their submission. In response, partisan staff mailed out a "half-bulletin" containing only the save-Diablo side. Club president George Marshall rewrote the editorial offered by Hugh Nash. Even the front cover was associated with controversy: cartographers had allegedly exaggerated the size of Diablo over Nipomo. Marshall accused Nash of engineering "a good propaganda piece." Similarly, members bickered over the wording of the petition. While save-Diablo members wrote the original petition, granting members the simple choice to either work to save Diablo or accept its sacrifice, pro-dealers adapted the final version so that Sierrans could only reaffirm or reject club policy over both Nipomo and the southern Pecho Coast. Hence voting to save Diablo emerged as tantamount to both losing the dunes and sullying the club.[31]

When the vote was finally counted, 11,341 members reaffirmed the original deal with PG&E, while 5,225 opposed it. The membership of the Sierra Club supported the sacrifice of Diablo in order to save Nipomo, although issues of club loyalty, tradition, and consistent policy also swayed opinion. After the count, pro-dealers (and many other club members) assumed that the Diablo controversy was officially over.

However, in April 1968 the membership voted several new directors onto the club board. All were known to support David Brower, and the issue of

Diablo Canyon soon resurfaced. Representing a majority on the board, eight save-Diablo directors signed a note to the president of PG&E warning him that Diablo was about to be reconsidered by the club. The letter featured an official Sierra Club stamp. Pro-dealers lambasted the letter as "back-handed" and something that "can do nothing but impair the Club's image." The Los Padres Chapter labeled the action a "devious maneuver." Club president Edgar Wayburn called it "a hell of a way to run a railroad." In December 1968 the board also voted to protect Diablo Canyon.[32]

Having suddenly reversed policy, save-Diablo directors sought the approval of the club membership for their about-face. The *Bulletin* again presented the two sides of thought. Siri and Adams produced a piece entitled "Diablo Canyon Again—And Again, and Again," while Litton and Eissler chose to go farther back into Sierra Club history for inspiration, claiming that "John Muir Would Have Voted YES" to protecting Diablo. Despite *Bulletin* pictures of sandy dunes and rocky canyons, the issue of Diablo Canyon had become more a matter of club politics than of ecological evaluation. As early as March 1967 the Toiyabe Chapter newsletter, the *Toiyabe Tattler,* had declared: "Somewhat obscured by this rather local but complex problem are bigger problems bearing on the basic executive, administrative, and conservation policies of the Sierra Club. It is clear that the main issue is not the intrinsic merit of Diablo Canyon." The transformation was complete. The Pecho landscape had been lost beneath a multitude of conservation questions and organizational disputes. Conservationists had rendered "Diablo" into an argument over club philosophy.[33]

■ CLUB PHILOSOPHY: ■
FROM CONSERVATION TO ENVIRONMENTALISM

The 1960s represented a time of change for the Sierra Club. For several decades the organization had focused on hiking activities and traditional, conciliatory conservation. Gathering momentum in the mid-1950s, the club gradually expanded its activities. Hoping to save Echo Park inside Dinosaur National Monument from damming, Sierrans embarked upon their biggest campaign since Hetch Hetchy. By the mid-1960s the club was fighting the U.S. government over its tax status and clamoring for a Redwood National Park in northern California. Sierran conservationists adopted controversial tactics. "Should we also flood the Sistine Chapel so Tourists can get nearer the ceiling?" read a club advertisement (1966) to save Grand Canyon from being dammed and damned. Despite seizing the proverbial higher ground and winning handsome conservation victories, some members expressed concern over the new club stance. This was new territory, after all, and older members were wary of the push by David Brower toward more radical paths of organizing. The Diablo Canyon controversy appeared at this difficult time. The canyon came to symbolize two conservation visions for the club, two choices of route that appeared in the mid-1960s. An unofficial mailing by the Grand Canyon Chapter explained: "Basically at issue are two philosophies of conservation—whether to compromise with the opposition or pursue the objectives of conservation without equivocation." While pro-dealers usually identified themselves with a well-trodden conservation direction, most defenders of Diablo Canyon preferred to climb up to the supposedly "higher ground."[34]

For Brower and Litton, preservation was essentially a pure, resolute, and uncompromising act. With reference to the defense of the Grand Canyon from damming, Brower explained simply, "We have no choice." Never giving in to industry, fighting battles to win protection for wilderness, and always putting nature first were hallmarks of a new style of conservation, later to be renamed environmentalism. Such ideas had already gained precedence in the club, providing victories including the halting of Echo Park Dam. The 1966 Diablo land deal represented a stinging affront to, even a rejection of, new environmental principles. It was "a mistake of principle and policy," reeking of compromise and unnecessary sacrifice. Shocked at the deal, one member strongly argued against such trade-offs: "When both alternatives, in any given scheme, are unacceptable, you reject *both* of them"; else, "What would you do if the Bureau of Reclamation asked the club whether it preferred a dam in Yosemite Valley or Yellowstone?"[35]

That the deal had been entered into with PG&E made it even worse. Member Betty Hughes wrote to Will Siri: "I remember taunting you in September with sounding like a PG&E man, but I thought I was mostly kidding. I begin to think its true. Candidly, I also begin to think you should resign from the Board. I do not see that the Sierra Club as a conservation organization has any need to fraternize with PG&E, or any other commercial enterprise as much given the uglification of our landscape and the utter disregard of our natural beauties, in pursuit of the almighty dollar." Another member simply asked Dick Leonard: "Do you work for PG&E?" Antipathy toward Pacific Gas reflected growing skepticism toward commerce and industry in conservation circles. Director Eliot Porter suggested that "compromise with private interest and industry will save no wild areas; it will only lead to their gradual loss. Industry is not concerned to preserve conservation values; its concern is profits."[36]

The save-Diablo lobby also had reservations over atomic power as an energy resource. Frederick Eissler read antinuclear literature. As early as June 1966 he called for a Sierra Club committee to examine "the pros and cons of fission, fusion, etc." in the aftermath of Bodega and in light of the Diablo deal. For others, working to save Diablo led them to uncover the dangers of the atom for the first time, from thermal pollution to radiation concerns. Brower himself had previously accepted atomic fission but changed his mind between 1966 and 1969. The North Group Redwood Chapter feared that PG&E did not intend to end its nuclear program with Diablo Canyon, claiming, "There is a long list of other outstanding coastal areas earmarked for a nuclear disaster."[37]

Nuclear plants also became associated with economic, industrial, and population growth. In the late 1960s a number of Sierrans came to look upon growth in all its guises as the antithesis of nature conservation. David Brower took note of Paul Ehrlich's *The Population Bomb* (1968). He duly connected Ehrlich's ideas with his own conservation ethic. Brower explained that "just about a decade ago" he and others had begun to realize something: "*Suppose we simply didn't* keep believing the myth that some divine law requires unending growth in the number of people, in their appetite for using up resources, and in their proclivity in fouling nests. . . . Suppose, in short, we simply didn't try to kill a Golden State." Members linked Diablo with other nascent environmental concerns. Local conservationists compared the Santa Barbara oil spill in late January 1969 to a potential accident at Diablo Canyon. The eruption at a Union Oil platform in the Santa Barbara Channel polluted the Central Coast with thick black oil just as the Diablo nuclear plant could vent an invisible—but even more deadly—cloud of radiation throughout the same region. Local campaigners drew pertinent comparisons between the polluting effects of different types of energy extraction. To the Scenic Shoreline

Preservation Conference, a small group of conservationists (including Sierra Club members) local to San Luis Obispo and Santa Barbara counties, the oil spill appeared "another tragic demonstration of the high risks from the rush of uncontrolled technology." Scenic Shoreline members predicted that oil disasters such as the Santa Barbara spill, along with the earlier *Torrey Canyon* accident off the English coast in 1967, might soon have atomic bed-fellows, that "similar precipitate action leading to technological blunders . . . will result from the hasty promotion of nuclear power." Club member Sue Schmitt, from British Columbia, Canada, interpreted Diablo as an example of government policies that "favor commercial enterprises and profits, and not the health and welfare for people now and in the future," and placed the canyon's development alongside Canadian examples of pollution, pesticides, chemical effluents, and clear-cutting. Schmitt also associated concern for Diablo with the growing role of ecology in environmentalist work. To Marshall and Brower she suggested, "Those of us who understand ecology must fight these things on all sides," and drew attention to the burgeoning view among environmentalists and independent scientists: "Radiation is dangerous and there is no threshold for safety." The less than positive response to the Diablo nuclear plant indicated an increasing skepticism toward science and big technology. Rachel Carson's environmental warnings about synthetic pesticides in *Silent Spring* (1962) also influenced popular debate. While commenting on the unknown consequences of the Diablo plant on local marine life, Brower noted that during "the pesticide controversy" there had been a "tendency in case of doubt to use pesticides first and study later." Fearing unforeseen damage on the Pecho Coast, Brower motioned for the Sierra Club to "make clear that Diablo should wait."[38]

The proliferation of confrontational tactics within the Sierra Club indicated that the organization had begun to shift direction. There was something fresh and dynamic concerning even token gestures. Member Stewart Ogilvy planned to cheekily "sneak in early" at a meeting of the Conservation Society of America and place copies of a save-Diablo pamphlet on chairs before "the PG&E man, A. E. Smith gets up and gives his spiel on industry's role in the beautification of the California Coast." Recent successes at Grand Canyon and Echo Park suggested that the club was ready to lead the way toward a modern environmental era.[39]

To the save-Diablo lobby, the Sierra Club was nothing without a pure conservation philosophy, and modern environmentalism carried this notion forward. Litton was dedicated to assuring preservation above compromise. To one concerned member he replied: "Let me assure you that we are not going to write the Sierra Club off. But 'a number' of us will strive to make it and keep it an uncompromising, consistent champion of wilderness and nature, always appealing to a higher tribunal than that of the exploiters we oppose, and ever wary of 'deals' offered by commercial or bureaucratic vandals." A modern environmental approach was rarely seen as divergent from past club ideals. In fact, Hugh Nash welcomed the revival of the coastal question in 1968, suggesting that "the club, which mortgaged its soul on the Diablo issue, has a chance to recover it. Even a pro-forma reversal would put the club comfortably back on the side of the angels."[40]

Save-Diablo Sierrans also presented their actions as true to the spirit of John Muir, cofounder and "patron saint" of the club. Contemporary, ethical environmentalism was tied to the distant past of the Sierra Club. Brower explained: "We worked with an old religion—Muir's—and new techniques—books, films, ads, TV, and we grew as we never had before." Brower himself was likened to the grandfather of the club—Leonard was not alone in calling him "reminiscent of Muir." In the 1969 *Bulletin* article on Diablo, the plea for membership support by Litton and Eissler was appropriately entitled "John Muir Would Have Voted YES." The article mused, "Can Diablo be saved? John Muir would not have asked; he would have rejoiced in the conviction that what must be done can be done. Let us do the same." When Kathy Jackson disagreed, claiming that, in fact, "John Muir would vote no," she received a reply purportedly from the man himself (most likely via Litton), now residing at the "Third Pew, Second Row, Nature Corner, Heaven." The mythical Muir was shocked by her comments: "Someone, (I suspect a departed PG&E official from across the hall,) has either been forging my name on fiery rocks or has bribed your medium." Seeming to have inside knowledge of the Diablo Canyon controversy, no doubt one of the benefits of higher ground, he explained: "If I were still fortunate (?) enough to be a voting member of the Sierra Club, I can assure you that I would, as Mr. Litton suggests, vote YES on this proposition."[41]

The save-Diablo lobby further drew attention to Muir's valiant work to save Hetch Hetchy from damming in the early 1910s, even though a large number of Sierrans had supported the engineering project. Brower literally rewrote club history by editing an extract from Holway Jones's *John Muir and the Sierra Club* (1965) that dealt with Hetch Hetchy. By simply replacing mentions of "Hetchy" with "Diablo," "San Francisco water" with "PG&E," and "national park" with "coast," Brower demonstrated how similar the two controversies were. He entitled the piece: "Need History Repeat Itself So Soon?"[42]

While recognizing that the save-Diablo group exhibited "a pure approach to conservation," pro-dealers such as Will Siri and Dick Sill cautioned that the Sierra Club was also heading toward disaster. The fate of Diablo paled alongside "the most important problem facing the Sierra Club at this time . . . to maintain its fine public image and momentum unweakened by dissension." The pro-dealers portrayed the save-Diablo Sierrans as leading an assault on the club, with the fear that such a laudable organization could be "destroyed from within." Save-Diablo directors were commonly portrayed as "club dissenters" even during their majority reign on the board. The determination of Litton and Eissler to reverse policy was taken as a veiled threat to club democracy. Pro-dealers expressed unease over staff loyalties on the Diablo matter. Brower's open support for saving Diablo led to a crackdown on staff actions by President Marshall. Diablo became a question of club authority. Increasingly, the issue focused "not [on] Diablo Canyon but who was going to run the Sierra Club, the board or the paid staff." By reviving the debate in 1968, the save-Diablo group appeared to reject not only the wishes of the previous board, but also the vote of the general membership. George Marshall repeatedly called for club unity on the issue, although he, like others, envisaged concord solely in its guise of unanimous support for the original 1966 deal.[43]

The split within the club had its greatest impact on those best referred to as the "old guard." Veteran members including Marshall valued the club for what it was, not what it could become. Although receptive to some of the changes Brower and his ilk instigated, Marshall proved wary of losing the hiking organization of old. In the 1966–69 period the "old guard" attempted to regain authority both inside and outside the club. The fracas over Diablo led them to publicly promote their vision of the club and the danger posed by "extremists." The "old guard" stood for a traditional conservation philosophy based on compromise. Ansel Adams portrayed the purists as rebellious idealists like those that, in his youth, he had related to. But Adams now had a "better perspective," whereby to "co-operate with reality" could lead to major victories such as saving Nipomo Dunes. For him, protecting Nipomo by sacrificing Diablo signified a conservationist's victory rather than an environmentalist's loss. Traditionalists only partially linked Diablo Canyon with wider environmental debates. To members such as Dick Leonard, industrial growth and technological progress were simple realities. Although sometimes reticent over the loss of open space, Adams and his allies did not consider it their (or the club's) duty to question wider forces. Adams elaborated: "We would, of course, like to see all of the beautiful coast saved as wilderness, but that is a rather impractical dream in view of the increasing demands of growing population." Challenging development at Diablo was considered tantamount to challenging California's growth and progress. Whereas saving Nipomo was tied to "reasonableness," saving Diablo was associated with "blind obstructionism."[44]

At a time when the dangers of nuclear power were not widely accepted, traditionalists had few qualms over an atomic plant on the Pecho Coast. Nuclear power represented a welcome alternative to unsightly dams. The Mother Lode Chapter supported the sacrifice of Diablo Canyon, explaining: "If we are to save scenic resources such as parks and wilderness areas from being seriously damaged by hydroelectric development, conservationists must encourage the development of alternate sources of power whether they are steam or nuclear produced." An editorial in the *San Francisco Examiner* warned the club against opposing nuclear plants along the coast: "It is a fact that nuclear technology offers the best hope for avoiding construction of large hydroelectric dams, including those proposed for the Grand Canyon. . . . Conservationists, of all people, should be eager to see the production of electric power shifted to nuclear piles as soon as possible." With little evidence of damage, the threat of atomic power proved hard for some members to accept. One Sierran noted: "I cannot conceive of a reactor near the ocean creating as serious a conservation problem as hydro-electric dams." Meanwhile, Will Siri worked for the Lawrence Livermore National Laboratory. Siri believed nuclear power to be statistically a lesser risk than flying and felt that claims of danger to public health would never hold on scientific grounds. For Siri and his allies, the Diablo nuclear plant represented an acceptable energy landscape in California.[45]

While the 1960s brought a shift in popular culture and growing criticism of institutions, corporations, and government, pro-dealers attempted to insulate the Sierra Club from wider social changes. They hoped to keep the club as a gentlemanly organization, happy to cooperate with business and industry and faithful to its origins as a hiking and camping outfit. For Adams and Siri the land deal over Diablo-Nipomo offered prima facie proof that old-style conservation still worked. A newspaper recounted how "Adams said . . . the co-operation demonstrated between the club and PG&E was one of the greatest steps ever taken by the club. 'It showed we're not against everything.'" Adams called it "a milestone in the progress of conservation." The land deal with Pacific Gas signified a conciliatory gesture to set alongside the fierce battles over Grand Canyon and Echo Park. The deal sent out a message that the Sierra Club had not become an unreasonable force in the 1960s, and that the possibility existed of a return to a more dignified approach to conservation lobbying. Diablo Canyon was a sacrifice to revive the "old" Sierra Club and traditional conservation values.[46]

■ THE BROWER CONTROVERSY ■

During prolonged debates over conservation philosophy, executive director David Brower became identified as the key proponent of radical environmental campaigning. His penchant for fresh ideas and new ecological causes alienated him from the "old guard." He also exercised too much power over club programs. Looking back, Siri claimed that the club's "internal problems began in the early sixties when Dave began to assert himself in a progressively more independent fashion, first in the publication program, then in conservation activities, and the club's financial affairs." Brower's financial "irregularities" particularly worried directors such as Dick Leonard, who liked to think of the club as his own well-run business. Brower appeared a growing threat to the traditional hiking club.[47]

Brower had also emerged as an eminent conservation figure. Traditionalists felt uneasy over claims that "David Brower is Sierra Club [sic]." When Brower placed advertisements for Earth National Park in national newspapers and planned to set up a London office before asking for club approval, pro-dealers considered the club's mandate to be threatened by one man. Although members thanked Brower for modernizing the organization in the 1960s, a number of directors resented being dragged (against their will) into a new era of radical environmentalism.[48]

Brower's motivation on the Diablo issue partially derived from his regret at losing Glen Canyon to damming interests in the late 1950s. Diablo, like Glen, signified an unknown landscape, whose fate had been decided by a combination of club ignorance, compromise, and dogmatic pursuit of conservation victory elsewhere. Sierra directors had failed to visit Glen Canyon before sacrificing the region in a bid to save Dinosaur National Monument. A Sierra Club exhibition book later referred to Glen Canyon as *The Place No One Knew* (1963). Brower no doubt empathized with one member who commented on the Diablo controversy: "We cannot allow another Glen Canyon, no matter how small we may think it is." Instead of upholding the original board decision on Diablo, Brower threw his support behind the save-Diablo lobby. Such partisan behavior placed him in a reckless position. As one member pointed out, an executive director (or any staffperson) was meant to be neutral on such matters, rather than side with club dissidents. Prior to Diablo Canyon, critics had remained quiet on the role of Brower within the organization. From 1966 onward, rumors circulated of schemes to restrict the activities of the executive director. Previously close friends of Brower's, Adams and Leonard turned against him. There were even suggestions of a conspiracy behind plans to discharge the executive director. However, Brower's uncompromising attitude had also gained him a dedicated support network of people who saw him as a true environmentalist. One member commented: "If it is felt he has acted too independently of the Board, perhaps the Board has invited this independence. I think the Diablo Canyon matter may be a case in point."[49]

▨ AT THE CHAPTER LEVEL ▨

The Diablo controversy affected all levels of the Sierra Club, not just the highest echelons. For several years, individual chapters debated the Diablo-Nipomo question and pondered which candidates to support at election time.

Los Padres was the chapter closest to the Pecho Coast. In 1966 the Sierra Club board of directors made their decision on Diablo-Nipomo without soliciting an official statement from the local chapter. Such ignorance of regional opinion outraged Robert Hoover, a county biologist who went on to campaign on behalf of saving Diablo. Hoover interpreted the board's actions as showing "contempt for members." In a less than sympathetic reply George Marshall suggested Hoover was "extraordinarily emotional" and "misunderstanding." However, Hoover made an important point in insisting that "the Directors have the duty to consider the interests of the members who elected them before making any public pronouncements" when such a decision clearly affected a local chapter's domain. Such splendid advice was nonetheless colored by Hoover's open admiration for the Pecho Coast. In response to the 1966 deal, the Los Padres Chapter passed its own resolution challenging the sacrifice of Diablo and called for members to be consulted on conservation issues relevant to their region. Chapter secretary Delee S. Marshall duly informed club president Marshall that "Diablo Canyon is of much concern to Los Padres Chapter." The club president replied with a persuasive letter applauding "the vigor with which different points of view are maintained by members of the Club and this is healthy" but also warning that such difference of opinion jeopardized the Sierra Club as a working organization. Taking note of the president's plea for club loyalty, Los Padres then rescinded its resolution and stood by the board.[50]

The majority of chapters affirmed the pro-deal stance on Diablo Canyon at the time of the first referendum. Sixteen out of nineteen chapters passed resolutions supporting the Nipomo-Diablo transaction. Chapter newsletters recommended, in no uncertain terms, that their members needed to affirm board policy for the sake of the club. Diablo was consistently portrayed as a test of member loyalty, rather than a deeper question of conservation philosophy. The John Muir and San Francisco Bay chapters proved particularly vehement in their support for a pro-deal position. The John Muir Chapter called for its members to affirm the deal as "a desired means of retaining the integrity of the Club," ending on: "We trust that you will concur with the actions of your Executive Committee in the Diablo Canyon issue." Chapter committees seemingly imagined themselves as miniature versions of the Sierra Club board. Upholding the deal made sense to local executives who valued Sierran tradition and hierarchy. They felt no guilt in informing their members how to vote. Most chapter committees reneged on the opportunity to provide their members with truly objective information on Nipomo or Diablo. While geographical distance prevented visits to the region by chapter staff, Diablo was so subsumed in the vagaries of club politics that remoteness was never the deciding factor. After all, the most outspoken group in favor of saving Diablo from development happened to be the Atlantic Chapter.[51]

When the issue resurfaced in 1968, the San Francisco Bay Chapter's newsletter, the *Yodeller*, responded with five pages criticizing the new board. The piece claimed: "The unity of the voices speaking against the reopening is probably unparalleled in club history." The author of the article defended his work as simply showing the "perversion of the Sierra Club from a group controlled by the wishes of its members into an autocracy." The Loma Prieta Chapter argued that Diablo Canyon "should be considered a dead issue." The majority of chapters concurred.[52]

Individual members varied in their response to the land controversy in California. Some saw it in exactly the same light as their chapter committees. Others were understandably puzzled that an unknown place had consumed so much club time. Ruth Weiner from the Rocky Mountain Chapter, Denver, noted that "the whole issue is confusing, especially to those of us who don't live in California and never heard of Diablo Canyon until a few weeks ago. It is hard to know how to vote intelligently on the Referendum." In a rare allusion to popular culture in the 1960s, one member saw the Diablo revival as "the first case of the 'Establishment' rebelling against the people while many sections of the U.S. people are rebelling against the Establishment." Club members felt confused over the merits of nuclear power. Siri and Eissler were in the minority with their clarity of vision. While Diablo differentiated atomic backers from skeptics, the *San Francisco Examiner* was wrong to suggest that the atom alone was responsible for splitting the club. Chapters had their own regional dissenters on the Diablo-Nipomo matter, such as James Hupp, who criticized the *Yodeller* for its "biased—no, bigoted—reporting," and Betty Hughes, an active friend of Martin Litton. Hughes consistently defended Diablo Canyon in letters to Adams, Siri, and Marshall. Reflecting a desire for the Sierra Club to offer a mix of radical environmentalism and traditional conservation, members articulated their support for club visions offered by Siri and Adams *and* Litton and Brower. Hence, they affirmed the Diablo deal in 1967, showing their loyalty to the club, yet voted in save-

Diablo directors, showing their admiration for dedicated, confrontational lobbying. The matter of club democracy was also a contentious issue. The Sierra Club had traditionally carried an elitist badge, with sponsorship the only way to membership. However, the "new" club of the 1960s allowed anyone to join. One member saw the revolt against the 1966 deal as an example of letting people into the Sierra fraternity who lacked the necessary qualities. Some Sierrans preferred club directors to make conservation decisions for them. By contrast, one member noted his distrust of the club elite, remarking that the directorial infighting reminded him of "Congressmen" at work.[53]

▪ THE 1969 VOTE ▪

In the board elections of 1969, save-Diablo directors and pro-dealers represented themselves on separate conservation platforms. An ABC coalition, standing for Active Bold Constructive (also known as Aggressive Brower-Style Conservationists), promoted an internationalist and confrontational club, while the opposing CMC (Concerned Members for Conservation) group offered a traditional, well-managed approach to organizing. The ABC group spoke of unrelenting pressures on the environment and the need for the club to look beyond the Sierra Nevada and take up fresh campaigns. The CMC platform offered a more cautious approach to conservation, hinting at a return to the settled past, to the old Sierra Club.

Both the Diablo petition and the ABC platform were overwhelmingly defeated. Diablo lost by a vote of 10,346 to 30,579. David Brower tendered his resignation at the next board meeting, on May 3, 1969. In a farewell speech Brower remained true to his reputation as an uncompromising environmentalist, declaring: "We cannot go on fiddling while the earth's wild places burn in the fires of our undisciplined technology." Sierra Club stewards had cut Brower loose in the hope of securing less fiery times for the conservation lobby.[54]

The exit of Brower and the loss of Diablo (along with the success of the CMC platform) suggested that the Sierra Club was far from ready to embrace, let alone lead, the new environmental movement of the late 1960s and early 1970s. The club, on one level, appeared likely to remain tethered to its conservative, elitist roots, unprepared (and unwilling) to incorporate the radical, grassroots, and antiestablishment tendencies of modern environmentalism.

However, Brower and Diablo Canyon had fundamentally altered the course of Sierra Club conservation by encouraging members to adopt a more politicized and proactive environmental philosophy. As the environmental journalist Philip Shabecoff put it, Brower "led several victorious campaigns to save the land, helped rekindle the transcendental flame lit by Thoreau and Muir, and played a major role in pulling the old preservation movement out of the comfortable leather armchairs of its clubrooms and into the down-and-dirty area of local and national policy making." Despite the official defeat of the ABC manifesto in 1969, Brower's broader ecological mandate continued within the organization during the 1970s and beyond. Those who worked to save Diablo adroitly recognized that nature conservation encompassed the protection of anonymous, "representative" landscapes as well as famous tracts of "monumental scenery." Members found beauty, wildness, and ecological vitality in the little-known rugged canyons of the California coast as well as in the famed lofty ranges of the Sierra Nevada. Diablo Canyon compelled Sierra conservationists to reconsider their opinions on industrial and technological progress (particular in the guise of nuclear energy) and ponder the dangers of unbridled growth in California. However, at root, the debate over Diablo was always more concerned with nature—explicitly, the politics of landscape, the best conservation strategy toward the natural world, and competing environmental aesthetics—than with nuclear power.[55]

■ CHANGES AT DIABLO CANYON ■

In February 1969 the *Daily Commercial News* of San Francisco ran an article on Diablo Canyon. The *Commercial News* was keen to suggest that controversies over Diablo were comfortably behind it. "All the technical, economic, ecological, aesthetic questions were thoroughly settled long ago," the newspaper declared. A new nuclear landscape was about to be forged, and an attractive one at that: "The twin-domed structure will never become an American parthenon, to be sure, but it is a clean-lined, well-designed bit of industrial architecture, actually quite handsome in the canyon setting." Pacific Gas had even contacted William Siri over his views on the architectural design of the Diablo Canyon nuclear plant, and in an environmental report to the Atomic Energy Commission, the corporation stated: "Every effort has been made to design the plant in a manner compatible with the coastal site." For atomic backers, nuclear plants replacing existing flora symbolized human progress beyond nature's limited growth, with a healthy yield of energy in the offing. For a number of conservationists, record-sized coastal oaks' being replaced with power-line pylons indicated the exact opposite. Litton had confronted developmental optimism with pictures of barren soil circled by bulldozers, showing what he judged to be the harsh reality of PG&E's creative process. Although Pacific Gas consciously preserved a few of the larger oak "specimens" and claimed the architecture of the nuclear plant befitted its wild setting, the fundamental contrasts went ignored. Construction signaled a new beginning for Diablo Canyon whereby the natural world would have to fit in with the atom. To defenders such as Martin Litton, Diablo's nature had been lost.[56]

THREE

Local Mothers, Earthquake Country, and the "Nuclear Center of America"

Converting Diablo Canyon into a viable nuclear complex officially began in June 1968 after Pacific Gas received its construction permit for the Unit 1 reactor (the permit for Unit 2 followed in 1970). During the first year, the site area was leveled and paved, and land excavated where buildings would soon arise. Diablo Creek played host to the plant's switchyard. PG&E contractors laid a private access road between the plant site and the nearest public road, at Avila Beach. Due to the size of construction components passing through (specifically the Unit 1 and 2 reactor vessels), engineers designed a route with gentle slopes and gradual corners. PG&E workers had their own seven-mile drive to rival the finest of California's coastal highways. In a region where whales had once been caught and hauled to port, the "big catch" for Avila in the early 1970s became two reactor vessels brought in by barge. In March 1973 the installation of Unit 1 reactor marked an "important milestone" not only for Pacific Gas but also for Diablo Canyon. A new kind of energy landscape had started to take form.[1]

The first few years of the 1970s went well for Pacific Gas. PG&E promoted its project as an environmentally friendly energy source far superior to gas- or coal-powered plants. In July 1971 the corporation explicitly stated such a claim in its final Environmental Report to the Atomic Energy Commission (AEC): "Compared to fossil fueled steam plants, nuclear plants offer definite environmental advantages." While some localized impact was expected during plant construction, PG&E outlined extensive reseeding and restoration schemes to combat this. During operation, only "the release of small amounts of low level radioactivity," along with the discharge of warm water into the bay, would upset the ecological equilibrium. These effects seemed a small price to pay for a clean and much-needed energy source.[2]

Those seeking to "save" Diablo in the Sierra Club had considered nature lost with the arrival of bulldozers on the Pecho Coast. Despite the construction site's being a mess of vehicles, concrete, and machinery, many wild animals adapted to the noise and disruption. PG&E had anticipated that "the power plant will have a minimal effect on the land use of the surrounding area." Most work centered on the canyon itself, with surrounding acres remaining relatively undisturbed and ecologically intact. When construction processes despoiled hillsides close to the nuclear plant, employees literally painted Diablo Canyon green to cover up the damage. This cosmetic operation reflected the level of concern shown for the environment at Diablo. Such an act also reflected the desire of corporate America to sidestep environmental criticism and avoid becoming a target of protest action.[3]

Tapping into the new climate of popular environmentalism sweeping the United States, PG&E officials hoped to situate nuclear power as a fundamentally green product. Seeking to demystify nuclear energy in the public arena, as well as stress its benign environmental properties, staff used a "mobile van . . . with exhibits explaining atomic energy" to help Californians understand the advantages offered by nuclear power. It started out in San Francisco, with the aim of traveling elsewhere across the Golden State. The plant was presented as vital to California's energy independence. As PG&E explained, "in order to have capacity reserve margins adequate to maintain reliable service in northern and central California," the reactors had to go on-line. San Luis politicians were given atomic pins to wear, and most locals at least tacitly supported the nuclear enterprise. In 1973 Jim Hayes wrote a series of articles for the local *Telegram-Tribune* entitled "Our Nuclear Neighbor." Hayes relayed the enthusiasm of county supervisor John Freeman that "the new plant will bring in a great deal of money to San Luis Obispo—so much, in fact, that if other counties knew how much, they would all be clamoring for a nuclear plant all their own." According to Hayes some residents had already asked for more plants, a clear indication that "San Luis Obispo is no longer afraid of the nuclear age." Considering the county's reputation as a conservative, middle-class community, Hayes surmised that "there is little organized opposition" to PG&E's "generating 2,000 megawatts of electrical energy and shipping it over the two transmission lines that march two abreast across the landscape. Most people seem to regard the plant and its steel-tower army as fait accompli."[4]

With similar sentiments the *San Diego Union* printed a story headlined "San Luis Obispo Eagerly Awaits Nuclear Power Plant." The article described how "on a fog and rock bound beach in Central California the nation's biggest nuclear power plant is being built. The reactor looks like something straight out of an early science fiction movie. The sea dashes on the rocks below and the fog drifts around the big steel dome that will soon house 30 tons of nuclear fuel." By combining the natural features of Diablo Canyon with its nuclear constructions, the *San Diego Union* forwarded a new romantic vision for the coastal landscape. Rather than a conflict between the needs of industrial construction and native flora, as local conservationists had once expected, the newspaper implied something far greater would come from nature and the atom sharing the same abode. The paper described coastal fog swirling around the reactor as though in harmony with the radioactive elements. The nuclear dream, "straight out of an early science fiction movie," recalled a much older American vision of manifest destiny. At Diablo Canyon, Americans had made "progress" by exploiting "free" land. "The huge modern reactor on the edge of a primitive beach" symbolized how far manifest destiny had come, both geographically and technologically.[5]

In contrast, local nature conservationists recognized only the damage being done to the landscape. In 1966 Pacific Gas had entered into a legal agreement with the state of California's Resource Agency that "the physical appearance of the entire installation will be aesthetically compatible with the surroundings." Conservationists felt that the industrial countenance of Diablo in the early 1970s suggested otherwise. Somewhat predictably, PG&E's concrete plant seemed far from "aesthetically compatible" with native flora and fauna. The local Sierra Club's newsletter, the *Santa Lucian*, claimed that "mutilated wild canyons, great patches of orphaned soil, ghastly, unhealable cuts which PG&E cosmetically paints green" amounted to "in all, an upheaval almost unmatched since the age of the glaciers." To make matters worse, the fervent construction activities at Diablo contrasted with the slow pace of change at nearby Montana de Oro State Park. In May 1973 *PG&E Progress* magazine, in a series of articles titled "Parks of California," featured the protected landscape just north of the Diablo nuclear plant. *Progress* celebrated how, "relatively undeveloped, with primitive campsites, Montana de Oro has been little changed by time." Cognizant of new mainstream environmental sensibilities, the corporation promoted the unspoiled nature of California to its clientele, selling both wilderness and electricity.[6]

The fight to "save" Diablo nonetheless continued into the 1970s. San Luis Obispo's California Polytechnic State University (Cal Poly) had "the reputation of being a guardian to which parents could entrust their sons and daughters without fear of their becoming hippies or radicals," according to local resident Julie Krejsa (wife of county supervisor Richard Krejsa). It also drew the accolade of being Governor Ronald Reagan's favorite campus. During the 1970s a small but significant number of students and professors offered their own "counter-expertise" against that of Pacific Gas by questioning the credentials of the Diablo project. A student group, Ecology Action, intervened in early nuclear licensing hearings and picketed California Public Utilities Commission (CPUC) discussions on power line issues in 1971, flourishing the banner, "Mother Nature Has Rights Too." Both Richard Krejsa and Ralph Vrana, a geologist wary of nuclear power, taught at Cal Poly, and several members of a local antiwar group, the Mothers for Peace, had husbands there. Despite Cal Poly's maintaining the impression of "Reagan Country" throughout the period, several individuals launched protest actions against the Diablo nuclear plant.[7]

The conservation-led challenge failed to die despite the implosion of the Sierra Club. A number of local conservationists, under the title of the Scenic Shoreline Preservation Conference, challenged PG&E's project in nuclear licensing hearings from the late 1960s to the early 1970s. Leading members of Scenic Shoreline included Sierra Club radical Frederick Eissler, Harold Miossi, and the environmental historian Roderick Nash, who taught at University of California, Santa Barbara. The group questioned the economic and ecological claims of PG&E concerning the Diablo plant. Members criticized what they saw as the speculative choice of nuclear power above conventional energy sources. In stark contrast to Ansel Adams's declaration of the Diablo land deal as a "milestone in conservation," Scenic Shoreline claimed that "the nuclear plant will be a white elephant and nothing more than a millstone around the necks of Pacific and its ratepayers." Locally minded conservationists feared that thermal pollution would ruin the marine ecology of Diablo Cove. Restricting the physical damage caused by electrical power lines on their route out of the Diablo plant and across adjacent lands represented another challenge. Scenic Shoreline presented arguments at CPUC hearings over Diablo. However, with the exception of William Bennett (a vociferous antinuclear critic), the majority of attendees approved PG&E's plans. Scenic Shoreline attorney Bruce Sharpe meanwhile noted his disillusionment with attending AEC hearings at the time: "You could intervene in 600 licensing hearings and probably AEC would wind up granting 600 licenses. But you have to go on fighting, plant by plant, until you can come up with a better answer." To critics of atomic energy, the nuclear licensing process was intrinsically biased toward forward progress. However, not just AEC officials backed nuclear power in the early 1970s—the web of support stretched much wider. Local resident Ian McMillan reflected that "intervention was lonely at the time." He felt that "to testify against the plant was heresy. Opposing the plant was the equivalent of being called a Communist. Everybody at the hearings was against us."[8]

Members of Scenic Shoreline longed for other groups to get involved. In 1973 Frederick Eissler convinced members of Mothers for Peace to take over the challenge at licensing hearings. The Mothers quickly became the major opposition to Pacific Gas. In contrast to prior conservationist arguments that focused on damage to natural scenery, members articulated antinuclear concerns very much in tune with nascent fears over atomic energy in the wider community. The 1970s had started with Earth Day and the blooming of modern environmentalism. The decade ended with mass antinuclear protests and an atomic accident at Three Mile Island, Pennsylvania. The Mothers were part of an escalating turn against the peaceful atom.

■ **FROM VIETNAM TO DIABLO** ■

The Mothers for Peace had a background in antiwar protest rather than nature conservation. Toward the end of 1969 a young mother sent a letter to the *Telegram-Tribune* asking like-minded individuals to join with her in sharing sadness and frustration over the Vietnam War. Mostly educated, white, middle-class mothers went on to form an independent group based around protesting American involvement in Vietnam. For the next few years the Mothers provided local residents with draft information and a counseling center, visited schools, organized vigils and parades, and leafleted the local Greyhound bus station, where draftees assembled for departure.[9]

In 1973 a few members became interested in the construction of the Diablo Canyon nuclear power plant. The series of articles in the *Telegram-Tribune* by Jim Hayes sparked their interest. The articles seemed to downplay the dangers of atomic energy. One story related a plant engineer's comparison of the dangers of shaving with nuclear accidents, and Hayes himself seemed personally taken with a Geiger counter's slang industry name as "cutie pie" (after its technical initials, CP). His fifth article, entitled "Just Don't Call It Disaster," revealed the fine line between reassuring the reader of the good intentions of "our nuclear neighbor" and subconsciously arousing nuclear fear.[10]

Rather than taking PG&E's safety claims at face value, Mothers Sandy Silver and Liz Apfelberg decided to research the implications of atomic power for themselves. Their actions implied a level of distrust of corporate America from the outset. Rather than request materials from major U.S. corporations involved in the nuclear industry, they instead turned to John Gofman and Arthur Tamplin's highly critical evaluation of atomic energy, *Poisoned Power: The Case against Nuclear Power Plants* (1971). In questioning what they perceived to be "the gospel of the peaceful atom," former AEC scientists Gofman and Tamplin had chosen a path of nuclear dissidence. *Poisoned Power* described in emotive terms a "nuclear juggernaut" out of control, threatening human embryos and children while also colliding with "our democratic rights to the pursuit of happiness, in the form of a livable environment." With huge trucks loaded with reactor parts traveling along PG&E's private highway from Avila Beach to Diablo, the Mothers superimposed Gofman and Tamplin's image of a dangerous nuclear juggernaut to their predicament in San Luis Obispo County. Concerns over atomic weapons proliferation and the "cover-up" of bomb tests and radiation effects further magnified their worries. The Mothers were both cognizant of and influenced by antinuclear commentary that had just begun moving from the fringes of U.S. society into the mainstream. Cultural unease over the atom intersected with the new environmental era. Social criticism of the nuclear age suddenly found a niche in critical news reporting on television. In a 1971 documentary entitled *Powers That Be,* actor Jack Lemmon declared that "nuclear power is not only undependable . . . it's about as safe as a closet full of cobras." Lemmon's analogy seemed appropriate for Diablo Canyon.[11]

With America's gradual withdrawal from Vietnam, Silver and Apfelberg sensed an opportunity for the Mothers to move from antiwar protest to nuclear protest. For some members this change of direction seemed easy enough. Having protested the stationing of a naval destroyer at Avila Beach in September 1971, they turned readily to PG&E's nuclear plant just around the headland as another "threat" lurking in San Luis Obispo County. As a pacifist group, the Mothers came to Diablo with preconceptions over nuclear energy. They naturally situated the nuclear age within a broader discourse of arms races, weapon development, and human health worries. The atomic bomb provided a psychological bridge between opposing the Vietnam War and challenging the Diablo plant. Skeptical of the peaceful intentions of nuclear power, some members of the group found it only reasonable to show concern over their new neighbor. For others, however, protesting an electrical plant appeared a highly inappropriate cause for pacifists. An antiwar group did not necessarily translate into an antinuclear one, for the routine construction at Diablo Canyon seemed far removed from the exceptional horrors of conflict in Vietnam. In case the group withdrew from proceedings, Silver and Apfelberg registered both as individuals and as Mothers in their application to intervene in the plant's nuclear licensing process. However, hesitation soon gave way to determination, and one year later the Mothers for Peace represented the major opposition to the Diablo nuclear plant. With a paradoxical turn of phrase, the *Telegram-Tribune* announced in March 1974 that the "Mothers for Peace are fighting another war."[12]

The Mothers attempted to access the nuclear licensing process by listing their grievances with both the Diablo plant and the nuclear industry in general. Rather than rally against damage to coastal wilderness, they focused from the outset on the alleged threat to human life posed by the plant and on their rights as local citizens to challenge an atomic neighbor. In November 1973 a request sent to the AEC argued that the Mothers' status as "residents, property owners, and taxpayers of San Luis Obispo, dwelling within a 12 mile radius of Diablo Canyon . . . gives us the right to be concerned with the quality of the environment in the area which we live and work." With their focus on immediate human surroundings, the Mothers articulated similar concerns to those of social justice environmentalists who, in the 1990s, rallied behind the principle that "all Americans have a basic right to live, work, and play in a healthy environment." The social justice movement primarily focused on the exploitation of people of color and working-class communities. Despite differences in race and class, the Obispan Mothers viewed the environment in a similar way to social justice advocates by interpreting pollution as an infringement on human rights. The work of the Mothers also resembled that of Lois Gibbs, who rallied opposition to toxic dumping at Love Canal, New York, in the late 1970s. Like Apfelberg and Silver, Gibbs was a housewife turned community leader, committed to justice and a clean home environment.[13]

As outsiders confronting the nuclear establishment, it took time for the Mothers to discover how the licensing process operated. PG&E denied that the Mothers' list of problems qualified as "proper items for consideration by an Atomic Safety and Licensing Board," many being "matters not relevant to an operating license hearing." The AEC was understandably prepared to consider issues that solely applied to the plant under discussion, and on those grounds the commission accepted as valid only questions surrounding evacuation procedures. The rejection of broader concerns made little sense to the Mothers. Silver confessed that "we didn't understand the rules." However, a crack in the earth provided the Mothers with a significant opportunity to challenge what they perceived to be a flawed and biased licensing system. Despite the abundance of earthquake zones across California, the discovery of a fault line less than three miles from Diablo Canyon represented a highly significant feature of that nuclear terrain. Questions of a seismic nature immediately entered nuclear licensing hearings.[14]

DISCOVERING THE HOSGRI FAULT

In view of the established rationale of placing energy-providing industries close to areas of need, it always appeared likely that nuclear power plants would be built close to population zones. In the seismic state of California, the unpredictable natural environment itself represented a key dilemma for nuclear planners, complicating siting and construction decisions. The Diablo plant was not the first nuclear project to be located close to a fault line. With similar discoveries at the Humboldt plant, during planning for Bodega Head, and later at Point Arena, one critic highlighted "PG&E's uncanny ability to pick earthquake zones as sites for nuclear power plants." David Brower later quipped that "a nuclear reactor is a sophisticated device that enables utilities to locate earthquake faults." With the Bodega Head project canceled primarily because of the proximity of the San Andreas Fault, Pacific Gas hoped to avoid a similar setback at Diablo Canyon. Consultants carried out extensive surveys of the Pecho region, and PG&E proved keen to make sure that the Diablo site was earthquake proof. In a report dated January 25, 1966, a preliminary geologic investigation for PG&E noted: "Although there is evidence of old and inactive faults in the area, the Diablo Canyon location appears geologically suitable for a Nuclear Generating Plant." Issues of seismic design were also discussed during a meeting of PG&E, AEC, and Westinghouse officials on April 20–21, 1967, where Dr. Richard H. Jahns, a geologist consulting for PG&E, expressed his professional opinion that the location of the plant was "adequate." In its Environmental Report for the AEC, the corporation insisted that "seismic activity within about 20 miles of the Diablo Canyon site has been very low compared with other parts of California." However, seismologists failed to extend their studies offshore for signs of faulting. Wary of allocating more resources to seismic study, the corporation resisted calls for additional investigation in the late 1960s emanating from Scenic Shoreline and the United States Geological Survey (USGS). The Cal Poly geologist Ralph Vrana suggested the likelihood of faulting off the Diablo coast, but Pacific Gas remained confident in earlier surveys carried out by its own professionals.[15]

In 1969 two Shell Oil geologists, Ernest Hoskins and John R. Griffiths, discovered a fault line less than three miles from Diablo. They published the results in the *American Association of Petroleum Geologists Bulletin* (1971). The fault line was named Hosgri, after Hoskins and Griffiths. For several years the Hosgri Fault remained undiscovered in both pro- and antinuclear circles. The AEC overlooked Hoskins and Griffiths's findings. According to Vrana, Pacific Gas officials should have noticed the discovery but failed to read the work. A Cal Poly student, having been on a USGS field trip in late

1973, was the first person to inform the Mothers for Peace and Scenic Shoreline of the existence of the fault. Both groups felt they had the right to be notified of any findings relevant to Diablo Canyon at the same time that the AEC and PG&E were informed. Hearing about Hosgri four years after its discovery, and at least one year later than Pacific Gas, riled the opponents of the Diablo plant. If the fault had first been discussed in 1969 rather than in 1974, activists felt that there might have been a realistic chance of stopping the nuclear project.[16]

The Mothers for Peace attempted to employ the fault line as a weapon against Pacific Gas, but motions to halt construction at Diablo were refused. For the next couple of years PG&E, the newly formed Nuclear Regulatory Commission (NRC, successor to the AEC) and the USGS debated the fault's characteristics. The dispute focused on the gap between an estimate of the Hosgri Fault's seismic potential as projected by the USGS and the existing design specifications of PG&E's project. The Diablo plant was designed to withstand a maximum tremor of 6.75 on the Richter scale, but geologists predicted that an earthquake from the Hosgri Fault could measure 7.5, threatening a "major" seismic event around seven times more powerful than PG&E had planned for. The huge economic implications of retrofitting two nuclear reactors encouraged the company to resist the higher figure. The utility responded with alternative methods of evaluating the Hosgri Fault that questioned its significance. The NRC also challenged USGS figures. Consultant geologist Richard Meehan recognized "two kinds of geology: pronuclear geology and antinuclear geology" at work in NRC seismic hearings. The 7.5 Richter estimate nevertheless remained.[17]

The Mothers for Peace informed the *Los Angeles Times* of the existence of the Hosgri Fault. The newspaper sold well in San Luis Obispo and chose to headline the story the following day. Up to 1973, articles published in the *Telegram-Tribune* frequently promoted nuclear power for the county. Following the discovery of Hosgri, the local newspaper withdrew its unconditional support for the nuclear plant.

The earthquake issue renewed public interest in Diablo Canyon. The Hosgri story, with its attendant image of two nuclear reactors built on an earthquake zone, led many people to question the Diablo plant for the first time. A natural danger had awakened San Luis Obispo County to its nuclear fears. Suddenly the place of the Diablo plant in the local community seemed far from assured. The Hosgri Fault encouraged citizens to reconsider their trust in engineering. Concerns over earthquakes and atomic power gradually intertwined. Meehan noted how a geologist at Bodega Head "visualized the San Andreas fault as a kind of terrestrial reptile, lying deceptively still in the Californian sun, ready to strike a nuclear reactor." From 1973, a similar serpent apparently lurked close to Diablo Canyon.[18]

▧ CAMPAIGNING FOR AND AGAINST THE PEACEFUL ATOM ▧

When the Mothers for Peace intervened in Diablo's nuclear licensing hearings, they faced not only scientific and technological boundaries, but also what they perceived to be deeper prejudices lurking behind the atom. The format of the licensing hearings proved less than ideal for working mothers. Lacking an attorney, members ended up bringing their children to the hearings and requesting an end to the day's business on the grounds that "we need to go home, we have families." Liz Apfelberg felt that their involvement was considered "a joke" by some attendees. As she recalled it, "at the beginning they didn't take us seriously—they thought we were just a bunch of housewives with nothing better to do." Reliving the experiences of Scenic Shoreline, the Mothers for Peace found themselves caught up in a system that they believed existed purely to bring about (by licensing) the Diablo Canyon nuclear plant. Silver even felt that "the whole proceeding was a farce. It didn't take us long to learn that."[19]

Considering issues that related solely to the Diablo plant, rather than to nuclear power in general, the commission bypassed many attendee concerns. Although NRC officials conscientiously dealt with industrywide problems, critics were left with the impression of a biased forum at Diablo. The Mothers felt that the public deserved more recognition in atomic decision-making. As a legacy of the Manhattan Project, security issues and scientific complexities had successfully insulated the nuclear industry from public criticism for several decades. Open democracy was legitimately deemed inconsistent with national security. Yet by the early 1970s the increasing presence of the atomic projects close to densely populated environments, dissident scientists publicly voicing their nuclear concerns, and a growing distrust of government bred by Vietnam and Watergate had produced a climate more hospitable to the

Mothers' challenge. By 1977 the local women's group had become something of a nuisance to PG&E.[20]

That the Mothers intended to delay the licensing process aggravated local citizens keen to see the Diablo nuclear plant go on-line. In his testimony at NRC hearings, James Jones, an engineer from Santa Maria, portrayed the "bunch of frustrated housewives" as traitors to the nation, accusing them of jeopardizing the country's economic strength and employment figures. According to him, the group had manipulated "Lady Justice." For Jones, along with other pronuclear speakers, nuclear power at Diablo symbolized a strong America. The engineer, "proud of country . . . our flag . . . and what it stands for," interpreted ardent opposition to the Diablo plant as anti-American.[21]

While the views of Jones were likely extreme, a fair number of people associated nuclear power with American pride, abundance, and economic strength in the mid-1970s. In 1973 the United States suddenly faced not only an oil embargo implemented by the Organization of Petroleum Exporting Countries OPEC due to American support for Israel in the Yom Kippur War, but the further repercussions of a 400 percent rise in OPEC's prices. PG&E justifiably used the energy crisis to smooth over cracks in support for Diablo Canyon. *PG&E Progress* predicted that "a crisis is on the horizon . . . and will be upon us if our efforts to provide for future supplies are unsuccessful." The magazine warned: "We do not expect blackouts or brownouts in the immediate future. But we cannot avoid them in the years beyond unless we are permitted to begin construction well in advance of need." OPEC's raising of oil prices temporarily waived nuclear concerns in the light of a nationwide energy crisis. In an August 1975 poll of 1,046 San Luis County residents, 75 percent "strongly" or "somewhat" favored the Diablo plant. Of the total number interviewed, 57 percent were "very seriously" or "somewhat" concerned over the energy crisis.[22]

Linking PG&E's project with U.S. energy sufficiency revived its popularity at a critical point, when nuclear optimism in the county as well as nationwide had begun to flag. Juanita Knapps of Cayucos wrote to the *Telegram-Tribune* in support of PG&E's project. Noting how "for every development that has ever benefited mankind, there have been risks and undesirable effects," Knapps preferred to take a chance on nuclear power rather than return to the "old days" implied by the absence of the Diablo plant. While a nuclear landscape in the 1960s had epitomized futuristic progress, in the mid-1970s it was viewed as a defense of the American way of life in the face of impending crisis.[23]

Hardly wavering in the midst of an energy crisis, the Mothers for Peace saw only a need to offer Obispans an alternative viewpoint to those arguing for more nuclear power plants. In late 1974 they approached the county board of supervisors to sponsor a "nuclear forum," whereby locals could hear both sides of the atom. However, the board itself was split over PG&E's project. Three members advocated nuclear power, while the other two held serious reservations. The forum idea was thrown out by three votes to two. The Mothers reapplied in April 1975. The *Telegram-Tribune* quoted Apfelberg on the responsibility of the board to provide public information when San Luis Obispo County "has the potential of becoming the nuclear center of America." A group of ninety-five doctors gave their public backing to the meeting. To the editor of the local paper, the appearance of medical professionals demonstrated that "the people who made such a request are neither ranters or crazies." Despite the backdrop of the national energy crisis, criticizing commercial nuclear development had begun to be seen as a legitimate and rational action for citizens.[24]

The *Central Coast Times* described the October 1975 forum as "the day the experts came to town," providing citizens with "a chance to separate emotional appeals from fact" regarding nuclear power. This state of calm reason proved more difficult to achieve in practice than to describe in print. Locals were instead offered a choice between two groups and two competing visions, both sides contributing their share of hard facts and emotional appeals. Jane Swanson, a member of the Mothers for Peace, leveled criticism at the exceptionally gifted scientist Edward Teller, "father of the H-bomb," for his emotional and nonfactual delivery. As with technical issues concerning the Hosgri Fault, experts were split over the safety of atomic power at Diablo Canyon. The forum showed the fallacy of interpreting the contest as a battle between (pronuclear) logic and (antinuclear) emotion. Without common ground between the two parties, it was a question of which side to trust. Those citizens who expected a clear result were disappointed. And from most accounts, few people were converted to either side as a result of the forum.

However, at least the public had been offered two contrasting interpretations of the Diablo plant, one from prominent corporate and scientific figures, the other from dissident scientists and grassroots campaigners. For the latter group the forum provided what Sandy Silver dubbed "the coming out party for the anti-nuclear movement" in San Luis Obispo County, thanks to the publicity and media attention.[25]

By 1976 sympathies for the antinuclear agenda had become more widespread in the state of California. Citizens campaigned for a California Nuclear Safeguards Initiative (also known as Proposition 15) to be introduced into state legislation that would limit, if not stop, nuclear projects. The initiative indicated growing public antipathy toward the atom, along with the desire of Californians to take matters into their own hands. Although Proposition 15 failed, three bills with antinuclear measures were passed by the state legislature as an act of compromise. The Nuclear Safeguards Initiative demonstrated that well-organized antinuclear activists could have an impact on atomic developments in California. Meanwhile, in San Luis Obispo, the Mothers visited schools and held a four-hundred-strong rally attended by antinuclear celebrity Jane Fonda. Fonda noted that "just 2 or 3 years ago, a locally initiated antinuclear movement, such as this, could not have been possible," and welcomed the mushrooming of local groups.[26]

The Mothers also organized a "No More Hiroshimas" event. Activists decoupled older associations of Hiroshima with victory in World War II, instead situating the city as a monument of mourning. Powerful images of radiation burns, dead bodies, and a leveled cityscape showed the horrors of the past, human loss to be grieved for. The devastated Japanese city also indicated the dangers of present and future nuclear development. Hiroshima served as a potent symbol of atomic destructiveness for peace campaigners. The Mothers, with their background in anti–Vietnam War organizing and pacifism, were predisposed to recognizing links between atomic bombs and nuclear power. For them, Hiroshima tied to Diablo through the nuclear fuel cycle, through the simple atomic symbol. Their campaign for a nuclear-free world drew together two disparate locations and events. Hiroshima anniversary events amplified the sense of danger associated with the Diablo plant by asserting atomic negativity.

▪ CHANGING PERCEPTIONS OF DIABLO CANYON ▪
AND NUCLEAR POWER

In San Luis Obispo County the bond between nuclear power and Diablo Canyon strengthened in the public image during the 1970s. Despite the presence of oak woodland and western rattlesnakes, Diablo overridingly emerged as a nuclear landscape. The perceived dangers of nuclear power encouraged environmental activists to imagine Diablo as a derelict and despoiled environment. Atomic optimists hailed Diablo Canyon as part of America's energy future, part of the solution to the national energy crisis. Any lingering memories of a prenuclear landscape were overwhelmed by far stronger images of atomic energy. The coastal wilderness had seemingly disappeared.

For Pacific Gas the disappearance of natural features was something of a disappointment. The nuclear industry favored the promotion of atomic plants in keeping with their natural settings, with trees and water serving to offset the artificial qualities of nuclear energy production. In its keenness to boost public acceptability of the peaceful atom, the AEC had once used an advertisement recommending that Americans go and "play in the nuclear power park." The advertisement showed a landscaped garden next to an atomic information center, with a nuclear plant hidden behind abundant flora. The information center's garden, complete with a pond and fountain, was a manufactured paradise, while the building itself resembled a wooden bathing lodge. The invitation to "play" in the nuclear park was not altogether misleading; the advertisement explained that "it is possible, you know. The grounds adjacent to nuclear power plants are safe and clean enough for children's playgrounds." In advertising Diablo nuclear plant, PG&E deployed a similarly inviting photograph of the Vallecitos reactor "nestled among the hills of the Livermore Valley," with four ducks casually swimming in the lake next to the plant. At Diablo two reactors were to be "nestled" in the canyon setting, part of, rather than at odds with, the fine coastal view. To Pacific Gas, which later encouraged school trips to the operating plant, Diablo Canyon was as safe as any other place for children to frequent. The corporation's declaration that "atomic power best serves man and his environment" not only envisaged a nuclear park ably controlled by men, but also betrayed a belief in nature as man's own playground.[27]

Diablo Canyon nuclear power plant, 1997, aerial view. Photograph by author.

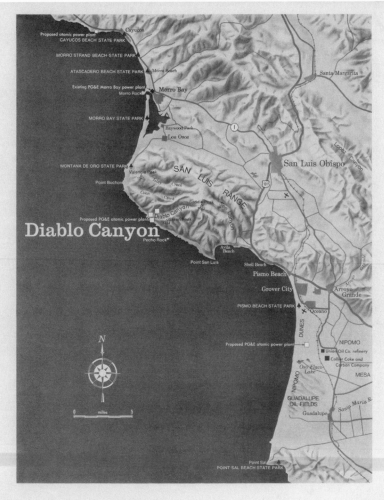

Sierra Club Bulletin
FEBRUARY 1967

Pros and cons of the Diablo Canyon issue,
which will be put to a vote of the membership

Front cover of the controversial February 1967 edition of *Sierra Club Bulletin*. Club president George Marshall claimed the map exaggerated the significance of Diablo over Nipomo. Author's copy, courtesy of Martin Litton, Portola Valley.

Mothers for Peace pamphlet. Courtesy of June von Ruden, Mothers for Peace.

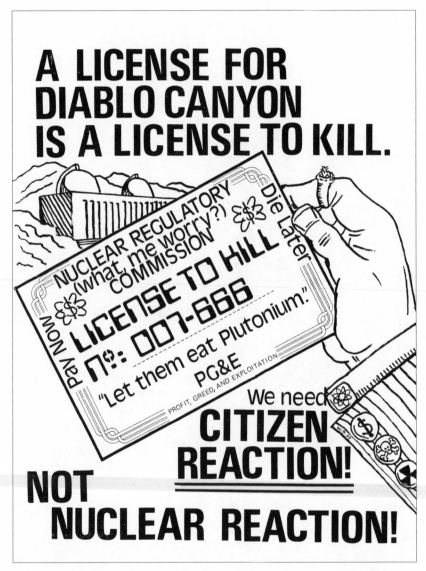

"A License to Kill," Abalone Alliance flyer, 1979. Courtesy of Abalone Alliance Safe Energy Clearinghouse, San Francisco.

The 1981 blockade. Backcountry protestors traveled across the Irish Hills to reach Diablo nuclear plant. Courtesy of Abalone Alliance Safe Energy Clearinghouse, San Francisco.

"Transform Diablo," Abalone Alliance flyer, 1978. Courtesy of Abalone Alliance Safe Energy Clearinghouse, San Francisco.

The Mutant Sponges affinity group. *It's About Times* (September 1980). Courtesy of Abalone Alliance Safe Energy Clearinghouse, San Francisco.

"Reagan's Arms Control Plan," *It's About Times* (May–June 1982). Courtesy of Abalone Alliance Safe Energy Clearinghouse, San Francisco.

"Peacekeeper on Earth," *It's About Times* (December–January 1983). Courtesy of Abalone Alliance Safe Energy Clearinghouse, San Francisco.

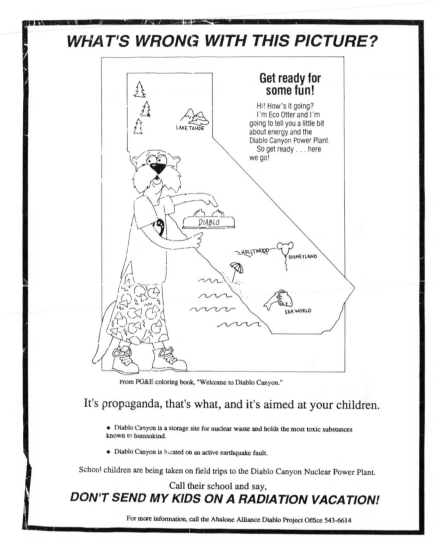

"What's Wrong with This Picture?" Abalone Alliance poster. Courtesy of Abalone Alliance Safe Energy Clearinghouse, San Francisco.

Diablo Canyon nuclear power plant. Photograph courtesy of Jay Swanson.

Images of nuclear nature parks failed to win over antinuclear activists. In their view, a nuclear landscape constituted a place of danger for nature and humanity. A vision of children on swings close to the Diablo plant represented a nightmare scenario. Meanwhile, Diablo's location served to amplify nuclear fears. Out of sight to all but passing mariners, Diablo's secluded position encouraged some residents to ignore construction, but others disliked the feeling of being unable to keep an eye on PG&E's activities. Critics took the choice of such a sheltered location as proof that Pacific Gas had something to hide. The atomic project also appeared dangerously near to San Luis Obispo. The Mothers feared a cloud of radiation would someday rise from Diablo Canyon and drift inland, engulfing towns in a deadly invisible mist.

For Californians who had harbored nuclear fears for some time, Diablo Canyon became a convenient landscape on which to focus their growing concerns. In the 1970s the prospect of global nuclear war gave way to the immediate danger posed by individual nuclear power plants. Test sites and missile silos were frequently far from population zones. Speaking on behalf of the Mothers, Sandy Silver explained how "all of us have been against nuclear weapons, but for most people nuclear weapons are an abstract issue. Fighting a nuclear power plant . . . all of a sudden it became tangible for people." In a sense Diablo provided a release valve for long-term nuclear anxieties, a place where concerns over radiation could be duly vented. PG&E's decision to build reactors on the Pecho Coast presented an opportunity for dissidence, a platform for debate of broader nuclear issues. This, in turn, cemented ties between the coastal construction site and older, more established nuclear venues and images. Antinuclear rhetoric asserted the common ground between nuclear swords and plowshares. Ultimately all things atomic derived from the original ground zeroes of Trinity and Hiroshima. Protesters saw the history of nuclear power as located firmly within the trajectory of nuclear weapons development. For some, Diablo undoubtedly seemed like a bomb waiting to go off in the backyard. Only the Irish Hills separated the atomic plant from residential gardens.[28]

▪ ECOFEMINISM AND PARENTING THE ATOM ▪

The Mothers for Peace challenged the nuclear plant on their doorsteps and, in so doing, highlighted the gendered nature of atomic development. Though

"Diablo Canyon" was a gender-neutral name, the design, construction, and future operation of the plant, not forgetting its licensing hearings, represented processes controlled overwhelmingly by men. The Diablo nuclear plant seemed part of a broader atomic patriarchy. On the deepest psychological level, the "limitless" quality of atomic energy referred not only to universal hopes of abundance, but arguably to breaking free of limits formerly imposed by nature—notably in granting women the exclusive right of reproduction and in the creation of new life. The nuclear bomb dropped on Hiroshima on August 6, 1945, was revealingly nicknamed "Little Boy"; the one detonated over Nagasaki three days later was "Fat Man." Edward Teller took the accolade of "father of the H-bomb," and AEC chairman David Lilienthal's sobriquet was "Mr. Atom." Nuclear images were often couched in terms connoting sexualized violence, with nuclear weapons being compared with the male sex organ and Hollywood starlets being described as "anatomic bombs," while atomic testing in the Pacific gave rise to name of the Louis Réard–designed bikini swimsuit. Nuclear power plants were similarly endowed with sexual references, from the "breeder" reactor to the analogy between a nuclear meltdown and a sexual climax. Diablo Canyon's reactors even resembled "breast-like domes" to some. Meanwhile, promotions of the peaceful atom reinforced the image of American women as domestic servants. The idea of futuristic kitchens with "nuclear powered toasters" tempted housewives to welcome the atom into their homes. Aimed largely at middle-class suburban homes, Disney's *Our Friend the Atom* and PG&E's description of the Diablo plant as a "good neighbor" suggested that a "nuclear family" was more than just a sociocultural ideal. Behind the stereotyping lay a belief that women could not, or need not, understand the actual science of the atom, but if nuclear power was packaged as a sleek and attractive electrical good, they could just about manage to plug it in and reap the benefits of man's work.[29]

With their suburban lives and well-appointed homes, many of the women who joined the Mothers for Peace were arguably the targets of such propaganda. The attractive prospect of a gleaming nuclear kitchen nevertheless proved insufficient to win over a middle-California "bunch of housewives" more committed to peace protests. The Mothers interpreted the nuclear-powered invasion of their homes as a radioactive threat rather than an atomic boon. PG&E's project signified a test of parental responsibility through its potential to violate the family environment. The Mothers focused not upon the promises of new schools or cheaper electricity, but instead on their own role as protectors of children. The group's motif of a motherly white dove holding a protective wing over her fledgling symbolized this parental duty. A 1976 poster of a mother and toddler read, "What do you do in case of a nuclear accident? Kiss your children goodbye."[30]

The Mothers were not the only women's group to challenge the atom. At Greenham Common, Berkshire, England, in the early 1980s, feminists gathered in camps along the fences of an American air base designated to receive cruise missiles with nuclear warheads. The antinuclear movement across the Western world attracted a strong contingent of women. However, in the early 1970s the Mothers were one of the first groups to openly challenge the nuclear hegemony. Yet they saw themselves neither as feminists nor as environmentalists. As Silver explained it, "you have to remember that this was kind of a very beginning scene. We had just come out of the 1960s. The Mothers for Peace were an anti-war group. We were no environmentalists as such, the feminist movement hadn't really started yet." Despite their title and largely, if not exclusively, female membership, the Mothers failed to see themselves as leaders of feminist thought and action. For Apfelberg the organization "was sort of like a group of friends." Looking back on the early 1970s, Silver remembered how it "definitely was not a feminist group then." She felt more concerned with civil rights at the time of joining the Mothers: "I felt very strongly for ethnic minorities, but women? I thought, we don't have any problems—how can you talk about women's problems when blacks can't vote, blacks can't drink water from the same fountain as a white." Although members such as Pat Noah raised feminist consciousness within the group, women's issues did not overwhelmingly dictate its path. The environmental tag equally seemed inappropriate. "It wasn't our tag. Our tag was there's radiation, radiation hurts children, in particular the fetus and young children, and that was our concern," explained Silver. The Mothers came from a background of civil rights and antiwar experiences, not from the Sierra Club. They were human preservationists, not land preservationists.[31]

Nonetheless, ecofeminist impulses drifted through the Mothers' meetings. Greta Gaard posits that modern ecofeminism derives from "peace movements, labor movements, women's health care, and the anti-nuclear, environmental, and animal liberation movements." At Diablo Canyon the Mothers for Peace pioneered an ecofeminist challenge to nuclear power, based on a heartfelt defense of nature, motherhood, and earthcare. Concerned women responded to the nuclear threat by coming together and sharing experiences and responsibilities. This almost unconscious, de facto female empowerment made them a "women's movement without knowing it" during the early 1970s. The Mothers also felt concerned for "Mother Nature." Their arguments were permeated with notions of technological dangers, artificial poisons, and human fallibility. "Radiation Blues," by a local woman, Jean Beauvais, articulated proto-ecofeminist concerns. The song begins: "Tell me mama, why the grass won't grow, at least it looks like its pretty slow, / ma please tell me why the grass won't grow, it worries me to death." Beauvais's melancholic story introduces a strong nature theme into the relationship between a mother and her child facing a slow death by radiation, presumably the result of an accident at the Diablo nuclear plant. In questioning why "the bird won't fly" as well as "why it's hard to talk," the child reveals a place quietly dying by radiation, very similar to the one Rachel Carson describes in "A Fable for Tomorrow," the opening chapter of *Silent Spring*. Both Carson's and Beauvais's imaginary places carry a sense of foreboding, "a strange stillness," caused by an invisible poison that not only has killed birdsong but will soon engulf life itself. "This town does not actually exist, but it might easily have a thousand counterparts in America," warns Carson at the end of her "Fable." Beauvais indicates that San Luis Obispo might soon become one of them. "Radiation Blues" forecasts the atom's role in both the death of nature and the death of children. The child, on behalf of nature, asks: "well if you could do it again, would you really TRY to save this earth before I DIE??"[32]

The indication of a link between ecological responsibility and parental responsibility suggested that the Mothers for Peace were well suited to environmental protest. Meanwhile, the Mothers no doubt respected and empathized with Rachel Carson, who herself had been patronized, condemned, and smeared by a male-dominated scientific community in the 1960s. The Mothers printed an extract from *Silent Spring* in their handbooks: "By acquiescing in an act that can cause such suffering to a living creature, who among us is not diminished as a human being?" The two strands of feminism and environmentalism gradually came together within the Mothers for Peace.[33]

▪ LOCAL FALLOUT ▪

Over a ten-year period the local opposition to the Diablo Canyon nuclear plant changed significantly. At the beginning of 1967 Pacific Gas faced a challenge from conservationists concerned about landscape despoliation. By the mid-1970s a group of women worried about radiation had become PG&E's foremost critic. Local attitudes had also changed. Citizens faced up to the realities of having a nuclear neighbor for the first time in the 1970s and also began to dwell on the dangers it posed to the region. The work by the Mothers for Peace, the discovery of the Hosgri Fault, and growing nationwide doubts over nuclear safety caused citizens to gradually reconsider a nuclear plant in their "backyard." As a useful barometer (and stimulant) of changing public sentiment, the local *Telegram-Tribune* went from enthusiastically supporting nuclear power in San Luis County in 1967 to openly criticizing it by 1977. While relaying the industry-held view—"We have a pretty good handle on all of this"—Jim Hayes had also compared the running of a nuclear plant at Diablo Canyon to "the very serious business of holding a king cobra by its hood while milking its venom." The golden optimism that had accompanied plans for PG&E's project in the 1960s ebbed during the 1970s. While many locals still accepted the Diablo plant, they did so with notable reservations.[34]

A wary public was just one of the problems PG&E encountered at Diablo Canyon. The corporation had hoped for its nuclear plant to begin commercial operation in 1972. The construction process took much longer than expected. Dilemmas arose in quality control and design schematics. During 1974 an estimated one million man-hours were lost in labor disputes. The cost of the project continued to rise. While plant systems were tested in early 1976, an operating license was delayed by disagreements concerning the Hosgri Fault.[35]

PG&E also became involved in a legal battle concerning the Diablo property. Rancher-developer Robert Marre originally leased 585 acres for the plant site (as well as land for a transmission corridor and access road) to Pacific Gas in return for "a possible $20 million line of credit." In 1974 Marre declared his holdings bankrupt. PG&E contended that it was owed $11 million. In 1977 a federal court awarded the utility a ninety-nine-year lease not only on

Diablo Canyon itself, but also on the Marre land surrounding it, amounting to an extra 3,875 acres. PG&E's assets stretched from Point San Luis to
Diablo Rock, representing over half of the Pecho Coast. The additional acres
provided the utility with its own nuclear buffer zone. The area immediately at
risk from a plant accident now came under the company's control.[36]

Another challenge surrounded the uncertain impact of plant operation on
the local environment. The passage of the National Environmental Policy Act
(NEPA) in 1970 led to PG&E's presenting an Environmental Impact Statement
on a half-finished nuclear plant. Eager to avoid delays in the licensing process,
PG&E successfully argued for construction to continue, pending NEPA review.
Officials claimed that ongoing building work would "not give rise to a significant adverse effect on the environment" but instead would "improve the
units' effect on the environment because it will lead to completion of partially
completed structures resulting in a continually improving visual effect as the
architectural goal is achieved."[37]

Further questions emerged over the plant's long-term effect on marine
life. The power plant's cooling systems had been designed to take in millions
of gallons of ocean water, which, after passing through the nuclear edifice,
would return to the Pacific around 20 degrees Fahrenheit warmer. Predictions varied over the effects of this warming on the chosen discharge area
of Diablo Cove. PG&E's Environmental Report to the AEC in July 1971 suggested a "change in species composition" from cold- to warm-water species
but asserted that "the end result could be a richer, more dense association
of organisms than now present." Based on AEC testimony that "much of
the marine plant and animal life would benefit from the discharge of heated
water," the *Telegram-Tribune* in September 1973 claimed: "Diablo to Benefit
Ecology." However, some feared that the immediate region would be significantly harmed by the change in temperature. In 1974 a local abalone diver,
William Cornwell, intervened in the licensing hearings, citing his concerns
for marine life along the Pecho Coast. Cornwell claimed that Pacific Gas had
already destroyed the cove immediately to the south of Diablo Canyon. By
installing the plant's intake systems, PG&E had allegedly created a "silt laden
grave yard" there. Having attempted to minimize disturbance of Chumash
burial sites at Diablo during construction activities, PG&E was now charged
with creating offshore cemeteries of its own.[38]

Pacific Gas tested the plant's cooling system for the first time during the summer of 1974. California Department of Fish and Game staff, along with PG&E's own biologists, later discovered two hundred dead abalone in Diablo Cove. By January 1975, estimates of the death toll ranged from two thousand to ten thousand black abalone and two thousand to three thousand red abalone. Officials blamed the use of copper in the cooling pipes for contaminating the discharged water. Fish and Game staff expressed further concern that the high level of toxicity might render local abalone unfit for human consumption—a reminder that Pacific Gas was not alone in killing sea life: a whole industry depended on it. PG&E then received a citation from the Environmental Protection Agency threatening action if the company further violated its permit to construct and test the Diablo plant. At a cost of over $5 million, copper pipes were replaced with titanium ones. The state attorney general's office negotiated a $375,000 contribution by Pacific Gas to the Department of Fish and Game, although a figure exceeding $1 million had been rumored. A biologist on contract to PG&E had monitored an increase in sea otter numbers along the Pecho Coast during the time of abalone loss. Otters display a voracious appetite for abalone. The discovery that local fauna as well as nuclear construction had contributed to a decline in abalone numbers probably saved the utility a few dollars. Nonetheless it was PG&E's role in the kill that a new environmental protest lobby highlighted by choosing "Abalone Alliance" as its name.[39]

FOUR *The Showdown*

I n the summer of 1976 a new style of environmental protest surfaced on the East Coast of the United States. A collection of citizen groups and local environmental organizations formed the Clamshell Alliance in response to plans for a nuclear plant at Seabrook, New Hampshire. Legal opposition had failed to dampen the enthusiasm of the Public Services Company for two 1,150-megawatt reactors on the coast, and with construction about to begin, the Alliance chose nonviolent direct action as the most suitable means to halt the Seabrook plant. Within the antinuclear coalition, members developed a consensus-based decision-making process to enable each group to participate fully. The motif of the clamshell meanwhile reflected a desire to protect marine ecology as well as "to honor Seabrook clamdiggers who were the first to reject the nuclear project, and the Native People who for three thousand years clammed there and cared for the estuary." The Alliance embarked upon a series of protests. During April 1977, Clamshell activists staged their first mass occupation of the Seabrook construction site, reclaiming the land under the title of "Freebrook."[1]

In February 1976 a Continental Walk for Disarmament and Social Justice passed through San Luis Obispo en route to Washington, D.C., from San Francisco. Several walkers visited Diablo Canyon and held a silent vigil within PG&E property. The act of civil disobedience impressed Raye Fleming, a resident of San Luis Obispo County and member of the Mothers for Peace.

Disillusioned with the constraints of legal intervention, Fleming welcomed the idea of direct action at Diablo Canyon. The Continental Walk highlighted the possibility of a network of activists working together to protest against the plant. The Santa Cruz Resource Center for Nonviolence and the San Francisco office of the American Friends Service Committee (AFSC) offered support for such an antinuclear alliance. AFSC co-workers David Hartsough and Liz Walker helped set up People against Nuclear Power (PANP), later renamed People Generating Energy (PGE), in the San Luis locality. By February 1977 approximately fifty people had joined.[2]

PGE, along with six other antinuclear groups from across the state, formed the Abalone Alliance at a conference at Rancho El Chorro, close to Camp San Luis, in June 1977. The California coalition bore more than a passing resemblance to the Clamshell Alliance, replicating the grassroots organizing, consensus process, and nonviolent civil disobedience practiced at Seabrook. Californians at Camp San Luis also chose a similar name to activists in New Hampshire. Diablo Canyon started out as "Seabrook West," an extension of the campaign against the peaceful atom in the East. Grassroots opposition to atomic power emerged across California during the late 1970s, and the Abalone Alliance grew from its initial seven member groups to twenty-four by 1979, reaching a peak of more than sixty by 1981. Participating antinuclear groups from across the state managed their own campaigns but came together at the California mid-coast for protest actions. Conveniently located just off Highways 1 and 101, the Pecho Coast proved accessible to activists traveling from San Francisco and Los Angeles. The Alliance established offices in San Francisco and San Luis Obispo, where opposition to the plant proved strongest. Newspapers described a white, middle-class movement, a mixture of students taking part in their first protest and seasoned veterans of earlier peace and civil rights crusades. Backed up by photographs of twenty-something protesters arm-in-arm singing pacifist songs at the gates of Diablo, the image stuck. Alliance members nonetheless claimed that the open structure and wide geographical spread of the coalition attracted a fair cross-section of Californians. Former Abalone William Miller remembers how he "was just amazed . . . at the variety of people who were involved, extreme differences from teenage anarchists to aging hippies to straight conservative people." Some local citizens also lent their support to civil disobedience events. By

1979 much of California seemed caught up in an antinuclear magnetic storm, with Diablo Canyon the conductor. People interested in grassroots organizing and nonviolent action, the mechanisms of protest, relished the opportunity to attend the first large-scale demonstration on the West Coast. Attendees voiced concerns over nuclear power, the environment, consumerism, authority, and government. After a brief respite in the mid-1970s, a time when social and environmental issues took second stage to Watergate and the energy crisis, "people were ready to get involved" in popular crusades again and some even hoped to resurrect the protest culture of the 1960s. For politically radical Californians, visiting Diablo resembled an act of civic duty, protesting simply "because that's the kind of people we are here."[3]

The Abalone Alliance held its first civil disobedience action at Diablo Canyon on August 6, 1977. The county sheriff's department arrested forty-six protesters for trespass on private property and failure to disperse. On arrest, demonstrators placed abalone shells on the road in their places. Those who illegally walked the Pecho Coast included local conservationist Ian McMillan (at seventy-one years of age) and a member of the Mothers for Peace, Mary Gail Black. Their presence served as a reminder that the Abalone Alliance, while bringing new tactics to Diablo, also continued a tradition of protest against the plant. Meg Symond, one of the 1,414 protesters arrested at Seabrook earlier in the year, also joined the Abalone action. The Alliance hosted a rally at nearby Avila Beach. Between 1,000 and 1,500 individuals took to the sand to hear the likes of ecologist Barry Commoner and nuclear critic Daniel Ellsberg highlight the dangers of the Diablo plant. The *Santa Barbara News and Review* predicted that "a major escalation in the battle over the nuclear reactor" would follow the event.[4]

Around three thousand people attended a similar gathering a year later. The *San Francisco Bay Guardian* named the event the "Diablo Canyon Anti-Nuke Beach Party Bonanza and Energy Fair." David Brower returned to Diablo, addressing a crowd far more receptive to antinuclear principles than his Sierra Club colleagues in the late 1960s. Ian McMillan and county supervisor Richard Krejsa spoke out against PG&E's atomic project, while former Atomic Energy Commission scientist John Gofman gave his view as to the scientific dangers of radiation. A giant plastic blue whale floated above protesters. Waves washed away a sand-castle version of the Diablo plant on

Avila Beach, while Abalone members hoped for a greater tide a few miles to the north. Officials arrested 487 Abalone activists. Upon arraignment, many used their courtroom appearances to argue an antinuclear case. "I am not on trial—nuclear fission is," declared county resident Bill Denneen.[5]

As well as organizing protests in San Luis County, the Abalone Alliance regularly picketed PG&E offices across the state during the late 1970s. The Alliance published a newspaper, *It's About Times,* that provided a forum for activist-led debate. Separate groups within the Abalone coalition developed their own foci and protest styles.

In March 1979 movie audiences followed the intrigues of corporate power, atomic danger and press manipulation in *The China Syndrome,* a Hollywood thriller focusing on unsafe practices at a fictitious American nuclear plant. During the same month, a partial meltdown at Three Mile Island (TMI) atomic power plant near Harrisburg, Pennsylvania, caught the attention of the nation. For several days of the crisis few appeared to understand what had gone wrong at Metropolitan Edison's Unit 2 reactor on the Susquehanna River. Rumors of a follow-up accident persisted, and thousands of families evacuated the region. Public confidence in the American nuclear industry plummeted. The Abalone Alliance had planned a rally in San Francisco for April 7, long before the problems in Pennsylvania. The combined impact of *The China Syndrome* and Three Mile Island spurred 25,000 people to attend the "Stop Diablo Canyon" protest outside San Francisco's city hall. Antinuclear activity reached a crescendo on the East Coast when 200,000 participated in a rally at New York City's Battery Park. Abalone staffperson Pam Metcalf noted: "Three Mile Island confirmed our worst fears, which was tragic," but the incident "also gave us what was needed to try to stop that from happening in California."[6]

▪ *THE CHINA SYNDROME,* "TMI 2," AND DIABLO CANYON ▪

Although a number of books and films had touched on the dangers of atomic power, the most notable being John G. Fuller's investigative report *We Almost Lost Detroit* (1975), mainstream success had eluded works of antinuclear fiction in the 1970s. Coinciding with Three Mile Island and sporting a capable script and cast, *The China Syndrome* proved the great exception. The movie relates dangerous cover-ups at a fictional "Ventana" nuclear plant in California "near" the San Fernando Valley. While filming a promotional segment on nuclear power at Ventana, TV news reporter Kimberly Wells (Jane Fonda) and her cavalier cameraman Richard Adams (Michael Douglas) witness scenes of panic following an unplanned reactor "scram." Unbeknown to officials, Adams captures the event on tape, but broadcasting moguls refuse to air the story. Undaunted, Wells and Adams convince one of the plant's shift supervisors, Jack Godell (Jack Lemmon), to look into the matter. On finding evidence of corporate malpractice, Godell, in desperation, locks himself inside the control room, promising to stay there until somebody takes notice of his story.

The China Syndrome's unusual mixture of Hollywood-style accessibility, gritty realism (Mike Gray's screenplay drew on an accident at the Dresden II nuclear plant near Chicago in 1970), and sense of foreboding made it a minor *Silent Spring* for the antinuclear cause. Similar to the victimization of Rachel Carson by pesticide conglomerates, *The China Syndrome* faced a barrage of criticism by nuclear industry officials, even prior to its release. Nine days before the opening, an executive of Southern California Edison, without seeing the movie, charged that *The China Syndrome* had "no scientific credibility and is, in fact, ridiculous."[7]

For antinuclear activists it was easy to superimpose the fiction within *The China Syndrome* onto the reality of Diablo Canyon. The Ventana plant, amongst "surrounding sand and chaparral," windy roads, and rolling hills, partially resembled Diablo Canyon and the Pecho Coast. The corporation owning Ventana, "California Gas and Electric" (CG&E), served as a fictitious twin to Pacific Gas and Electric. The *Village Voice* associated the spate of welding problems at Diablo with similar problems at Ventana. The newspaper's description of nervous PG&E workers, keen to avoid the attention of the press, resembled *The China Syndrome*'s portrayal of CG&E employees and their own guilt-ridden silence in response to the investigative advances of Kimberly Wells. Among Obispan cinema attendees, violent tremors at Ventana due to the near-failure of pump supports, threatening to "blow Southern California sky high," no doubt conjured images of a Hosgri-induced earthquake at Diablo Canyon. Richard Adams even shouts "Earthquake" in response to the shudders at Ventana. The film's companion novel described Adams as "a regular organizer of civil rights marches, Vietnam protest marches, free speech movements, campus disturbances, Greenpeace demonstrations, liberation movements of every kind and of every persuasion." The Abalone Alliance would have fitted nicely amongst that list. Members of the film crew also supported nuclear protest in the region. Mike Gray notably attended a press conference in San Luis Obispo and "charged that Diablo is a real-life example of the corporate irresponsibility dramatized in the film." Jack Lemmon endorsed requests for donations to the Center for Law in the Public Interest, a legal group working with the Mothers for Peace against the Diablo plant. Pacific Gas employees who queried construction standards at Diablo reminded Lemmon of the role he played in *The China Syndrome*. "Diablo Canyon," he declared, "threatens every Californian—my family as well as yours." Meanwhile, grassroots groups belonging to the Abalone Alliance took advantage of the alarmist tone of the Hollywood thriller. Activists leafleted Californians exiting movie theaters, hoping to tie the still-fresh image of the fictional plant with popular perceptions of Diablo Canyon.[8]

The nuclear accident at Three Mile Island boosted *The China Syndrome*'s attendance figures across the country. The film offered the American public a useful, albeit sensationalized, insight into the real-life drama in Pennsylvania. The movie explained the basic workings of an atomic reactor, translated a few key phrases of nuclear jargon into common English, and provided a virtual tour of a nuclear plant. Moviegoers searching for answers behind the accident at Three Mile Island found the film's portrayal of a corrupt and inefficient atomic industry, ineffectual government regulation, and all-consuming profit motive entirely plausible. In San Luis Obispo protesters carried a coffin from the local movie house to the regional office of Pacific Gas. Images of *The China Syndrome*, Three Mile Island, and Diablo Canyon temporarily merged.

Wary Californians even anticipated a follow-up to Three Mile Island on the West Coast. Protesters feared that Diablo Canyon would become "TMI 2." One Abalone placard imitated a movie trailer blurb, promoting events on the Pecho Coast as the next installment in a Hollywood-style disaster trilogy: "If you liked Hiroshima . . . were thrilled by Harrisburg—you're gonna love Diablo Canyon!!" An Abalone flyer warned: "Three Mile Island: An Accident without End—Diablo Canyon: An Accident Waiting to Happen." Ralph Nader declared, "We all live in Pennsylvania," at an Abalone rally in

San Francisco in April 1979. Similar phrases associating Diablo with Harrisburg adorned antinuclear T-shirts. Two distant landscapes were momentarily joined in their atomic associations. Newspapers deliberated the connections between West Coast and East Coast nuclear plants, joining disparate states together in their common dose of nuclear fear. Given that "the Diablo Canyon plant is a product of the same technology which failed at Three Mile Island," the *Central Coast Sun Bulletin* advised the Golden State to do without nuclear power. "If the system didn't work in Pennsylvania or if it tried to work and was thwarted by human error," the *San Luis Obispo County Telegram-Tribune* feared that "the same pattern could be repeated at Diablo" and argued for the NRC to deny the Diablo plant a permit to operate.[9]

In his staff report to the American Friends Service Committee, David Hartsough stated that the Three Mile Island accident "has awakened people as nothing before has, to the dangers and problems of nuclear power." As a result, said Hartsough, "the anti-nuclear movement is now much larger than we ever dreamed of two years ago." Although the Abalone Alliance had grown significantly between its inception and March 1979, Three Mile Island proved a "huge catalyst" for nuclear protest on the West Coast. On the local scene, folksinger Ede Morris chose the apt analogy that "Three Mile Island set off a chain reaction of opposition in San Luis Obispo." The American nuclear industry struggled to come to terms with what seemed like public paranoia. Atomic corporations underlined the lack of fatalities or serious consequences in the Harrisburg accident. In an advertisement paid for by Dresser Industries (manufacturers of the faulty valve blamed for causing the accident), Edward Teller asserted that he had suffered a heart attack from arguing against Jane Fonda and other antinuclear activists in the aftermath of the reactor scram. "I was the only victim of Three Mile Island," claimed Teller. Diablo Canyon seemed another casualty of the social fallout drifting from Harrisburg.[10]

▪ THE NUCLEAR THREAT ▪

The popularity of *The China Syndrome*, impending investigations into Three Mile Island, and a temporary licensing moratorium, along with national protests, denied the U.S. nuclear industry respectability in the public arena. The U.S. government had failed to convince many people of the merits attached to nuclear energy production. Childhood memories of "duck and cover" class-room exercises and the destruction of Hiroshima and Nagasaki resurfaced in the popular consciousness. All of sudden, Americans everywhere turned their back on "our friend the atom."

Diablo Canyon served as a focal point for those Californians eager to show their disaffection with atomic energy. As Abalone William Miller explained, "I think there was a pretty strong resentment to nuclear material in our gen-eration. I think it was a very fertile ground for an issue like this." Where once PG&E officials had presented a place of optimism and promise, Alliance members speedily fashioned Diablo Canyon into an icon of environmental destructiveness. Cartoon images of cracked reactors and radiation clouds at Diablo imparted themes of slow death, ecological decay, and a fragile and contaminated planet. Activists doctored images of the gray, stolid industrial site to convey a sense of impending doom. On posters and placards, protest-ers created visual danger by showing nuclear missiles exiting the plant or jagged fault lines running underneath it. An Abalone poem entitled "Clear Beginnings" compared the "nuclear core" of Diablo with the apple picked from the tree of knowledge by Eve, a dangerous and forbidden fruit.[11]

While atomic advocates heralded the creation of a chain reaction as the discovery of one of nature's last secrets (Winston Churchill referred to the first atomic bombs as "a revelation of the secrets of nature, long mercifully withdrawn from man"), nuclear protesters projected a clear divide between nature and the atom. The Alliance theorized that at "the heart of the matter, the matter of nuclear energy, is the distance between nature and us humans. It's a distance we're trying to bridge." Behind the cardboard placards and anti-nuclear aphorisms was a common belief that the Diablo plant (and nuclear power in general) posed a danger to ecological vitality. Abalone Elizabeth Whitney saw a "nuclear threat . . . to the common source: our land, our water and our air." Diablo, claimed one Abalone protest handbook, amounted to "a statement: We don't care about the weather, we don't care about the sun or the moon." For activists, the nuclear plant epitomized the loss of contact with the natural world endemic to twentieth-century industrialized society and illustrated how technological progress could encourage a divide between humans and nature. Abalone Don Eichelberger interpreted nuclear protest as "a response to the increasing technicalness of environmental degradation that you're seeing. Its easy to quantify a clear-cut . . . an open pit coal mine . . . the effects of building a dam on a beautiful pristine area, but its really not easy to quantify the effects of radiation which is odorless, colorless, tasteless, invisible." Popular environmental ideology thus informed Abalone protest motivations.[12]

Eichelberger had read Rachel Carson's *Silent Spring* (1962) at an early age. Carson employed images of atomic fallout to dramatize the long-term effects of pesticides on a rural American community. As *Silent Spring* became an icon of the modern environmental era, so too did the "modern environmental threat" appear quintessentially invisible, hard to contain, and all-encompassing. Nuclear energy fitted the picture perfectly. Abalone activists quickly drew attention to the potential danger that the Diablo plant posed to southern and central California. Concern grew for agriculture downwind of the plant. Citizens feared that an atomic meltdown "would contaminate the state's Central Valley whereon is grown nearly half of America's fruit and vegetables." Despite their failure to recognize a land area already heavily contaminated by pesticides, radiation was, metaphorically speaking, covering similar ground.[13]

Members also feared for coastal ecology. An antinuclear pamphlet urged readers to look beyond the superficial, warning that "PG&E intends to treat wildlife and sea life around Diablo in a manner far different from that depicted in the beautiful displays of plants and animals in the PG&E 'nuclear information center.'" The Sonoma County group SONOMOreAtomics even predicted the "eco-rape" of the coastal estuary. For many Abalone protesters, the Diablo plant represented an immediate threat to the environment where they lived and worked. One protest song followed the tune of "Don't Throw Your Trash in My Backyard." Meanwhile, veteran ecological campaigner Mary Moore emphasized the interrelatedness of environmental dangers: "The message we're trying to get across is that if you live at Love Canal it's related to Diablo Canyon."[14]

Abalone protest further reflected unease over the direction of modern technology. The San Francisco Society against Blatantly Obnoxious Technology (SABOT) protested alongside Abalone activists in 1981. The group's acronym conjured images of angry French workers sabotaging factory machinery with their wooden shoes in the early nineteenth century. Meanwhile, *It's About*

Times recast the atomic industry advertising icon "Reddy Kilowatt" as a crazed character with a plutonium habit by the name of "Unreddy Killer-watt." In a similar vein a protest poster portrayed "Nukes" as a cigarette brand, a "choice blend of berserk technology, radioactive crud, and 100 per-cent American bureaucracy," with a health warning underneath. Protesters also challenged the expertise of American nuclear engineers by comparing claims as to the safety of the Diablo plant with the faith of British shipbuild-ers in the "unsinkable" *Titanic*. On a more thoughtful note, Don Eichelberger situated the Alliance as being generally "concerned about the promises made by science to end all our problems" and thus recognizing "the need to be criti-cal of all new technology that comes and holds itself as the panacea." Anxiety over the path of modern industrial society situated the antinuclear movement within a broader environmental movement keen to tackle existing economic priorities and technological imperatives.[15]

In response to the environmental dangers posed by the Diablo plant, Alliance members fervently promoted themselves as nature's defenders, and thus rekindled some of the sentiments articulated by Sierra Club members and local conservationists before them. Tita Caldwell suggested she had been "summoned" to Diablo by "the pelicans, butterflies / and tiniest ants" along with her "human family / at Nagasaki and Hiroshima." Another poem pleaded: "let children grow up in nuclear free light, / saving the environment, that's what's right / ecology should be sought / let's let the fish swim in the waters, / without the reactors turning." Naturalistic namesakes denoted a basic environmental consciousness within the antinuclear movement. Affin-ity groups included the Friends of the Fish (NoFission), Friends of the Sun, Spiderwort (a flower sensitive to radiation), and the Radioactive Rock-Cods from Mendocino.[16]

▪ THE SOCIAL THREAT ▪

Along with the prospect of radioactive particles in the atmosphere and other potential nuclear disasters, the Abalone Alliance considered the spread of nuclear facilities as synonymous with a fast-decaying society. Members asso-ciated Diablo with authoritarianism, militarism, abuses of power, and the loss of core American values. Antinuclear activists accused both the nuclear industry and the federal government of frequently operating outside the realms of democracy and accountability by pushing through atomic schemes. The newspaper *It's About Times* jokingly "exposed" a redesign of the White House along atomic lines (complete with reactor dome), suggestive of the pronuclear bias of leading American politicians. Abalone activists felt that nuclear developments were tied to a dereliction of trust in society and politics. The willingness of the Alliance to openly engage in social criticism marked its difference from the Sierra Club and Scenic Shoreline, organizations that ultimately felt more comfortable dealing with nature rather than with society.[17]

Seeing Diablo as a social threat had consequences within the Alliance. Members felt persecuted, even at personal risk, for taking a critical stance. The local sheriff's department infiltrated the organization in 1977. Two undercover deputies, Richard Lee and Charles Douglas, were accidentally arrested during the August 1977 protest. Rumors circulated that PG&E paid for surveillance. The spy theme found artistic fruition in the Abalone poster "License to Kill, no. 007-666," with PG&E being awarded the license by the head of the NRC, the supposed counterpart of James Bond's "M" (and sporting a fancy line in "atomic energy" cuff links). In response to pronuclear campaigns led by small groups such as Citizens for Adequate Energy, the Alliance felt under personal attack. One *It's About Times* headline read, "Corporate Nostalgia for the McCarthy Era Seems on the Rise." Likened to remote U.S. military sites, the Diablo headland itself hardly helped matters. Off-limits to the public, it was imagined as a place beyond control or assurance. Conspiracy theories prospered in a fearful climate.[18]

Abalone campaigners felt particularly uneasy over corporate America. In a regular feature entitled "Corporate Lies Department," *It's About Times* targeted such nuclear stewards as Westinghouse and Bechtel, poking fun at how such companies sought to link patriotism, progress, and nuclear power. In response to a claim by Westinghouse that in "every energy shortage nuclear plants have kept the electricity flowing" and the American flag flying, the Abalone newspaper criticized the idea of energy independence, claiming that the American flag would reach only half-mast with nuclear power. A Christmas play organized by Bechtel wives received the attention of the January 1980 issue. The play documented the struggle of town residents to light their community tree during a power failure. Even "Father Fossil Fuel" proved unable to help out, so "Reggie the Real Great Reactor" stepped in to save the day. *It's About Times* used the play as evidence of corporate America's still being in love with nuclear fairy tales.[19]

In interpreting an association between nuclear power and corporate power, Alliance members articulated radical left-wing concerns over American capitalism. Protest songs bore nuances of an antidollar culture. To the rhythm of "Dry Bones," protesters recounted "The Connection" between "power," a "nuke plant," a "utility," and "money." In cartoons of Diablo Canyon, dollar bills traveled by conveyor belt or construction truck, feeding the growth of PG&E's plant. A sketch captioned "Members of the board of a utility considering all aspects of building a nuclear power plant" showed an executive pointing to one huge dollar sign on his otherwise bare blackboard. Calling for a broad alliance against corporate capitalism, the March–April 1979 edition of *It's About Times* declared, "Everybody who fights against corporate profit fights against the same thing we do in our anti-nuclear movement." A "Smash Capitalism, Not Atoms" banner adorned the side of a van at the July 1979 Abalone rally.[20]

However, for most Abalone activists the nuclear issue superseded the traditional politics of the far left. U.S. senator Jeremiah Denton of Alabama included the Alliance on his list of "communist organizations" operational within the United States. Despite accusations by the senator, the Abalone Alliance proved far from communist. At the 1981 blockade camp, Alliance representatives threw out San Francisco's Revolutionary Communist Party for that group's incitements to violence and dogmatic recital of Marxist rhetoric. As with most environmental organizations, the Abalone Alliance maintained independence from official political parties. Members reacted with very mixed opinions to offers of support from California governor Jerry Brown, a politician renowned for his liberal leanings. Abalone protesters chose direct action at Diablo as their primary means of political struggle to indicate their distaste for traditional channels of involvement in the nuclear process. The Bay Area activist Roger Herried felt that "the government lied to the public" over the dangers of atomic energy: "Nuclear power along with Watergate created an environment where you couldn't trust the government because the government does what it wants." Conventional politics seemingly had little to offer.[21]

Abalone distrust of established political channels had a lot to do with Watergate, Vietnam, and the behavior of local police departments toward civil rights campaigners in the 1960s. According to the *Washington Post*, the Abalone blockades provided a "measure" of "the strength of an antinuclear movement that has appeared to replace civil rights and opposition to the Vietnam War as a magnet for college youth and older political activists." Veterans of civil rights protests such as David Hartsough and Mary Moore proved early converts to the antinuclear cause. The Abalone anthem, "No Diablo! No Diablo! No Diablo over me! / And before I'll be oppressed / I'm gonna stand up and protest / For the love of the human family," as a deliberate reference to the sixties song "Oh Freedom over Me," epitomized the inclusive sense of civil rights within the Alliance. The language of protest frequently relied on references to the civil rights struggle. During one Abalone play, protestor Chuck Knerr revised Martin Luther King's "I have a dream" into a nuclear "nightmare." The activist newspaper *Radioactive Times* quoted another King speech in its call for people to attend Diablo protest: "We are now faced with the fact that tomorrow is today. We are confronted with the urgency of now." However, antinuclear marches attracted mostly white Americans, rather than a multiethnic crowd. In a letter to *It's About Times*, black protester Sylvanus DeVoe regretted the marginalized status of people of color in the movement, despite, according to him, a common factor of greed encouraging racism and atomic development alike. Abalone activists struggled to understand why the antinuclear cause, which many considered a civil rights and survival issue, failed to attract people of color. Attendance partially reflected the demographic character of San Luis Obispo and its middle-class white suburban majority, but the lack of nonwhites in the antinuclear movement ran deeper. Diablo Canyon ultimately signified a remote danger compared with the everyday experiences of African Americans, Native Americans, and Hispanics in a racially divided nation.[22]

The Vietnam War meanwhile instilled notions of an untrustworthy government and the dangers of militarism in Californians who went on to protest against Diablo nuclear plant. At the April 1979 rally, consumer rights advocate Ralph Nader proclaimed nuclear power to be the "technological Vietnam." *It's About Times* compared how the Three Mile Island accident and the Tet offensive (1968) had both precipitated times of reflection and doubt in American life. Protesters used "Vietnam" as a metaphor for self-inflicted failure. "The Diablo Canyon nuclear plant is the Vietnam of the nuclear power industry and PG&E in particular," claimed Barbara Levy of San Francisco. That civil disobedience (by demonstrations, draft dodging, and public education) helped end the Vietnam War inspired hopes of similar success at Diablo Canyon. Nevertheless, for the majority of Americans the issue of nuclear power lacked the sense of urgency and potency common to wartime conditions. The dormant appearance of the Diablo plant hardly matched footage of military action in Vietnam. Abalone Louise Billotte understood that "what we are responding to is still to a large degree potential, while the war in Vietnam was sickeningly actual." The potential dangers of home-grown atomic plants paled alongside both the threat of communism and the body bags arriving back on U.S. soil.[23]

At its most positive, the antinuclear movement responded to the errors of past protest movements, particularly in terms of gender relations. Radical groups of the 1960s frequently upheld traditional gender stereotypes. Male leaders of civil rights, black power, student, and antiwar movements typically resisted the rise of women to positions of influence or authority within "their" organizations. Don Eichelberger explained how in "the sixties and the anti-war thing . . . there was mostly a machismo thing going on—a lot of men jumping off on things, talking a lot and throwing molotov cocktails with sorts of values. . . . In the anti-nuclear movement, it was a lot more decentralized, a lot less male-dominated, there were men and women working closer than I'd ever seen before." Mary Moore considered the Alliance "a real attempt . . . to level the playing field."[24]

Both the Mothers for Peace and the Abalone Alliance honored Karen Silkwood as a female antinuclear martyr. A technician at a Kerr-McGee plutonium plant in Crescent, Oklahoma, in the early 1970s, Silkwood criticized the nuclear industry for poor safety standards. In the process of gathering evidence against Kerr-McGee, Silkwood was exposed to plutonium and died in a car crash en route to a meeting with a reporter from the *New York Times*. Abalone protesters arrested for nuclear misdemeanors frequently gave Silkwood as their surname. Alliance members proved more vocal (and articulate) in their feminist associations than most Mothers. Abalone Elizabeth Whitney congratulated women speaking up for natural cycles in defiance of the "potential destruction machine" of the Diablo plant. Protest handbooks claimed feminism as a "biophilic philosophy" and "a positive vision of the world in which we want to live." Handbooks also attributed the historic exploitation of women and nature alike to the treatment of both groups as "alien, or *Other*." The nuclear landscape of Diablo Canyon signified a dangerous example of patriarchy at work. By undermining atomic machismo, feminists within the Alliance symbolically reclaimed the lands surrounding the plant. As one activist, Jane Miller, put it, "For me, Diablo was a place to be to develop new forms and attitudes of political expression that were congruent with myself as a woman."[25]

■ LINGERING SEISMIC PERILS ■

Like the Mothers for Peace and Scenic Shoreline before them, the Abalone Alliance cited the Hosgri Fault as a key reason to shut down the Diablo plant. Cartoons depicted a jagged fault line emerging from the sea, running directly beneath the facility, cutting the two reactors apart. People Generating Energy paid for billboards in the San Luis area carrying the simple message "Diablo Canyon. On Shaky Ground." A multiplicity of fault lines had successfully thwarted a number of other atomic schemes in California. PG&E's Humboldt Bay nuclear plant, on the northern coast near Eureka, had been shut down in July 1976 for refueling but never restarted due to the discovery of three fault lines close to the site. Don Eichelberger remembered fishing as a boy at Bodega Bay during the time of the corporation's failed attempt to construct an atomic plant on the headland.

The Hosgri Fault elevated the Diablo project above its contemporary atomic peers in terms of press coverage. Events at Diablo were considered unique due to the scale of protest and the curious amalgamation of natural and nuclear hazards. Jack Anderson of the *San Francisco Chronicle* compared the Diablo plant to the Teton Dam in Idaho. Ignorant of geological warning signs, "the government built a monster called Teton," which failed on June 5, 1976, killing fourteen people and leaving thousands homeless. "Now a worse disaster may be in the making on the Californian Coast," cautioned Anderson.[26]

Living in a seismic state no doubt heightened the concern of Californians over the idea of operating a nuclear plant next to an active fault line. Earthquake stories in state newspapers reminded readers of the possible danger lurking at Diablo. "Because there are earthquakes here, and you experience an earthquake, you take them more seriously," explained Bay Area activist Jackie Cabasso. Protester Lauren Alden nevertheless detected a sense of denial in the broader California malaise. Earthquakes had become second nature to many Californians.[27]

▪ BUILDING UP TO BLOCKADE ▪

The year 1979 proved a good one for the Abalone Alliance. A rally at Camp San Luis, just north of Diablo, on June 30 attracted between 35,000 and 40,000 Californians, including Governor Jerry Brown. In his speech to the crowd Brown referred to the Alliance as "a growing force to protect the earth." Other speakers included John Gofman, David Brower, and Bill Wahpehpah from the American Indian Movement. Performers such as Bonnie Raitt, Jackson Browne, and Graham Nash merged popular hit singles with antinuclear song. Pam Metcalf remembered the buzz surrounding the June gathering: "It was our rally. It was incredible to feel that kind of power about people's concerns about a single environmental issue." Momentum appeared firmly on the side of nuclear protest. The specter of Diablo was unavoidable: The *Santa Rosa Press Democrat* simply called San Luis Obispo "Diablo Country."[28]

The NRC temporarily suspended all licensing of nuclear plants in response to Three Mile Island and the subsequent rise in public concern. Abalone activists welcomed the delay imposed on PG&E's plant but pondered how best to take advantage of a nuclear project in limbo. Peter Lumsdaine from the Resource Center for Nonviolence in Santa Cruz saw an opportunity to build on the successes of 1979 by escalating protest activity. However, a more cautious approach prevailed within the group. Alliance members preferred to wait until PG&E's project appeared close to operation before amassing forces outside the gates of Diablo.[29]

Almost two years later the NRC approved low-power testing at Diablo Canyon. The enforced delay had cost PG&E millions of dollars in interest charges on the capital put into the plant. The corporation had also had to source alternative electrical capacity. As the *New York Times* explained, "The plant's unrealized output is equivalent to what would be produced by burning about 20 million barrels of oil." The two reactors could have supplied electricity to a population of around 1,700,000, but instead the power turbines rested inactive. In response to the NRC announcement, the Abalone Alliance called for a full-scale blockade of the site. Activists prepared camp in Los Osos Valley, eight miles northeast of Diablo Canyon. State officials anticipated vast numbers of protesters arriving in the region. Five hundred National Guardsmen and 270 officers from the California Highway Patrol bolstered the forces of the county sheriff's department. Two thousand members of the press descended on the area. On Tuesday, September 15, the first group of Abalone campaigners approached PG&E's entrance to Diablo Canyon. Other protesters hiked across backcountry hills to reach the plant. A few landed at Diablo Cove by boat. Diablo Canyon resembled a battleground between two armies. The *Daily Californian,* the student newspaper at the University of California, Berkeley, headlined, "Diablo Siege: 300 Arrested. Protesters Invade by Land and Sea," and backed up the military metaphors by quoting the contentions of Berkeley activist "Ellen M." that the development of the "peaceful atom" in fact "directly related to how they're getting ready for World War III." Newspapers noted the warlike determination of San Luis Obispo County sheriff George Whiting to circumscribe protest activities. *Newsweek* declared: "Showdown at Diablo Canyon."[30]

It's About Times celebrated the 1981 blockade with the visual capture of PG&E's plant as backcountry hikers unfurled their antinuclear flag to celebrate "Mendocino County against Diablo" next to the reactors. Not all press coverage was so positive. The *Daily Californian* described the blockade as being "like an intriguing soap opera" and criticized the Alliance for spending too much time on symbolic acts and gesture politics. While Jackie Cabasso remembered a "big model of Diablo Canyon, made of dry ice with black smoke coming out of it," being placed at the plant's gates, where the police "smashed" it, reporters remained unimpressed. Vigorous antinuclear chants prompted the *Telegram-Tribune* to describe a "fervor bordering on religious fanaticism" inside the Abalone camp. The *San Francisco Chronicle* meanwhile depicted the "anti-nuclear faith" as "one of the fastest-growing cults in this cult-ridden country." Over 1,900 went to jail during the two-week-long protest, a record for arrests outside an American nuclear plant. Whatever the interpretation, Diablo Canyon had become a statistical landmark in nuclear protest.[31]

Protest activities at Diablo provided Californians with a rare taste of both the natural and nuclear sides of the Pecho Coast. Unlike courtroom battles or congressional lobbying, direct action as an environmental tactic assumed some level of physical interaction between people and place. Abalone activists blocked the public road along Avila Beach in an attempt to stop workers arriving at Diablo. They clogged Diablo Cove with a sea blockade, including the use of Greenpeace's rented schooner *Stone Witch*. The Alliance also hiked across the Pecho Coast, turning the headland into a temporary protest landscape.

Backcountry hikers utilized what they judged to be old Chumash trails across Diablo country. Waiting for them, in the words of the *Oakland Tribune,* were "squadrons of law enforcement helicopters" and "troops" at the disposal of plant manager E. C. Thornberry, the appropriately titled "commander under siege." Common descriptions of the "hostile landscape" noted the alignment of natural dangers with security measures, one article allying high hills with barbed-wire fencing, and rattlesnakes with patrol Dobermans. PG&E released press statements warning of rattlesnakes and other hiking dangers. The *Los Angeles Times, Pacific Sun* (Marin County), and *Berkeley Gazette* followed suit by all drawing attention to the "rattlesnake-infested wilderness" of the Pecho Coast. It seemed history had been temporarily rewound in San Luis, back to a time when Americans feared the supposed evils of untamed nature.[32]

Hiding from helicopters and infrared scanners, "Jackrabbit" idealized the protesters as "ecowarriors going into the woods." When not avoiding capture, members had time to relate the landscape around them. Abalone Crystal enthused: "The country around Diablo is so . . . Californian . . . is there a better word? A hundred hues of gold, a handful of greens, the blues of sky and ocean." For Starhawk, the Diablo nuclear plant signified a "desecration" of a "beautiful place." With a firm "belief in nature as sacred," Starhawk saw the plant as threatening to upset the balance of ecology on the coast. Reminiscent of Sierra Club prose by Litton and Eissler, Alliance leaflets described the region as a "beautiful stretch of coastline." Once again Diablo was granted wilderness credentials in the fight against nuclear power.[33]

Native American links with the coastline also came to the attention of activists. One affinity group called itself "Friends of the Chumash" and protested to honor the "bodies buried on this property." The knowledge that Chumash bones rested at Diablo "helped to reinforce the idea that pagans had of it being sacred," explained Abalone Phoebe, a member of the Matrix affinity group practicing religious protest rituals on site. Fellow protester Brook remembered some success in pagan (as compared to PG&E) "energy work" at Diablo with the appearance of electrical problems at the plant following full-moon rituals in the surrounding hills.[34]

Most protesters responded emotionally to witnessing the plant itself. Barbara Levy, arrested at the main entrance gate, was taken by bus to the reactor site at night and remembered that the area "was lit very strangely." "It felt very spooky to me, and I was feeling nervous about radiation," she recounted. Yet no nuclear fuel had been loaded on-site. For Starhawk the visual appearance of PG&E's project matched its incompatibility with nature: "Below us lies the plant, square, hard-edged, and out-of-place, like a bad science-fiction fantasy cartoon imposed on the landscape. In this place where the earth stretches out her arms and rears her soft breasts, this plant is the emblem of our estrangement, our attempts to control, to impose a cold order with concrete and chain links." Seeing the plant signified the end of the trail for most protesters.[35]

▥ PROTEST TACTICS AND FORGING CHANGE ▥

By the time of the 1981 blockade the Abalone Alliance had established a flexible environment where protesters from across California channeled their actions toward a common antinuclear goal. Using a consensus decision-making process and affinity groups, the antinuclear coalition had spread out across the Golden State. The Clamshell Alliance on the East Coast traced the roots of such a system to Native American and Quaker thought. San Franciscan radicalism and counterculture was also a strong influence. The Abalone process further drew inspiration from a variety of past social movements, from struggles against slavery to peace activists' protests and other actions against America's war in Vietnam. A letter by People Generating Energy member Bob Wolf to the *Telegram-Tribune* in 1977 likened antinuclear activists at Diablo to the protagonists of the Boston Tea Party and those who participated in antisegregation sit-ins during the 1960s, all "small groups who broke the law to make moral statements." Wolf argued that "our non-violent statement should be considered not destructive, but restorative of democracy." The Abalone Alliance listed Henry David Thoreau's "Civil Disobedience" as "suggested reading" in its protest handbooks. Abalone members appreciated Thoreau's insistence on the duty to act by a higher moral law. One member recognized Thoreau's dictum "Let your life be a counter friction to stop the machine" as a highly appropriate phrase for protest against the Diablo nuclear plant. However, Thoreau, who coveted time for individualism and solitude, would never have been comfortable among the Abalone groups amassed at camps. Living alone at Walden Pond for two years represented his idea of a "utopian experiment," rather than choosing to join Brook Farm or any of the other radical communities that flourished in New England during the 1840s.[36]

The nonviolent tenets of Abalone civil disobedience attracted California radicals to the Alliance. Charlotte Davis was won over by the "transformative experience" of nonviolent action. People Generating Energy meanwhile saw "aggression" toward the natural world as "rampant through the work in chemicalized agriculture, strip-mining, and industrial pollution," predictably naming nuclear power as "the most violent form of violence against Nature because it threatens to destroy all forms of life." To Abalone protesters, nonviolence offered a way of life at peace with nature. Like the archetypal Sierran conservationist John Muir, they viewed nature as a wonderful, peaceful community, ignoring the fierce struggles involved in survival.[37]

The fondness displayed by Abalone members for nonviolence and consensus process reflected their belief that such systems would bring about fundamental social change. "Nothing short of changing the system, non-violent revolution," was the naive hope expressed by Abalone "Jayne." While activists primarily struggled *against* nuclear power at Diablo Canyon, those who experienced the Alliance also recognized its optimistic drive *for* what they saw as a better society. The social scientist Barbara Epstein suggested that this latter dynamic of the Abalone Alliance provided the measure of its true agenda: "The threat that Diablo posed to the environment was the occasion, rather than the impetus, for a movement that was fundamentally about social, communal, and personal transformation." Many activists dwelt on ideas of social change as opposed to purely environmental philosophy. The Alliance provided members with an alternate form of society (and utopian experiment) that members wanted to take further. It might also be considered significant that the crucial form and ideals of the Abalone Alliance, of non-violence and consensus, could be found in other social struggles, and were brought *to* protest at Diablo Canyon rather than emerging *from* it.[38]

However, a distinctive and idealistic social-environmental dynamic consistently infused Abalone thought. The "Declaration of Nuclear Resistance" issued by the Alliance articulated a desire to "build a more loving and responsible world for ourselves, our children, and future generations of all living things on this planet." According to David Hartsough, the act of rejecting PG&E's project, simply saying "'No' to Diablo," indicated that people were "saying 'YES' to building a beloved community, to caring for one another, to caring for the earth and future generations." Abalone David Martinez explained that "those who oppose Nuclearism work in the interests of poor and rich, women and men, all ages, all races, all nations, all religious groups, all species endangered or otherwise." Modern environmentalism, fear of nuclear energy, and the landscape of Diablo Canyon all indelibly shaped Abalone consciousness. Given the desire of activists for human society and nature in mutual balance, the Abalone conception of a social utopia inevitably included an environmental vision as well.[39]

In handbooks and on posters the social-environmental utopia played out as a rural-based, solar-powered collection of independent communities, heavily influenced by E. F. Schumacher's environmental treatise *Small Is Beautiful* (1974). One protest newsletter pondered a future of cooperatives based on "work places within walking/biking distance," along with radical ideas proposing common property, "regional consciousness," grassroots democracy, and "the re-establishment of rural culture." This future required reduced consumption complemented by careful conservation to an extent impossible for California in the late 1970s.[40]

An artistic sketch of the "ideal future" in the 1981 Abalone blockade handbook showed a patchwork of buildings, small-scale energy collectors, and crops intermingled with wild trees and plants, giving the impression of a random yet harmonious landscape crafted by an anarchic, organic civilization. The lack of hard lines in the picture symbolized citizen commitment to living as part of a natural and free-flowing landscape, of choosing a soft-energy path over the harsh and obtrusive designs associated with nuclear and coal plants. In the mingling of human and natural features, the Abalone picture contrasted with images of "static," untouched wilderness savored by traditional conservationists. Nature was something to interact with and shape, rather than isolated and protected from everyday living. A rural utopia suited the Abalone desire to balance the needs of nature alongside the requirements of society. Ultimately the Abalone vision represented a sort of middle ground between wilderness and urbanity.[41]

Given the antinuclear focus of the Alliance, it seemed fitting that alternative energy was a key feature of the social-environmental utopia. A solar future was an enticing vision throughout the global antinuclear movement. A beaming sun, with the message "Nuclear Power? No Thanks," became a popular motif of protesters worldwide. "Give me the warm power of the sun . . . but take all your atomic poison power away" was the deal offered in John Hall's antinuclear anthem of the time. Solar power seemed particularly suited to the Golden State.[42]

The Alliance vision drew on the fears and ideals of the nascent environmental era. As Abalone concerns over nuclear power were influenced by Carson's *Silent Spring* and Ehrlich's *Population Bomb,* so too were their hopes for a utopia coinciding with the ecofriendly ideals of new green politics. Articles such as William Moyer's "De-developing the United States through Nonviolence" tied environmental change with social progress in response to strains on the ecosphere. The Abalone utopia drew on the work of soft-energy advocate Amory Lovins. With the support of David Brower and Friends of the Earth, Lovins emerged in the late 1970s with a holistic plan for using renewable and environmentally benign energy sources (solar, wind) and conservation techniques, rather than what he dubbed "wasteful" oil, coal, and nuclear power plants. The AFSC "Energy Slideshow" of 1980 called for the end to the old American Dream dependent on "hard" energy, and the beginning of "a new vision based on values of: local self-reliance, democratic control of resources, harmony with the environment, strong sense of community"—in short, the "New American Dream (Soft Path)." The New American Dream of soft energy appealed to most environmentalists, but it lacked clout in real politics.[43]

By idealizing pastoral life, antinuclear activists unconsciously aligned themselves with past visions. The Abalone "rural community" resembled a suitable home for Jean-Jacques Rousseau's virtuous "natural man." Rousseau and intellectuals from the Romantic movement envisaged rural living as Arcadia, a rhapsodic mix of decent people, nature, and emotion, in contrast to the cold reason and alienation found in cities and industry. The Alliance's presentation of a rural future of honorable people also resembled the Jeffersonian pastoral ideal. Thomas Jefferson had idealized agriculture in the West as marking the true "Republic of Liberty," promising an end to the dirty workshops of the Old World. The nuclear-free utopia similarly suggested a fresh start, freedom, and an escape from polluting industry. However, it hardly represented a realistic option for California state planners.

As if to prove otherwise, Abalone activists transformed their campsite in Los Osos Valley into a testament of antinuclear ideals and ecophilosophy during the 1981 blockade. Solar generators supplied power for the sound system, hot water, and lighting. With theater, flags, balloons, and frequent song, the camp bore a festive and countercultural atmosphere. To Starhawk the camp "seemed magical—like a medieval fair from the past or a premonition of a better future. When you were in it, the space had the kind of order found in a messy room . . . an order like that of an Arabian bazaar, a gypsy camp, or an Indian village." Protester Miki Sanders recounted meeting his mother, Bea, at the camp: "Years of work, civil rights, anti-war and anti-nuke were culminating at Diablo for both of us and this seemed a time to rejoice, to revel in our commitment that spanned decades." The *San Francisco Examiner* described the camp as "a sort-of eco-activist Hooverville," while the liberal-leaning *San Francisco Chronicle* opted to call it "a little Woodstock West." For Elizabeth Whitney, the setting of the camp, amid "the serenity of the on-going natural world," appeared ideal for Abalone protesters making their "stand to shape and change human activities, not only here, in California, in America, but in the whole world." However, the stand lasted only two short weeks, hardly enough time to forge a cohesive or sustainable social model.[44]

■   **THE INTERIM PERIOD**   ■

The September 1981 blockade ended on a high point for the Abalone Alliance with the announcement of a blueprint error at the Diablo plant. Engineer

John Horn found that safety supports in Unit 1 reactor had been installed backward. The timing of the discovery led the Alliance to declare a short-term victory. The following month eighty California Indians held a day-long prayer vigil at Diablo Canyon to mark their disapproval of the nuclear project. In recognition of having built on sacred Indian ground, Pacific Gas accepted the "sincere objection" by Native Americans as a legitimate pro-test act, in contrast to efforts of the Abalone Alliance. On November 19, in response to the blueprint issue, the NRC suspended PG&E's low-power testing license for the Diablo plant.[45]

Other construction problems surfaced in the months that followed. The activities of the Abalone Alliance added to a list of errors, costs, and delays that the *New York Times* declared "a paradigm of nuclear power troubles." The plant gradually underwent earthquake retrofitting so that it could handle 7.5 rather than 6.75 on the Richter scale. "U.S. Lists 111 Problems at Coast Reactor," headlined the *New York Times* in March 1982, while *It's About Times* exploited the situation by printing a photograph of the Diablo plant accompanied by the tagline, "Find the 125 mistakes in this picture."[46]

Despite the errors, Pacific Gas officials remained confident in the nuclear project. "The Diablo Canyon plant has been compared in strength and stability to the strongest manmade structures in the world, even to non-manmade structures like the Rock of Gibraltar," claimed one promotional leaflet. Because of enforced delays, Diablo Canyon far surpassed the standards of facilities such as Three Mile Island. The Diablo project would go on-line, despite an anticipated delay of two to three years.[47]

Affinity groups of the Abalone Alliance had always maintained an interest in issues other than Diablo Canyon. The interim period granted coalition members the chance to develop campaigns in places outside San Luis Obispo County. The Pelican Alliance campaigned against oil leasing near Point Reyes, while SONOMOreAtomics protested the Rancho Seco nuclear plant near Sacramento and highlighted the conspiratorial activities of the Bohemian Club. The all-male Bohemian Club represented an elite selection of American politicians, industrialists, financiers, and military muscle. Dating back to 1872, "Bohos" annually met at a retreat on the Russian River, just north of San Francisco. Only Americans considered important to the country made it to what "Boho" Herbert Hoover described as "the greatest men's party on earth." Psychology professor William G. Domhoff described the 2,700-acre retreat as "a summer camp for overgrown Boy Scouts." At a ceremony entitled the "Cremation of Care," Bohos were asked to leave their worldly pursuits outside the camp. However, SONOMOreAtomics suspected that most club members discussed shady "Politics among the Redwoods," while the burning of "care" actually denoted ignoring "responsibilities" for the majority of attendees. Protesters conspiratorially claimed the decision to manufacture an atomic bomb had originated in discussions on the Russian River, and even ventured that campfire chats revolved around Diablo in the 1980s.[48]

Abalone activists also protested on the streets of San Francisco. In 1982 a number of protesters led a "Hall of Shame" rally through the city business district. Participants toured "corponuclearmilitary businesses that operate downtown," including PG&E and Bechtel. Urban activists uncovered what they judged to be myriad nuclear threats on their doorsteps. The Abalone's Mutant Sponges named themselves after marine sponges found growing on radioactive waste barrels dumped near the Farrallon Islands, eighteen miles west of San Francisco. The Sponges appeared at many antinuclear functions dressed in foam rubber outfits. During February 1981 they played volleyball (the earth represented as the ball) with the "Plutonium Players" antinuclear theater group on a court on top of UC Berkeley's reactor. In a letter to It's About Times, Tori Woodard made an emotional stand against the nuclear-powered aircraft carrier USS Enterprise, stationed at Alameda; the warship was "a floating Diablo Canyon bristling with nuclear weapons" that "dares to call the San Francisco Bay its home!" One Abalone poster asked: "Did you know? There is plutonium at 8 sites in the bay area on earthquake faults." According to protest discourse, placing a nuclear project close to a fault line at Diablo appeared not a chance mistake, but a common error made by nuclear industries across California.[49]

Some Abalone groups singled out Pacific Gas for attack, arguing that the corporation had systematically destroyed public power in San Francisco ever since its purchase of Hetch Hetchy dam. Along with concerns over the spolia-tion of a sacred valley by flooding, John Muir, in his protests against the dam in the early 1900s, had attacked the entrepreneurial ethos that converted nature into monetary value. Abalone protesters interpreted Hetch Hetchy as the starting point of a corporate campaign to dominate regional energy resources, as well as marking the beginning of what they dubbed "the power-drunk, anti-nature sub-culture that controls our society." Protesters hyperbolized Pacific Gas as the worst of a "handful of gigantic corporations and government agencies" that "have conspired to bring us all to the brink of apocalypse."[50]

The period also saw *It's About Times* extend its coverage of political, social and environmental topics beyond the confines of nuclear activism, running stories of revolution in Nicaragua, European youth movements, and green protests against industrial expansion. The newspaper consistently targeted Republican president Ronald Reagan. In spring 1981, left-wing writers cast a critical eye over Reagan's planned economic reforms in an article entitled "So Long, New Deal—Howdy, Raw Deal." Caricatures of the president and his political leanings became commonplace. The SONOMOreAtomics monthly newsletter, *Nuke Notes,* referred to Reagan simply as "Pres. Raygun." In the May–June 1982 edition of *It's About Times,* the president appeared in full cowboy gear riding a nuclear missile as his pony.[51]

Activists also lambasted U.S. military projects and the continuing development of nuclear weapons. The emergence of the nuclear weapons freeze movement in California in the early 1980s represented on the surface a natural avenue for Diablo protesters to follow. In August 1981 Steve Ladd of the War Resisters League invited Abalone members to support the campaign calling for a halt to the nuclear arms race. However, using the forum of *It's About Times,* activists criticized the freeze movement for its overreliance on conventional politics, bilateral rather than unilateral rhetoric, and refusal to take a stand on nuclear power. Staff writers applauded the movement for at least putting "nuclear war in the headlines," but protesters seemed unable to find common ground on even the most likely issues.[52]

This seemed all the more bizarre given the extent to which Alliance members conceptualized Diablo as one link in a longer chain. In the documentary film *Dark Circle* (1982), filmmakers Judy Irving and Chris Beaver traced the nuclear fuel cycle, or "dark circle," to Hiroshima and Nagasaki, Rocky Flats (Colorado), and Diablo Canyon. By showing black brant geese passing radioactive sites on their migration route and concerned mothers threatened by the nuclear landscape of Diablo, *Dark Circle* imparted a sense of the nuclear fuel cycle as a danger to both nature and humanity. The vulnerable flight path of the geese symbolized a natural cycle of life threatened by the "dark circle" of plutonium. To maintain ecological stability, or the health of this life system, protesters felt the need to halt the nuclear fuel cycle at its various locations.[53]

In tracing the routes of the nuclear fuel cycle, antinuclear activists forged a unique map of the American landscape. Cartographers marked the locations of uranium mines, reactors, research centers, and test sites. Missile silos replaced mountains, while remote testing grounds, deliberately chosen to avoid public attention, suddenly became landmarks. Highways were only noted if identified as transport routes for the nuclear fuel cycle, while Hanford and Los Alamos signified the "big (atomic) cities." Nuclear cartography proved popular in the late 1970s and early 1980s as activists discovered what they considered to be a hidden country of dangers. The War Resisters League regularly updated a poster of "Nuclear America" with new discoveries of atomic facilities. A photograph in the *Berkeley Barb* highlighted a protester carrying two maps of the United States, one indicating the number of reactors circa 1975, the other showing proposed reactors by the year 2000. The protester's use of black dots to denote nuclear plants gave the impression of an epidemic spreading across America. Jointly published by Greenpeace and the Center for Investigative Reporting, *Nuclear California* (1982) provided the definitive "nuclear atlas" of the Golden State by documenting the pervasiveness of the atomic problem in major California cities and rural locations.[54]

Abalone affinity groups challenged atomic and military installations at a number of locations on this nuclear map during the early 1980s. Just thirty miles south of Diablo, Vandenberg Air Force Base made an obvious target for Alliance members. In 1982 and 1983, activists protested the deployment of mobile MX missiles at the base. A few hundred miles to the north, Abalone activists joined the Livermore Action Group (LAG) in opposition to nuclear weapons research at the Lawrence Livermore National Laboratory, east of Oakland.

In their studies of the nuclear landscape, activists discovered that American corporations sometimes used Native American terrain for atomic projects. Uranium mines often resided on or close to Indian reservations. *It's About Times* detailed one corporation's plans for Redwind Indian Community, just forty miles northeast of San Luis Obispo, along with claims of atomic pollution on distant Navajo homelands. The Alliance berated PG&E and other major U.S. companies for "threatening the land, lifestyle and lives of Native Americans." To Abalone members a Euro-American campaign against nuclear power and protests against uranium mines on Indian reservations represented associated struggles. The 1981 blockade handbook proclaimed that "Indians are our 'natural allies' politically and spiritually." Don Eichelberger believed in a "natural alliance that exists between the environmental movement and Native Americans" and that the Abalone Alliance had that kind of unspoken relationship with California Indians. However, Native Americans rarely attended Abalone rallies in any sizable numbers. While Dennis Banks, a leader of the American Indian Movement, spoke at the "No More Nukes" gathering held in April 1979, for most Native Americans there were more pressing issues than the defense of a largely white, middle-class coastal town from the clutches of corporate America.[55]

▪ RETURNING TO DIABLO ▪

The authorization of fuel loading at Diablo Canyon Unit 1 reactor during November 1983 prompted renewed protest on the Pecho Coast. With the very likely prospect of an operational plant, the Alliance launched the "Peoples Emergency Response Plan" (PERP) on January 13, 1984. PERP sought to "provide a vehicle for everyone opposed to Diablo Canyon to make the strongest statement possible." Resulting articulations often verged on the outlandish. Jackie Cabasso helped formed "the 'Save the Madonna Inn from Diablo Canyon' fan club and affinity group," defending the extravagant hotel and its themed bedrooms from nuclear decay. Over four months of sustained protest, 537 protesters were arrested. A smaller turnout than during the 1981 blockade reflected a measured loss of interest in both the dangers of nuclear power and Diablo Canyon. In contrast to the mass protests on the Pecho Coast during 1979 and 1981, Diablo no longer appeared the obvious focal point for statewide dissidence. By the mid-1980s a variety of environmental and social struggles, from Livermore to Nicaragua, vied for the attention of Californian activists. Nuclear energy no longer seemed the big issue that it once had been.[56]

In order to promote their cause, antinuclear activists had projected "the peaceful atom" as a priority among social and environmental problems. While such grandiose claims suited the climate immediately following Three Mile Island, the argument proved less convincing by 1984. Questions remained over the ties of the antinuclear movement to other protest groups. By shaping the atomic threat into a unique danger, antinuclear activists had unconsciously alienated people concerned with issues of racism, gay rights, inefficient welfare systems, and the exploitation of Native American communities. *It's About Times* rightly noted that "the biggest shortcoming" of the concert film *No Nukes* (1980) "reflected that of the U.S. anti-nuclear movement in general—a certain cultural and racial isolation." With its San Franciscan ties and bohemian sentiments, the Abalone Alliance was less isolated than most antinuclear organizations. However, Alliance members recognized (and regretted) their failure to reach out to a broader audience. The antinuclear movement was similarly at odds with traditional environmental campaigners. The perception of the atom as "an ultimate threat to the existence of life on this planet," as one protester put it, falsely elevated (and thus separated) the atomic threat from other ecological dangers. More significantly, the Abalone Alliance (and other antinuclear groups) offered radical forms of protest and demanded societal and economic changes with which more-traditional conservation groups such as the Wilderness Society and Sierra Club were far from comfortable.[57]

In 1981 the *New York Times* had commented that "the no-nuke movement" was being "seen as the potential heir to the anti-war, civil rights and environmental conservation movements." While antinuclear activism, with its pacifist stance, civil disobedience actions, and "save the planet" motifs drew on all three movements for its organizational structure, it cannot, in hindsight, be considered a perfect heir to any of the three. Nuclear protest never achieved the stature, the victories, or the mass appeal that the prior three movements engendered. Abalone visions of a nuclear-free utopia failed to enthrall everyday Americans in the way that Martin Luther King's dream did. That is not to say that the movement amounted to little, just that the *New York Times* exaggerated its overall resonance. By emphasizing grassroots organizing and equality between the sexes, the antinuclear lobby did solve some of the problems of its forebears. Although Abalone protesters failed in a practical sense to bridge the gap between white wilderness conservationists and African American activists, they adroitly illustrated that social and ecological ideas (and protest) could be part of the same rainbow. Abalone veterans also popularized ways of organizing, such as consensus process and feminist structure, that were taken up by later California movements. For California and Diablo Canyon, nuclear protest was more vocal and carried more media coverage than at most other locations across the United States. In a sense, California radicalism gave the antinuclear movement more clout in the Golden State than elsewhere. By the mid-1980s Diablo had become an energy landscape based not just around ecological growth and atomic progress, but also on the energies of citizen-led protest and a dynamic California zeitgeist.[58]

FIVE

Living Alongside the Machine

"**S**HE'S BACK!!**—but only to face . . . disaster at diablo reactor!" read the front cover of a 1982 Marvel comic. A menacing combination of a nuclear plant waiting to go on-line, a pile of uranium, and an evil masked man known as "The Negator" heralded the return of Marvel superheroine She-Hulk. The Negator planned to "destroy LA in atomic holocaust" by sabotaging the nuclear plant on the Pecho Coast. "Diablo reactor shall encounter—the China Syndrome," the masked man threatened. Atomic matters were hardly new to the pages of Marvel Comics. The Fantastic Four, with their special powers forged by cosmic radiation, started off the comic franchise in 1961. Atomic rays spawned a veritable nuclear family of cartoon heroes in subsequent years, from Spiderman and the Incredible Hulk to the X-Men, self-proclaimed "children of the Atom." Diablo Canyon joined the coveted comic-book pages of atomic-bred folklore as a dangerous nuclear landscape. As if to acknowledge the years of confrontation between Abalone protesters and PG&E officials, Marvel cartoonists created their own kind of showdown at Diablo. She-Hulk, joined by The Thing, a suitably aberrant cohort, traveled to the canyon to face the maniacal Negator. With the nuclear plant about to go on-line and disaster imminent, the two superheroes dispatched the Negator and jet-packed the uranium into space. California was saved from atomic abomination by two Marvel mutants.[1]

No superheroes interfered in the start-up of reactors at the real Diablo plant. The NRC granted PG&E a low-power testing license for the Unit 1 reactor on April 13, 1984. PG&E officials started a nuclear reaction at Unit 1 for the first time on April 29, with full capacity achieved in May 1985 (Unit 2 started in August of that year). The Abalone Alliance ended its People's Emergency Response Plan (PERP). Activists from northern California returned home despondent. The Alliance was over. Those with enough energy immediately moved on to protest U.S. intervention against left-wing regimes in Central America or joined the nascent green political movement in California.

The Mothers for Peace desperately searched for legal precedents to halt the production of nuclear electricity at Diablo. In August 1984 the Mothers gained an injunction against the NRC from the U.S. Court of Appeals for the Ninth Circuit, based upon the failure of the commission to consider a seismic event in evacuation planning. The injunction lasted until the end of October. Then, in January 1985, San Francisco's KRON-TV revealed secret NRC transcripts concerning the Hosgri Fault. The transcripts revealed the apparent willingness of NRC commissioners to sideline earthquake issues in their haste to license the Diablo plant. At a closed meeting held in July 1984, NRC chairman Nunzio J. Palladino had pondered the possibility of granting a license while leaving the seismic quandary over evacuation to a later date: "What if we do nothing? Suppose we don't put—I think it's been asked before, but I don't remember the answer—suppose we don't issue an order [to fully consider earthquakes in evacuation planning] now and just go ahead." Commissioner James Asseltine, who argued against Palladino throughout the session, gave a harsh indictment of NRC policy, claiming that "the Commission's decision was motivated solely by the objective of avoiding delay in issuing a full-power license for the Diablo Canyon plant." The Mothers recontacted the U.S. court of appeals in the hope of a favorable investigation but were ultimately disappointed. The court reached its verdict in April 1986, ruling 5-4 against a full investigation into the Diablo licensing process as requested by the Mothers for Peace. The court refused to consider the NRC "secret transcript" as an "extraordinary intrusion" into nuclear regulation. Plant operation continued.[2]

Firmly rooted in the local community, the Mothers for Peace saw few avenues to escape the specter of Diablo Canyon. Many Abalone activists had long since returned to homes several hundred miles from the Pecho Coast.

The immediacy of the Diablo issue receded for those living far from San Luis, and the Alliance itself disbanded. For the Mothers, tied into lengthy legal proceedings and with nowhere to go, it seemed only natural to continue working against their atomic foe. With the onset of commercial operation, the nuclear threat was arguably more tangible than ever before.

The reality of an operational plant fueled elaborate fictions of impending disaster. For nervous activists the Central Coast of California resembled the doomed Australian shores in Nevil Shute's novel *On the Beach* (1957), where locals lived out superficially normal lives while waiting for radioactive clouds from the Northern Hemisphere to reach them following World War III. The nuclear threat from Diablo merely replaced the death sentence wrought by sparring superpowers. Having identified what they claimed were flaws in state evacuation plans, the Mothers remained pessimistic over the possibility of escaping a toxic plume emanating from the Pecho Coast. Fears of radiation and the distance it could invisibly travel challenged traditional conceptions of local geography. Diablo Canyon appeared to move ever closer to the suburbs of San Luis. Anxious residents believed that their day-to-day lives could be disrupted at any moment. Found in unexpected, everyday places such as California Polytechnic library restrooms, "Radiation Alert" signs reminded antinuclear folk of their insecurities and of lurking dangers in the backyard.

For other residents of San Luis Obispo, the Diablo plant's going on-line hardly seemed momentous. Aesthetically, the nuclear landscape seemed little different from before. Public fears were allayed as months passed without any calamities. The lack of problems on-site gave legitimacy to the assertion by PG&E staff that Diablo Canyon had become "by far, the most thoroughly scrutinized nuclear power plant in the United States." Nonetheless, the *San Francisco Chronicle* found some evidence of lingering nuclear anxieties during interviews with "the closest human residents to the power plant," Gordon and Virginia Bruno, on their ranch just north of Diablo. Gordon relished his rural setting and ranching enterprise. Stopping his jeep for a "stalled cow," the rancher mused: "Since we've been here, I've learned to respect cows. . . . They shelter their young." However, the Bruno family continued to be wary of their nuclear neighbor, the "domesticated" atom.[3]

Hopes of winning perfect countywide acceptance of the Diablo plant were thwarted in April 1986 by news of an accident at the Chernobyl nuclear plant in Ukraine. The distant Soviet atomic disaster reignited fears over nuclear energy production in the state of California. In a survey immediately following the Chernobyl accident, 49 percent of 277 San Luis Obispo County residents voiced their opposition to the Diablo plant. Doubts resurfaced over the ability of Pacific Gas to operate its nuclear project safely. Rancher Joann Warren of Cambria, on the county's northern coast near San Simeon, compared the situation at Diablo to "turning 5-year-olds loose in a barn with a bunch of matches." William Loran of San Rafael, a town 250 miles north of Diablo, wrote a letter to David Hartsough. Loran expected an earthquake to strike the San Luis region shortly and warned: "Should Diablo crack, the Chernobyl accident will seem exceedingly minor." He predicted that a nuclear catastrophe would render a third of California uninhabitable and kill half the population of the state. Loran's doomsday prophecy seemed both farfetched and premature, but it captured the worst anxieties of the period. In Ukraine, the settlement of Chernobyl, described by the Ukrainian physician Iurii Shcherbak as "a pleasant little provincial Ukrainian town, swathed in green, full of cherry and apple trees," had been contaminated by radiation from its nuclear neighbor, cordoned off from civilization by military barriers and Geiger counter readings. The town of Pypriat had also been evacuated. A week after the accident its children's park lay deserted, the swings and Ferris wheel ominously silent. Pypriat had developed in the 1970s and early 1980s as a service town to the nuclear station, while the rural village of Chernobyl dated back to the twelfth century. For those of an antinuclear disposition, the Diablo project similarly threatened the existence of San Luis Obispo, a historic Spanish settlement.[4]

However the political, geographical, and economic distance between the Soviet Union and the United States helped many Californians overcome their fears. Contractor Don Ritter interpreted Chernobyl as endemic proof of poor-quality Soviet technology: "It's typical of the Russians. They steal our

ideas and can't make them work. Their tractors fall apart. Their plants leak."
Local businessman Bill Burriss proudly proclaimed, "We've got the dome."
While Russian plants lacked containment domes, the majority of American
reactors featured thick concrete walls to insulate atomic reaction. Nuclear
reactors served as emblems of the dueling communist and capitalist economic
systems. The failure of Chernobyl substantiated the nationalistic reflections
of an American public already sure of the inadequacy of the Soviet experiment vis-à-vis U.S. enterprise. True to the competitive spirit of the cold war,
Uncle Sam's reactor claimed victory over a shoddy Marxist design.[5]

In contrast, the Mothers for Peace attempted to link Chernobyl with Diablo. In an August 1986 letter alert, the Mothers claimed that "PG&E plans to
store spent fuel (high level radioactive waste) at Diablo Canyon in the same
way that it was stored at Chernobyl." As with Three Mile Island, the Ukrainian accident offered the Mothers a frightening image to superimpose on
Diablo Canyon. The group wore badges declaring, "Remember Chernobyl:
It can happen here." William Bennett, a former member of the CPUC and a
longtime critic of the Diablo project, despaired at what he saw as complacency within the American nuclear industry. Bennett felt that an in-house
attitude of "it couldn't happen here" predominated. To him, the congruities
between Russian and American reactors were far more obvious than the differences: "Steel, nuclear energy, the housing, the personnel, the engineering,
the mentality: they're all the same. They don't fail because of political ideology." He also posited that a comparable accident at Diablo would ruin much
of central California.[6]

Chernobyl briefly rekindled antinuclear sentiment across the state. Roger
Herried, working at the Abalone Clearinghouse, San Francisco (a repository
of nuclear information that survived the breakup of the Alliance), remembered being inundated with phone calls from concerned citizens. "Diablo
Canyon, the devil's reactor, gets licensed, there's no further opposition available, and then Wormwood," recounted Herried, referring to the American
translation of the word *chernobyl*. The description, found in Revelation 8—
"A great star, blazing like a torch, fell from the sky on a third of the rivers and
on the springs of water—the name of the star is Wormwood. A third of the
waters turned bitter, and many people died from the waters that had become
bitter"—presented an outlandish doomsday scenario vaguely appropriate

to contamination in the nuclear age. Suddenly the Soviet accident carried nuances of religious wrath. However, Chernobyl failed to ignite the protest zeal of previous years, and few, if any, considered re-forming the Alliance.[7]

■ THE LOCAL WATCHDOG ■

The Mothers for Peace eased into the role of a nuclear Cassandra or atomic watchdog group during the late 1980s, independently monitoring events at Diablo Canyon on behalf of the local community. The sisterhood of activists remained eminently distrustful of the nuclear industry. Fearing that a corporate desire for profit would inevitably gnaw away at safety procedures and eventually lead to an accident, the Mothers appeared wary of leaving PG&E staff to their own devices. Acting on rumors of safety violations, the Mothers brought issues to the attention of the Nuclear Regulatory Commission. They also liaised with Consumers Organized for Defense of Environmental Safety (CODES), a local whistle-blower support network. CODES claimed to offer disenchanted PG&E employees a truly confidential refuge where they could air grievances concerning the plant. One ex-employee saw at Diablo a pronuclear mindset that he nicknamed "Gung-ho Diablo" and regarded as responsible for a "false sense of security" in the workplace. According to this individual, concern over criticizing the nuclear machine led to pressure on supervisors not to tag ("speeding ticket") poor-quality work. By encouraging employees to register their disaffection with plant protocols, CODES and the Mothers evoked the memory of Karen Silkwood, the nuclear industry's most famous whistle-blower.[8]

The Mothers enlisted the help of the Sierra Club in their 1986 campaign to prevent PG&E from storing quantities of radioactive waste, an inevitable by-product of nuclear power plants, on-site at Diablo. In contrast to its position on Diablo in the mid-1960s, the conservation group now steadfastly opposed PG&E's plans for development. Ultimately, the waste required long-term storage at a safe location. Sierrans and Mothers alike castigated the proposal by Pacific Gas to extend its own storage system, warning against a "high-level radioactive waste dump" being added to Diablo Canyon. The vivid imagery of an atomic garbage heap on the picturesque San Luis shoreline offended citizens who prided themselves on a well-kept county. An editorial piece in the *Telegram-Tribune* ran under the headline "Hats off to Sierra Club, Mothers for Diablo Action." Despite the cooling-pond storage system's resembling a clean and sparkling swimming pool, the Mothers for Peace and Sierra Club resolutely argued that nuclear power was intrinsically dirty.[9]

The Mothers initially resisted involvement in the rate case over Diablo Canyon, held by the California Public Utilities Commission in the late 1980s. The local group primarily saw their role as defenders of public safety rather than financial prosecutors. Rochelle Becker attended the hearings of her own accord, until she convinced fellow Mothers to support her actions. Becker, along with Laurie McDermott, the consumer advocacy group Toward Utility Rate Normalization (TURN), and the antinuclear Redwood Alliance challenged the idea of ratepayers' meeting the $5.5 billion construction cost of the Diablo plant. The CPUC initially appeared keen to pass the majority of the bill onto Pacific Gas. However, in June 1988, state attorney general John Van de Kamp, PG&E chairman Dick Clarke, and CPUC director William Ahern reached a private settlement. The deal shifted $3.4 billion of the plant's cost onto ratepayers. In typically angry mood, the *San Francisco Bay Guardian* charged that "the deal effectively censors the entire history of the plant, and wipes it off the public record as if it never happened." An accompanying cartoon portrayed the Diablo plant as a dilapidated motor vehicle with an atomic energy symbol as its official hood ornament. "Test Drive the 1989 PG&E Diablo! No Warranty, Pay Now, Pay Later," read the sale sign, with a "fat pig" salesman muttering, "Financing? Sure—You got a blank check on ya?" Whatever the fairness of the Diablo deal, the bigger issues of California electricity rates and energy regulation had yet to be sorted.[10]

▪ **MONKEY-WRENCHING '89** ▪

In May 1989 an FBI SWAT team chased three members of Earth First! across the Arizona desert. The radical environmental group had earned a reputation for subversive activities, its members famed for stealing into forests and spiking redwoods to dissuade loggers. Activists Mark Davis, Marc Baker, and Peggy Millett had instead decided to trim the man-made electrical forest. Davis, Baker, and Millett, along with FBI informant "Mike Tait" (real name Mike Fain), attempted to cut down a power line near Salome, one of many entrails of the Central Arizona Project (CAP), a canal system redirecting water from the Colorado River to the cities of Tucson and Phoenix.

Impeded by thick goggles and wooden boards worn on their feet to disguise prints, Davis and Baker were swiftly apprehended by federal officials. Millett eluded agents in the bush, turning herself in the following morning. The FBI also arrested Dave Foreman, prominent cofounder of Earth First!, at his Tucson home. During a three-month trial in Prescott, Arizona, in 1991, federal agents insisted that the CAP sabotage prefigured a larger plan to disable the electricity cables of three atomic projects: the Palo Verde plant (Arizona), Rocky Flats weapon-processing facility (Colorado), and PG&E's Diablo Canyon project. Earth First! sympathizer Susan Zakin colorfully recalled that paralyzing the nuclear triumvirate represented the "bigger enchilada."[11]

In the 1970s and early 1980s opponents of atomic energy rarely considered ecosabotage as a justifiable course of action for stopping nuclear power. Typical protest scenarios involved plants yet to go on-line, with direct action by activists designed to impede construction, garner press attention, and on occasion demonstrate the vulnerability of nuclear projects to "real" saboteurs. Sam Lovejoy, who with a simple crowbar toppled a utility weather tower at a proposed nuclear plant site near Montague, Massachusetts, during February 1974, represented an early hero of the direct-action antinuclear movement. However, the majority of activists preferred less confrontational forms of protest. The Clamshell Alliance considered the occupation of the Seabrook nuclear plant a valid activity yet split between "hard Clams" and "soft Clams" over the issue of fence cutting as a means of entering the site. The contentious matter of property destruction remained unresolved. In the Abalone Alliance a prevalent atmosphere of nonviolence reined in those willing to consider dismantling parts of the nuclear machine. Sneaking through wild grasses, protest groups deliberately avoided security forces on backcountry routes to the Diablo plant but had no intention of physically damaging the two atomic reactors. The only person close to sabotaging the plant belonged to neither the Abalone Alliance nor the Mothers for Peace. John Junot from Los Angeles was arrested by FBI agents on Pismo Beach, just south of Avila, in December 1982. Officials charged him with intent to blow up the Diablo plant. Junot related his desire to expose the full vulnerability of nuclear projects to terrorism and, in the process, highlight the broader danger of developing atomic energy. Junot told the *Telegram-Tribune*, "Nuclear power is the only thing that the more I studied, the more scared I was of it."[12]

"Radical Environmentalists Held in Plot against Diablo," read the head-line of the *Telegram-Tribune* in response to the Earth First! fracas in the summer of 1989. The local newspaper noted that Mark Davis had inspected power lines connected to the Diablo plant just six weeks prior to his capture. The ensuing Arizona court case nevertheless paid only incidental attention to Davis's wanderings in San Luis Obispo County. During the three-month trial the nuclear landscape faded into the background, a hazy mirage in the heated disputes between desert saboteurs and government prosecutors. Diablo, Rocky Flats, and Palo Verde simply provided the legal settings for entrap-ment, the atomic snares of "tree huggers." Press accounts of the case duly ignored the atomic landmarks, and for many readers Diablo Canyon merely represented an anonymous place on a list of targets. Newspaper coverage instead homed in on the colorful personalities in the dock.[13]

Court proceedings revealed the determination of the FBI to shackle Dave Foreman and, in so doing, send a warning to the radical environmental move-ment. Roger Dokken, first assistant U.S. attorney at Phoenix, painted Fore-man as the boss of the eco-Mafia, who "always send their little munchkins out to do the dirty work . . . A mind guru and a leader, and that's even more dangerous." The FBI case against Foreman rested on a small financial dona-tion to Davis and a conversation with the informant Fain, monitored by a low-flying federal plane. Discussing ideas for ecosabotage, Foreman sug-gested to Fain: "I think it's got to be real targeted and be directed at targets that will have some kind of impact. . . . Like the nuclear thing, that might help prevent additional plants." The FBI took Foreman's commentary as a verbatim endorsement of the 1989 Davis plan.[14]

The serious implications of sabotaging three nuclear facilities helped the government flesh out a picture of radical environmentalists crossing the boundaries of acceptable behavior. In a pretrial hearing, U.S. attorney Steven Mitchell admonished Earth First!ers as lunatics, pointing out that by propos-ing to cut the transmission lines to the Diablo Canyon plant, Davis, Baker, and Millett endangered California with a nuclear meltdown. Mitchell used the testimony of NRC senior project manager Terrance Chan to support his argument. In stark contrast to the assurances made by regulatory officials concerning the safety of the plant in prior decades, NRC staff explored the vulnerability of PG&E's project to terrorism, even meltdown, and argued the unreliability of its backup generator.

Attorney Gerry Spence represented the accused. Spence had successfully brought a lawsuit against the Kerr-McGee Corporation on behalf of the Silkwood family in 1979. Refuting attempts by the FBI to tarnish Earth First!ers as "violent terrorists," Spence portrayed the likes of Foreman as "ordinary, decent human beings who are trying to call the attention of America to the fact that the Earth is dying." The trial lawyer from Wyoming further noted that federal treatment of Earth First! in the 1980s appeared "very similar to the procedures the FBI used during the 1960s against dissident groups," invoking the Bureau's mistreatment of civil rights and anti–Vietnam War campaigners. The Prescott judge eventually sentenced Davis, Millett, and Baker to six years, three years, and six months, respectively. However, Foreman eluded jail time by his peripheral role in sabotage planning.[15]

The appearance of Diablo Canyon in the Earth First! plot indicated that PG&E's project had retained at least a touch of its former notoriety. The nuclear plant scarcely provoked levels of rage comparable to the heady days of Abalone protest or Sierra discord, but environmentalists in the 1990s still regarded the project with disdain. The reputation of the atom as a harbinger of ecological catastrophe persisted, its destructive capabilities cemented by years of campaigning. For environmental radicals the Pecho Coast clearly marked the dangerous excesses of human invention, and Earth First! hooked the power lines of Diablo into a broader assault on industrial society. Atomic projects embodied the worst in technological tomfoolery, not only failing to live up to their economic and social promise but threatening the survival of whole ecosystems. Foreman hoisted monkey-wrenching as "our fundamental strategy for dealing with the mad machine." The Diablo plant seemed an appropriate target. The Earth First! episode further demonstrated the nucle-arization of the wild coastline. Ecoactivists, like many other Americans, rec-ognized the reactor domes rather than the rolling hills of Diablo. The atomic-spiced "bigger enchilada" thus bespoke the side of Earth First! dedicated to sabotaging human industry, rather than its deliberative defense of American wilderness. In essence, however, the two approaches were related. A spanner in the machine resembled the spiking of a redwood to ward off loggers. Both tactics sought to wear down the industrial monolith and, according to radical environmentalists, enable the survival, or recovery, of the natural world. Nevertheless, the Pecho wilds remained a mere backdrop to the contrivances of Mark Davis. The temporary disabling of the Diablo plant seemed to fall a long way short of restoring the region to wilderness status. Ultimately the reinstatement of wild nature on the Pecho Coast would have to come from other sources.[16]

■ NATURE STRIKES BACK? ■

In October 1990 journalist David Helvarg, using a backcountry route, infiltrated the Diablo property unseen by security forces. "Climbing through dry grass and thistle toward the Diablo Canyon power plant," Helvarg, reporting for *California* magazine, noted "the drought-parched hillside hums with a low, insectlike sound from 2 million kilowatts of electric current coursing overhead." Planting Silly Putty on a PG&E tower, the reporter nonchalantly boasted how "if this *were* C4 [an explosive compound] I could easily blow up the main power lines leaving Diablo." Helvarg had surmounted nuclear defenses and claimed success where Earth First! had previously faltered.[17]

Rather than an invincible coastal fortress, the Diablo plant resembled a remote, automated outpost. Although the nuclear landscape reminded Helvarg of "Dr. No's secret base in the first James Bond movie," it lacked the elaborate defenses and thousand-strong private army that 007 traditionally toyed with. The San Francisco reporter instead discovered that "PG&E has just three people cruising its 11,000-acre spread, and one of them is unarmed." Security presence had relaxed following the withdrawal of Abalone protest in 1984. High technology had filled the gaps, cameras and underground sensors replacing watchtowers and hourly patrols. There was another factor that the intrepid reporter noted during his visit. Helvarg related how TV security monitors had apparently begun "to blur out in heavy rain and the microwave detectors can also be set off by rainstorms as well as sea gulls, raccoons, skunks, cats and other local residents." Ecological forces presented problems for the nuclear installation.[18]

While Helvarg merely set putty under Diablo pylons, weather extremes physically tested the plant. In May 1989 hot and dry summer conditions were blamed for igniting a fire that got within a quarter mile of the two reactors.

The brushfire spread to sixty acres, blazing beneath transmission lines carrying 2,500,000 volts. One hundred and fifty firefighters, along with air tanker support, rushed to the scene.[19]

Other trials emerged from the sea. "Kelp Attack at Diablo," read the *Telegram-Tribune* headline of September 27, 1995, the article explaining how drifting kelp had compromised power generation by blocking the flow of water through the plant's cooling system. PG&E spokesperson Jeff Lewis acknowledged that "unusually large swells of 7 to 9 feet" had "damaged screens used to keep the seaweed out of ocean water intake tunnels" in Diablo Cove. "Diablo Hobbled by Heavy Surf," ran the colorful headline for another *Telegram* story. Similar to the effects of a tsunami, eighteen-foot swells wrenched kelp from seabed moorings and bombarded the intake cove with floating debris. Pacific storms and weather changes ushered seaweed into Diablo Cove. Mussels and algae also gathered at the nuclear gateway. The oceanic ecosystem had inadvertently challenged the atomic leviathan. To combat the buildup of organic forces, PG&E staff devoted extra time to cleaning the intake system during preplanned reactor shutdowns.[20]

The kelp "attacks" formed part of a weather-system bombardment of the central California coastline during which winter storms unleashed high waves, strong winds, rain, fog, and sea debris upon Diablo Canyon and nearby Avila Beach. In March 1995 the local town found itself flooded by storm waters. Just nine months later an approaching storm system led PG&E to shut down both of its reactors as a precautionary measure. PG&E staff also monitored the progress of El Niño during late 1997 and early 1998. In November 1997 oceanographer John Lindsey reported six-foot swells off Diablo. By January the figure had risen to eighteen feet, with twenty-five-foot waves crashing against nearby ocean buoys. On February 3 the *Telegram-Tribune* anticipated thirty-foot swells buffeting Avila and Diablo. Debris collected in Diablo Cove and compromised water intake, reducing the performance of Unit 1 by half. At nearby Avila Port, El Niño forced ships into harbor before huge waves and unsettled seas. The Pecho Coast temporarily regained its semblance of wildness and remoteness.[21]

As the point of interface between a self-enclosed nuclear system and the natural world, the water intake system experienced the most setbacks. However, while fences blew down and boats capsized at nearby Avila, the Diablo plant remained steadfast. The huge dark brown turbine building conveyed a sense of sturdy permanence as though physically stamped into the coastal shelf. Concrete reactor domes, designed to confine atomic chain reactions, seemed equally capable of keeping out nature's stormy intrusions. Neither did seismic tremors unsettle the plant. In February 1990 an earthquake measuring 4.1 on the Richter scale transpired thirty-three miles southwest of San Luis Obispo. An accelerometer at Diablo Canyon noted the movement, but according to the local paper, only one PG&E employee "reported feeling the quake." The headline "Quake at Sea Triggers Diablo Alert" exploited all the excitement it could muster from such a minor event. In January 1992 an unidentified fault line just two miles east of Point Buchon produced an earthquake rated at 2.6 Richter. PG&E workers and electronic detection systems registered the movement, although both reactors continued to generate electricity at full capacity. In 1995, ten years after the Diablo plant's inception, PG&E seismic expert Lloyd Cluff gave a ninety-minute presentation to the Independent Safety Committee set up to monitor the nuclear project. Cluff buoyantly declared that earthquakes posed "absolutely no threat" to Diablo, describing the power plant as "the most conservative structure in the world." Even if a sizable tremor struck the region, Cluff remarked, "there's no place I'd rather be than inside the plant." The seismic threat fostered in the early 1980s suddenly seemed in danger of slipping into a meaningless social construct of antinuclear alarmism. The earthquake that followed Cluff's presentation a fortnight later hardly suggested otherwise, rating merely 2.4 to 2.7 on the Richter scale.[22]

The United States Geological Survey adopted a more cautious stance on the relationship between Diablo Canyon and seismic activity. In October 1989 an earthquake measuring 7.1 on the Richter scale struck Loma Prieta, causing extensive damage to San Francisco. Six months later, aftershocks were felt at Diablo Canyon, 230 miles south of the earthquake epicenter. Sounding an air of caution, USGS official Robert Brown described the Loma Prieta event as a "living example" of the hazardous geology found off the Pecho Coast.[23]

However, USGS staff represented the minority in terms of their sensitivity to natural hazards and seismic complications. The far more usual refutation of natural danger at Diablo Canyon embodied a steadfast belief in human control over the physical environment. Such a view was hardly uncommon in the state of California. South of Diablo, the Los Angeles megalopolis appeared a much greater example of engineering prowess. A thriving, sprawling city had been built on arid land thanks to gigantic water projects. Arguably, control of the L.A. environment signified a more dangerous illusion than that of PG&E's containment of danger at Diablo. "Once or twice each decade, Hawaii sends Los Angeles a big, wet kiss," noted the historian Mike Davis, describing the Kona storm system, also known as the "Pineapple Express." Davis commented on the sizable risks posed by Kona floods and storms, which, along with regional earthquakes and fires, threatened to turn the "former Land of Sunshine" into "a Book of the Apocalypse theme-park."[24]

The "undoing" of the human landscape was not to be welcomed at Los Angeles, Diablo Canyon, or anywhere else. Humans preferred to have control, or the illusion of it, rather than work within ecological limits. By defying accurate prediction and absolute understanding, earthquakes, fires, and storms highlighted the finite boundaries of scientific knowledge, assuring nature a degree of mystery and self-determination. Natural agents emerged as unexpected vandals, eminently capable of upsetting industrial schemes. At the Idaho National Engineering Laboratory, scientists in the early 1990s searched for ways to prevent harvester ants from disrupting nuclear waste storage. The *High Country News*, a biweekly Colorado newspaper devoted to western topics, described how "Low-tech Ants Give a High-tech Idaho Lab Fits," the small insects jeopardizing the long-term containment of radioactive waste at the site by their earthmoving skills. The paper deemed the contest between the invertebrates and the Department of Energy "nature's equivalent of David versus Goliath." By interpreting the actions of harvester ants in terms of "battling" insects, nature emerged as a surreptitious enemy of the nuclear industry. Abalone activists had once hoped for an earthquake to sabotage PG&E's plans for the Pecho Coast, to force a seismic monkey wrench into the workings of the atomic machine. While ground-shaking fissures and soil-moving ants conveyed a notion of natural agency at work, the sense of nature as an exemplary ecosaboteur remained hazy. Despite the comments by Abalone activists and Department of Energy officials, earthquakes and ants hardly presented unmistakably antinuclear forces.[25]

■ **FALLIBLE DIABLO?** ■

During the 1990s a number of minor incidents at Diablo suggested to nuclear critics the continued dangers of human and technological fallibility. In February 1997 shift foreman Neil Aiken alleged a number of safety violations at the plant in a report to the Diablo Canyon Independent Safety Committee. In October 1995 worker error caused a transformer to explode on-site. The *San Francisco Bay Guardian*, by now famous for its anti-PG&E rhetoric, drew attention to a "list of safety violations worthy of Homer Simpson" that had resulted in a $50,000 fine for the electrical utility. Homer's accident-prone antics at Springfield nuclear power plant beggared belief. From doughnut feasts and sleeping spates in the control room to bringing nuclear fuel rods home from work, Simpson regularly flaunted nuclear safety procedures. The owner of the Springfield nuclear plant, Mr. Montgomery Burns, similarly ignored protocol, but in the pursuit of endless profit rather than idle relaxation time. During civic events Burns, with a sardonic smile, addressed the amassed crowds of Springfield as his "nuclear family," yet willingly risked their lives in haphazard money-spinning schemes. By comparing Homer with PG&E employees, the *Bay Guardian* invited its readers to superimpose the cartoon world of *The Simpsons* on San Luis Obispo and Diablo Canyon. Whether the cartoon series actually bred nuclear fear appeared questionable. Even Mr. Burns had a likable side, while Homer always recovered from his dangerous atomic exploits. The nuclear industry had little to fear from clever cartoons, although the American Nuclear Society saw things differently, organizing an educational tour of a California atomic plant for the creators of *The Simpsons* in an attempt to change the program's slant.[26]

Alongside questions of human fallibility lay the specter of unexpected technological failure. In an article entitled "PG&E Readies for Y2K Woes at Diablo," the *Telegram-Tribune* noted that dozens of technicians had begun "working to debug Diablo Canyon nuclear power plant" in preparation for the year 2000. Hoping to avoid computers crashing in the control room on the eve of a new millennium, Pacific Gas expended significant time and money on checking its high-tech systems. The lack of public concern over computer malfunction at Diablo (along with other nuclear installations) reflected a nation dulled to the threat of machines rising against their masters. Hollywood movies had already explored the drama of the sentient machine at great length. Celluloid provided a visual critique of technological progress, portraying riotous robots and defiant computers as the inevitable results of unchecked experimentation. *Colossus: The Forbin Project* (1970) saw the nuclear defense computer systems of the USA and the Soviet Union joining forces to hold the human race to ransom while they took over the globe. The immensely popular *WarGames* (1983) similarly expounded on the bewildering power of the machine. The movie's plot centers on a young man enamored of computer games who inadvertently accesses the U.S. military's mainframe for simulating nuclear hostilities, thereby threatening to foist the machine's warring projections on the real world by unleashing missiles by digital consent. The virtual innocence of the NORAD computer's asking, "Do you want to play a game?" translated into deadly implications for the public domain. The cold war rhetoric that pervaded films such as *Colossus* and *WarGames* nevertheless seemed inappropriate to the depolarized international climate of the 1990s. At Diablo Canyon the primary issue involved poor programming rather than lurking artificial intelligence. Thus the scheming HAL 9000 system in *2001: A Space Odyssey* (1968), responsible for murdering its space crew, and the devious SKYNET computer in *The Terminator* (1984) that pitted machines against humans (following a digitally inspired nuclear judgment day) had little in common with their seemingly antiquated counterparts at Diablo. The control room of the Diablo plant, with its 1970s architectural design and simple switches, hardly bespoke mechanized sentience.[27]

▪ GROWING CONFIDENCE IN THE MACHINE ▪

That few Obispans concerned themselves with the Y2K compliance of the Diablo plant suggested residual confidence in the ability of PG&E engineers to correct machine problems. Given the cost overruns, construction errors, and blueprint mistakes that plagued Diablo in the 1970s and 1980s, such acquiescence suggested that the corporation had significantly improved its performance output. One employee felt that "after 15 years of safe operation, some people have overcome their initial fear of the plant." The Y2K "woes" failed to materialize. With the arrival of a new millennium, PG&E spokesperson Diana Gapuz explained to the local paper: "The rollover for

Y2K has gone very well. . . . We did not have any outages in the San Luis Obispo area."[28]

The Diablo plant garnered a high reputation among nuclear industry commentators, with its day-to-day running regularly yielding impressive results. In 1994, officials refueled Unit 2 reactor in a record thirty-three days. In September 1998, Unit 1 reactor broke the industry record for a continuous period of operation, with 484 days of electricity production. PG&E's Jeff Lewis declared the sixteen-month feat a "significant milestone" in the history of Diablo Canyon. The NRC typically rewarded Diablo operators with "good" or "superior" ratings in Systematic Assessment of Licensee Performance reports. "Everyone is very competent here," Morris Branch of the NRC told local reporters in autumn 1997, following an eight-week design inspection of the Diablo plant. The *San Francisco Chronicle* noted that PG&E could have easily lost money by operating an inefficient facility, but the corporation had "instead turned Diablo Canyon, which cost $5.5 billion to build after years of planning mishaps and regulatory delays, into one of the world's most reliable nuclear plants." The Diablo plant had become a working testament of faith in the nuclear enterprise. The plant proved to be safe, efficient, and eminently praiseworthy.[29]

In an article entitled "Diablo Experts Radiate Confidence in Nuclear Power," Joel White, a senior health physicist at the plant, nonetheless complained that "a small, vocal minority" of antinuclear protagonists received "a lot of press attention," in comparison with few positive stories on Diablo's performance. That neither the local press nor public openly enthused over the Diablo plant puzzled White. Having "given up trying to convince antinuclear activists that Diablo is safe," White still longed "to see the community take more pride in Diablo's safety record and staff." While his own three children "frequently wear Diablo Canyon T-shirts," the father hoped more people would take a positive interest in the nuclear landscape. In a sense, White's lament reflected the disempowered status of nuclear enthusiasts in the 1990s. With the American public relatively skeptical of atomic-powered schemes, the nuclear industry was forced to defend its existing projects from criticism. The beleaguered pronuclear community, or atomic faithful, was metaphorically, if not literally, holed up in nuclear bunkers and domes across the country. The remoteness of these locations, along with electric fences and concrete walls, insulated them from a prevalent atmosphere of social inertia and distrust. Diablo Canyon had become one such island of atomic confidence, with Lawrence Livermore, Vandenberg, and other stations marking the 1990s American nuclear archipelago.[30]

▪ LOCAL RELATIONS ▪

At the same time, local anxiety over the operation of the Diablo plant had mostly dissipated by the early 1990s. Visions of atomic doomsday on the Pecho Coast receded in the light of several years of safe electricity generation. A nuclear accident became a distant prospect, scarcely considered by the local populace. Reflecting a lack of interest in nuclear issues, California newspapers rarely carried stories on the plant. The region no longer seemed exciting or newsworthy. The nuclear landscape represented just another local industry, and citizens accepted Diablo as part of the county scene. The possibility arose of the Pecho headland's regaining its prenuclear anonymity.

When Native Americans first established residency on the Central Coast, they acclimatized to living in the shadow of a series of dormant volcanoes (the Nine Sisters). The modern-day county treated two reactor domes on the Pecho Coast as similarly quiet volcanoes. Californians assimilated, or naturalized, nuclear fear itself. Concern over the Diablo plant resembled sentiments toward underlying dangers native to the far-western landscape. Obispans treated the two nuclear reactors like thousands of Californians treated fault lines—as unavoidable risks. They acknowledged the existence of danger but also recognized that, on a day-to-day level, the nuclear neighbor posed little practical nuisance. Locals adjusted their images of a nuclear disaster to that of a natural disaster, akin to an "act of god" and thus out of their hands.

Former antinuclear activists had little choice but to reluctantly accept their atomic nemesis. That statewide protest failed to stop the plant in the early 1980s implied little chance of shutting the operation down in the 1990s. The passing of time helped ease their fears. Ex-Abalone Bob Wolf explained: "It's strange, I have to admit I hardly think about it anymore. Other times I try to decide either to move away, stay here and be pissed off all the time, or stay here and kind of put it out of my mind. I've kind of put it out of my mind—which I think a lot of people did." A 1991 survey of 188 California Polytechnic students found that 50 percent of them "rarely" considered the nuclear danger, while 19 percent had not even heard of Diablo Canyon. The lack of concern partially reflected the cocooned life at the university, yet the same California campus had produced a number of antinuclear activists during the 1970s. The remote geographical position of the Diablo plant meanwhile enabled locals to put to one side any lingering nuclear concerns while casually shopping in peaceful downtown Obispo. The county landscape bore few reminders of its nuclear lineage. Electricity cables crossed Highway 101 but hardly betrayed their atomic source. The Irish Hills (San Luis Range) comfortably blanketed San Luis residents from their nuclear neighbor. The nuclear plant invariably appeared an unreal danger, remote, hidden, and visually at odds with both its natural surroundings and everyday reality. Events at the Diablo plant mostly remained in the backdrop to contemporary county life. Dick Krejsa noted that PG&E's project remained "out of sight, out of mind" for the majority of Obispans.[31]

Local apathy further reflected the passé status of the atom in U.S. popular culture. The appropriately titled movie *Blast from the Past* (1998) showed Adam (Brendan Fraser) entering chaotic and contemporary urban California for the first time after growing up inside a nuclear bunker. As a response to the Cuban missile crisis, Adam's parents had taken to their well-stocked family fallout shelter on mistaking a nearby plane crash for nuclear holocaust. For several decades the shelter protected them and their son Adam from social change as opposed to radiation sickness. On leaving the safety of the bunker Adam initially struggles to interpret the complex "real world" of Los Angeles. Good old-fashioned notions about relationships and manners applied only inside the concrete atomic coffin. As identified in the movie, the atom endures only as a relic of a paranoia-stricken cold war society. It seems out of touch with American life thirty years on.

Burying plutonium, dismantling weapons, and shutting down reactors in the 1990s related a corresponding desire to leave behind a difficult period in global relations. In a local context, controversies over Diablo Canyon belonged to a former era of county history—the turbulent late 1970s and early 1980s—rather than the less impassioned nineties.

Nuclear nomenclature, meanwhile, lost some of its meaning by being assimilated into mainstream American discourse. The U.S. government traditionally mitigated the dangers of the atom by using a range of phrases, or "Nukespeak," that described accidents as "events" and lost weapons as "broken arrows." By the 1990s nuclear language had proliferated into public life, losing its tinge of secrecy and surreptitiousness in the process. *Meltdown* related political, financial, or personal collapse, but rarely atomic catastrophe. *Chain reaction* morphed into a musical hit for Diana Ross. Environmental doomsdays similarly lost their salience in U.S. society, and this, too, influenced local attitudes toward Diablo Canyon. The "population bomb," "limited" Earth, and nuclear apocalypse all seemed distant ruminations of 1960s and 1970s doomsday culture. The immediacy of a number of ecological issues receded, while environmentalists turned to face fresh, but longterm, challenges such as global warming, the invasion of genetically modified organisms, and corporate malpractice. Atomic catastrophe accordingly dropped on the ecological danger list from Defcon 4 to Defcon 2, perhaps even 1. The Diablo plant no longer represented the potent threat that had once inspired thousands of environmentalists to act.[32]

▪ MONEY, DEREGULATION AND DIABLO CANYON ▪

The financial aspects of the Diablo plant had always remained of interest to residents of San Luis Obispo. Back in the 1960s county officials had welcomed the atomic project partly for its economic promise. During the 1970s and 1980s huge construction costs associated with the plant placed doubts on anticipated financial gains. Citizens questioned whether the nuclear project could ever be cost-effective. Nonetheless, in the 1990s PG&E established itself as an important patron of county life, with the Diablo plant providing the region with significant tax revenue, employment opportunities, and even the occasional corporate gift. In 1997 the *Telegram-Tribune* calculated that "Diablo's parent" contributed approximately $225 million to the local economy every year. The tax returns generated by the operational nuclear plant provided essential funds for county schools. As a large employer in the area, the electrical utility assisted a plethora of local businesses. Diablo workers helped keep the Fat Cats Café at Avila Beach open twenty-four hours a day. Pacific Gas made sizable donations to local charities. Where once Abalone cartoons indicated trucks of dollar signs traveling into Diablo Canyon, arguably the picture most appropriate to the 1990s was one of "Diablo dollars" fueling the local economy.[33]

Environmentalists berated the power and influence held by corporate America. "People look at Diablo now as money," Raye Fleming observed in 1997. Geoff Land, of the Environmental Center of San Luis Obispo (ECOSLO), lamented that the Diablo plant "has sacred cow status now" in the broader community, with PG&E almost untouchable due to its financial contributions. Another activist felt angry that the "almighty dollar" had won out. In April 1994 the *Telegram-Tribune* printed a cartoon showing "PG&E distributing its 'political influence' in San Luis Obispo County" with the two Diablo reactors as giant octopuses. For the artist the nuclear plant represented two devilish sea monsters tightening their grip on the county. In an article for the *Telegram-Tribune* in May 1996, Dick Krejsa related the need to avoid over-dependency on atomic handouts. During his term as county supervisor in the early 1970s, Krejsa had recommended the creation of a special fund in order to avoid becoming reliant upon Pacific Gas contributions for the everyday running of the county. Angered by paying 11.589 cents per kilowatt hour to power his ecofriendly home, Krejsa drew attention to the significant contributions county residents made to the plant as electricity consumers, arguing that the high cost of electricity from Diablo "should be everyone's business." On the same page as Krejsa's admonitions a cartoon criticized the billions of dollars pumped by the U.S. government into the Star Wars defense project. With a giant missile pictured protruding from the White House, the punch line read, "This thing won't backfire on us, will it?" As environmentalists saw it, Californians only partially recognized the dangers involved in relying on an atomic plant for long-term prosperity.[34]

During the late 1990s the California Public Utilities Commission introduced the deregulation of electricity provision across the Golden State, generating a wave of concern in San Luis Obispo over the continued survival of the Diablo plant. PG&E faced the difficult prospect of downscaling its more inefficient operations in order to provide competitively priced energy to California customers. The *Telegram-Tribune* responded to the climate of uncertainty with stories anticipating the early shutdown of Diablo nuclear plant. "Closure Would Send Out Ripples" warned the headline of the first article in a three-part series on the relationship between Diablo reactors and the local community. Retail commerce, the construction industry, fast-food joints all had "a stake in Diablo." Reporter Silas Lyons detailed the fate that befell the Rancho Seco plant outside Sacramento following its shutdown in 1989. All that remained of Rancho Seco was "the gutted carcass of a nuclear reactor." In contrast to sentiments displayed in 1984, locals feared the shutdown of the Diablo plant, rather than its operation. The financial importance of PG&E's project outweighed any lingering doubts over its nuclear personality. In order to gain regional competitiveness, Pacific Gas reassessed its energy projects, selling the Morro Bay, Moss Landing, and Oakland plants to Duke Energy Power Services of North Carolina in a $501 million deal. However, PG&E remained adamant in its intention to keep the Diablo project alive by using a number of cost-cutting maneuvers. Under the headline "A Fiscal Meltdown," the *San Francisco Chronicle* detailed PG&E's plan to accelerate the depreciation of the Diablo plant, thereby reducing its corporate tax bill.[35]

However, a sudden decrease in revenue threatened to deal a blow to the finances of San Luis Obispo County. Silas Lyons reported on PG&E's aim to "squeeze more efficiency out if its staff" by reducing their number to 1,300. (The nuclear department of Pacific Gas, spread between San Francisco and Diablo Canyon, at one time employed 3,000.) In April 1998 Jeff Lewis announced the closure of the on-site marine biology laboratory, although he noted a continuing desire "to work with all those who used it to find a way to give it a life outside Diablo." The corporation traditionally detailed emergency information concerning the Diablo plant in the form of a glossy annual calendar featuring black-and-white photographs of picturesque county scenes, which was sent out free to energy users. In 1999 PG&E chose to provide the same information on an insert in the local Pacific Bell phone book, saving $100,000 in publication costs. Carmen Girardi of Shell Beach lamented the loss of the calendar: "You would be seeing it all the time and know where it is." Just as San Luis residents had become accustomed to their nuclear neighbor and its annual mail, the position of the Diablo plant within the local community seemed threatened by California energy deregulation.[36]

▪ MOTHERS FOR PEACE IN THE 1990s ▪

The Mothers for Peace had few qualms over the unexpected closure of the Diablo plant. The local group was more worried by the idea of PG&E compromising safety procedures in the pursuit of cost cutting and increased electrical output. In response to the refueling of the Diablo plant in record time during 1994, the Mothers argued that significant sacrifices had been made in the race to restore power. June von Ruden, in a letter to fellow members, claimed that "during this hasty refueling: the cooling system was shut off; radioactive water was spilled; defective fuel rods are leaking radiation; and power to monitor radioactivity in the control room was cut off. . . . Let's face it, money talks and PG&E loses $3 million every day the plant is shut down." Local writer Jeff Wheelwright expressed a similar point of view on the refueling episode, comparing the "life" of the Diablo plant to "a shark that must never stop swimming." The lifeguard role remained taken by the NRC, along with the Diablo Canyon Independent Safety Committee set up by the CPUC in 1988 to monitor plant procedures (it disbanded in 1997). Citizens most skeptical of Pacific Gas looked to the Mothers for a critical assessment of plant operation. Rochelle Becker suggested that "when there's a problem at the plant, the community turns to the Mothers for Peace for a solution." Meanwhile, those residents who expressed confidence in PG&E's ability likely dismissed the Mothers' complaints as antinuclear propaganda.[37]

That the Diablo plant maintained a level of proficiency led to occasional calls for the Mothers for Peace to shift their gaze away from the Pecho Coast and toward other local landmarks. Walt Reil, from Atascadero, wrote to the *Telegram-Tribune* in March 1997 declaring that "it is time for this group to get on with life and do something truly beneficial for San Luis Obispo County." The Mothers had nevertheless broadened their activities during the 1990s. Members protested American involvement in the Gulf War during 1990–1991. The *Telegram-Tribune* described a move from "anti-Vietnam to anti-nuke to anti-war. Some people might say the Mothers for Peace has come full circle." In 1994 seven Mothers helped build houses on the Cheyenne River Sioux reservation as part of the Habitat for Humanity program. The group organized an annual ecotour of environmentally friendly Obispan homes and funded a scholarship for ecologically aware local students. A mission statement reflected broad, inclusive notions of environmental responsibility, noting that the Mothers focused "on the interconnected issues of the need for peace, social justice and a safe environment."

■   GREENING DIABLO   ■

A Chumash story recorded by John Peabody Harrington told of a "man at La Purisma long ago" who bargained the latter portion of his life in return for "ten or twelve years" of riches. Failing to confess his sins, the man, who "always had plenty of money," died beneath his "beautiful big horse" when the animal "stumbled and fell." Harrington entitled the story "A Pact with the Devil." It opened with a question: "Do some Americans also make friends with a devil?" In a brief résumé of San Luis Obispo circa 1995, Mike Steere, writing for *Outside* magazine, promoted a "town where you can have a real job, a real life, and still get to move in with the scenery." However, Steere noted two "prices" of the Central Coast "paradise." One drawback concerned the "grudging, inept college-age help in stores and restaurants," the other a covert county deal whereby the "same city that works so hard to keep its liveable virtue has a quiet pact with an environmental devil, Diablo Canyon nuclear plant." According to Steere, behind the lush grasses and green policies of San Luis lurked a malevolent, dirty force.[38]

PG&E's plant embodied the hidden, ugly side of county life in the modern fairy tale. It appeared to make the paradise possible but also represented its major flaw. Yet the deal with an atomic leviathan was not unprecedented. San Luis Obispo County officials had invited other industrial and energy-related projects that, in the 1990s, had become equally, if not more, disturbing than the Diablo plant. One of the worst offenders resided just a few miles south of PG&E's reactors, at nearby Avila Beach. If the Diablo plant was an environmental boondoggle, what of Union Oil (later Unocal), which had used Avila Port for crude extraction activities since the early 1900s? Union had turned the southern hillside of Avila into an ugly "tank farm" for oil storage. While PG&E's concrete domes remained hidden from public view, few could miss the oily blot on the landscape of Avila. In 1995 officials recognized for the first time the full scale of ecological damage. Spills of gasoline, diesel, and crude oil had leaked into the groundwater below the beach, roads, and buildings of the small coastal town. Much of the shoreline had been contaminated with petroleum hydrocarbons. Unocal responded with a public relations campaign and a cleanup operation, including the removal of Avila's tank farm. Oil excavation work closed the Lighthouse Bar and Grill, local hangout of Diablo employees.

The future of Avila appeared uncertain. The *Telegram-Tribune* pondered the loss of the county's "funky" beach town to the disruptions of the decontamination process, while locals feared that "an expensive condo resort" would rise up from the scrubbed and sterilized sands. The *New Times,* a San Luis Obispo news and entertainment weekly, foresaw a $327 million theme park, "Oilworld USA," taking advantage of Avila's natural resources. "We've taken an environmental disaster and turned it into a one-of-a-kind theme park," explained a fictional Unocal spokesperson, "Dennis Lamb." "Expected to rival Magic Mountain and the recently opened Legoland," Oilworld would feature an oil-skating rink utilizing the *Exxon Valdez* tanker deck, "oilwrassling" (with adult-only shows past 7 P.M.), and an interactive museum where "an animatronic figure of oil well firefighter Red Adair will greet visitors and take them through an educational center designed to highlight the true glory of the Oil Age, unhindered by environmentalist historical revisionists." The *New Times* article came out on the morning of April 1.[39]

The geographical proximity of the Diablo plant to Avila bore mixed implications for local perceptions of nuclear power. Krejsa noted that with Avila "in the public eye now," the oil problem had become the priority concern in the region. "Waking up to smell the oil" each morning led Avila residents to look on their nuclear neighbor as a far less tangible threat. Yet the propinquity of the oil spill to the Diablo plant gave credence to the idea of the Central Coast as an overexploited energy landscape, an ecological hot spot courtesy of unbridled industrial activity. By the time Unocal finished cleaning up its mess, more dirty work loomed on the horizon. Krejsa foresaw the termination of the Diablo plant as "our bomb for the future. That's going to be another hit on Avila Beach when they have to dismantle the plant."[40]

The idea of the Central Coast as an industrial dumping ground gained currency among local environmentalists. Along with Avila and Diablo, numerous other examples of ecological despoliation could be found on the San Luis shoreline. On the Guadalupe Dunes, south of Avila, petroleum-coated dead animals were discovered suspiciously close to Unocal's Guadalupe oil field in 1988. Citizens complained of dune contamination, but Unocal denied responsibility. In 1992, following a raid at Unocal offices, state officials disclosed that the company had covered up in excess of two hundred leaks and thirty-one plumes at Guadalupe. An estimated 8.5 million gallons of oil had been spilled. At Morro Bay environmental malpractice dated back to the nineteenth century. Morro Rock, "the firm, grim guardian of the placid bay" as described in a poem by C. Elwoods during the 1800s, had "his head" unceremoniously decapitated for building materials in the 1890s. Elwoods's "bold sentry" was joined by a four-stack power plant, courtesy of PG&E, in 1954. In 1998 environmentalists, local ranchers, and Native Americans joined forces to protest plans by the Hearst Corporation to build a golf resort and hotel at San Simeon Point, a scenic peninsula on the north coast of the county. "Many are calling it 'the coastal battle of the decade,'" noted the *Telegram-Tribune*. The Hearst Ranch Resort represented "the biggest development controversy since Diablo Canyon." Rather than the Diablo plant standing alone as a symbol of industrial despoliation, a number of other "controversial" schemes marked a coastline under siege by corporate America.[41]

Both Unocal and PG&E presented their respective enterprises as ecologically benign in the hope of mitigating public antipathy. Unocal attempted to reshine its tarnished reputation with a handout entitled *Yesterday, Today, Tomorrow* (1996). A photograph accompanied each time period, with "tomorrow" depicted as a pristine dune wilderness, untainted by years of oil development. Unocal presented modern approaches to oil refining as in keeping with the natural landscape. A picture captioned "Pumping unit in Santa Barbara County, 1980" showed a single, clean pump in a bushy green field. The shot had been taken between two thick tree branches, giving the impression of nature guarding the machine, as if fondly wrapped around it. Pacific Gas and Electric had represented the Diablo nuclear plant as a green industry for several decades. Ex-Abalone Tom Athanasiou dated what he judged to be "the age in which ecological crisis met public relations, the age of corporate 'greenwashing,'" as beginning with PG&E's spraying of the denuded Diablo hillside with green paint in the early 1970s. In the 1980s and 1990s PG&E promoted the Diablo plant as an ecologically friendly neighbor. "Our universe is bathed in radiation," the Pacific Gas Community Center (formerly Nuclear Information Center) soothingly declared, hoping to assuage public fears over energy production at Diablo Canyon. Optimistic portrayals of nuclear power in the 1990s bore some resemblance to atomic information of the 1950s and 1960s. Handouts available at the Community Center explained that Americans soaked up far more radiation by watching television and eating food than from living alongside a nuclear plant. One booklet on Diablo Canyon used a graph to illustrate different radiation sources. While "living near site boundary of a Nuclear Power Station" represented a dose of 1 millirem per year, "natural radiation in food" weighed in at 17 to 22 millirem. Another pamphlet available at the Community Center, published by Westinghouse in 1990, equated the radiation of a nuclear plant with that of a television set. Pacific Gas nonetheless struggled to locate a truly effective "greenwashing" primer for Diablo Canyon.[42]

Perhaps in recognition of its failure to secure mainstream public support for atomic power, PG&E gradually played down its nuclear portfolio during the 1990s. In official brochures the corporation justified the Diablo plant as part of "a broad mix of energy sources, both 'alternative' and conventional." The onus was placed on an entrenched defense of the Diablo project, rather than heralding it as the harbinger of a new electrical age for California. Employees wanted the local community to accept and support Diablo on its own merits rather than linking it with a nuclear-fueled future. PG&E also demonstrated a philanthropic side to corporate America. In 1983 the marine biology unit at Diablo Canyon gave the Steinhart Aquarium at San Francisco two hundred mature abalone shellfish. In early 1987 Pacific Gas provided $420,000 for Golden Gate lights on the fiftieth anniversary of the bridge, a fitting gesture for an electricity provider. The corporation also published a pamphlet titled 30 Simple Energy Things You Can Do to Save the Earth. [43]

Critics predictably dismissed PG&E's ecological compassion as a public relations masquerade. The Mothers for Peace pertinently replied to the 30 Simple Energy Things booklet with their own "revised" edition entitled What PG&E Can Do to Save the Earth. The "alternative" green agenda included shutting down the Diablo plant, restoring "the land to its nature state prior to construction," and erecting "a modest plaque on the revegetated site honoring Mothers for Peace, the Abalone Alliance, People Generating Energy and the many others who spoke up and acted to protect their families, community and the earth." In 1991 PG&E set up a booth at the annual San Luis Earth Day fair. Organizers of the event initially asked the corporation to limit its brochures to energy conservation rather than atomic promotion, but later conceded on the issue. Booklets on Diablo duly appeared at the Pacific Gas stall. Company spokesman Brad Thomas explained: "PG&E is a utility and part of it is a nuclear plant in this area and that's part of PG&E. We're good corporate citizens and we're a green corporation and we're not ashamed of anything we're doing." Earth Journal later responded with a cartoon of a vulture holding a pronuclear banner, along with a report entitled "Gag Me with a Green Ad."[44]

Environmentalist cynicism toward PG&E reprised the sentiments of Thomas Turner in "Eco-Pornography or How to Spot an Ecological Phony," an article featured in *The Environmental Handbook* (1970), prepared for the original Earth Day in April 1970. In rebuttal to PG&E's claim that "We Keep a Smile on Mother Nature's Face," Turner had argued that activities at Diablo Canyon instead suggested that "Mother is having a miscarriage." PG&E leafleting at the Earth Day fair in 1991 represented an act of environmental blasphemy to the Mothers for Peace. For many activists corporate infiltration reflected the loss of Earth Day as a down-to-earth, spontaneous, and genuine occasion. However, businesses had always attempted to buy into Earth Day, with Dow Chemical and Ford both providing contributions to event organizers in 1970.[45]

PG&E tours of Diablo Canyon also remained controversial in the eyes of environmentalists. Opponents of nuclear power had always been uncomfortable with the utility's taking busloads of local citizens, children, and even tourists to the Pecho Coast. The Abalone Alliance mimicked PG&E's tour for schoolkids in the early 1980s. The Alliance reprinted a page from the coloring book that corporate executives handed out free to youngsters, in which a cartoon "Eco-otter" showed students the location of Diablo Canyon on a map of California. The otter mouthed, "Get ready for some fun!" while the other sites marked on the map—Lake Tahoe, Hollywood, Disneyland, and Seaworld—indicated that the Diablo plant, or perhaps Diablo atomic theme park, ranked alongside the best entertainment on offer. "It's propaganda, that's what, and it's aimed at your children," claimed the Abalone protesters on their version, which implored local residents to call their children's schools and say, "Don't Send My Kids on a Radiation Vacation!" In June 1992 schoolworker Kathy di Peri indeed refused to take her students on a prearranged trip to the Diablo plant's marine laboratory.[46]

PG&E had failed to convince the environmental lobby as to the worth of nuclear power. However, the corporation still had one card to play. During the 1990s PG&E officials focused on the resident wildlife of the region to promote their nuclear project as environmentally friendly. Arguably, the beauty of wildlife found on the coastline rubbed off on the concrete domes of the

Diablo plant. George DeBord, writing in the *Telegram-Tribune,* related: "The drive into Diablo is one of the prettiest in the county." *Sea Changes,* a promotional film made for PG&E by Patrick Mulvey, presented Diablo Canyon as an "ancient place" of natural wonder, with prehistoric survivors such as the bishop pine and horsehill fern still thriving on Pecho hills. Whales swam past the promontory on their nine-thousand-mile journey between Baja California and Arctic waters. Northern elephant seals hauled out on the rocky shoreline of Diablo Cove. By sidelining six hundred acres of atomic industry, and instead concentrating on ten thousand acres of relatively undisturbed coastline, *Sea Changes* provided a visual retort to those conservationists who considered nature lost at Diablo Canyon. Mulvey had fashioned a natural-history film, a celluloid celebration of the Pecho wilds. On environmental tours of Diablo PG&E guides highlighted the rich flora and fauna of the Pecho Coast, emphasizing the healthy natural environment surrounding the two reactors.[47]

People ventured to Diablo Canyon to marvel at organic *and* atomic attractions. The apparent dangers of the nuclear landscape faded behind a foreground of flourishing natural variety. Oft-touted criticisms of atomic energy seemed less salient in an environment resounding with ecological vitality. Meanwhile, the focus on local ecology suggested a degree of biocentric awareness within PG&E tour operations. Talk of sea otters and peregrine falcons pointed toward the possibility of seeing a nuclear reactor through nonhuman eyes. Nevertheless, the tour existed to win public support for the Diablo plant rather than to explore biophilic notions. As with national parks, the wildlife did not always appear on time for the watching audience. Sea otters often ate outside Diablo Cove, while peregrine falcons alighted on distant rocks. When the wildlife failed to show up, PG&E relied on the facilities of the marine laboratory for entertainment. Guides encouraged every tourist to touch and hold a native resident of Diablo waters, albeit a craggy crab rather than a furry animal. In the thrill of prodding and poking marine locals, visitors felt inclined to interpret the radioactive reactors humming nearby as harmless, if not irrelevant, additions to the natural environment. The proof of safe nuclear power lay in their hands.

However, living in an age predominantly critical of atomic progress, the combination of nuclear plant and coastal wilderness seemed too absurd for staunch environmentalists to contemplate. Deer munching on the well-kept lawns adjacent to the two reactor domes, below a sign announcing, "Welcome to Diablo Canyon Nuclear Power Plant," appeared a scene straight out of Yellowstone National Park. Yet at Diablo the instinctive reaction was to look for a rope tethering the resident fauna rather than reach for the camera. PG&E security officers, meanwhile, insisted that tourists refrained from photographing the local plant life. The seamlessness of nature and nuclear artifice in PG&E watercolor handouts generated distrust more than comfort with corporate America. Could the material environment really disprove a vision of Diablo manufactured by and believed in by thousands of Californian environmentalists over several decades?

▪ AN ENVIRONMENTAL BALANCE SHEET ▪

The deer eating on PG&E turf and the marine life housed in the laboratory ultimately failed to communicate the whole story of Diablo Canyon. While resident crustaceans endured the overeager fondling, local abalone populations suffered a decline arguably due to the operation of the Diablo plant. From 1988 onward, biologists noticed a substantial decrease in the numbers of red and black abalone surviving in Diablo Cove. The artificially heated waters in the cove encouraged "withering foot syndrome," a natural pathology triggered by high temperatures. Although no "three-eyed fish" similar to the one found at Mr. Burns's Springfield nuclear plant in *The Simpsons* surfaced, the mutated abalone nonetheless pointed to similarly unexpected side effects of an operational atomic project.[48]

As part of its obligations to state regulatory agencies, PG&E documented changes in the marine environment in and around Diablo Cove. The 1997 Thermal Effects Monitoring Program report noted the establishment of a warmer, southern-style environment in the cove, caused by the constant discharge of heated coolant water into the sheltered bay. Fish endemic to warmer ocean ecosystems, typically found off southern California, colonized the inlet, while native cold-water species vacated their Diablo homes. An artificial warm-water system supported an "unusual community" of fish, invertebrates, and algae. Leopard sharks, bat rays, and white seabass swam in Diablo Cove but proved rare elsewhere along the Central Coast. Black and yellow rockfish and painting greenlings did not venture into the bay, preferring to confine their activities to surrounding, cooler waters. The year-round operation of the

Diablo plant also created an artificially constant water temperature. Without the natural fluctuations in temperature caused by seasonal climatic changes, the reproductive processes of bull kelp were compromised. Bull kelp forests in contact with the thermal plume experienced premature aging.[49]

However, in comparison to the visible damage inflicted by oil spills at nearby Avila, the transformation of Diablo Cove to a warm-water environment seemed subtle and complex. Significant impacts of plant operation failed to emerge far beyond the cove itself. Environmental consultant Jim Blecha characterized Diablo Cove as "environmentally dynamic" by natural design, regardless of the nearby nuclear machinations. El Niño and Pacific storms, together with the migrations of sea creatures, refuted the existence of a static marine equilibrium. The emergence of ecological chaos theory— positing biotic conditions as naturally disturbed, changeable, and unruly— represented a useful scientific model for the nuclear corporation. However, PG&E had disturbed a complicated set of ecological relationships.[50]

In 1995 county supervisor Bud Laurent informed the California Regional Water Quality Control Board (CRWQCB) of data amiss in PG&E environmental reports. A subsequent investigation by state attorney general Dan Lungren and both state and U.S. Environmental Protection Agencies found that Pacific Gas had consistently failed to detail the negative effects of the water intake system on marine larvae over an eight-year period.

The corporation was duly charged with violation of the Clean Water Act. In May 1997 the California Environmental Protection Agency announced "the settlement of one of the largest environmental cases in California history." PG&E agreed to pay a $14 million fine for withholding information from the CRWQCB concerning its operation of the Diablo plant. U.S. EPA employee Cheryl McGovern described the deal as "one of the largest environmental settlements reached since the 1989 Exxon Valdez disaster." Significantly, radiation remained in the background of the ecological dispute over fish larvae data, with problems at the Diablo plant not greatly dissimilar to pollution incidents at other large-scale industrial complexes. However, the actual scale of ecological damage remained a contested issue. On the day of the settlement PG&E spokesman Jeff Lewis admitted, "We are happy to get this to a conclusion," but also emphasized, "We don't believe there has been any kind of impact to the environment." The exclusion of the data represented an administrative oversight. Officials had omitted information regarding fish larvae, deeming it "flawed" or "irrelevant." Lewis argued that the damage to "tiny larvae" hardly justified government press releases implying that the plant was "taking up everything from sea otters to whales. That's absolutely not true."[51]

In contrast, Michael Thomas of the CRWQCB stated that his agency considered the PG&E plant's "impact to be significant" in reference to the ecological changes at Diablo Cove. Research indicated a reduction of up to 90 percent in marine life passing through the cooling system. Felicity Marcus, regional administrator for the federal EPA's Western Region, saw the issue as one of trust, asserting that "PG&E is paying a hefty price for taking the wrong course here. This settlement sends a loud and clear message . . . that such conduct is just plain wrong. California's Central Coast is a national treasure." The $14 million fine did have its ecological beneficiaries. Morro Bay enthusiasts received $3.6 million for an estuary protection and improvement project, while Marcus declared the settlement "a win for the coastal environment."[52]

Acting on evidence of damage to the marine environment, the CRWQCB debated options for disciplining PG&E in late 1999. The agency considered modifications to the cooling system of the Diablo plant in order to mitigate adverse environmental effects. Alternatively, state officials raised the possibility of a land deal protecting the coastline following the decommissioning of the two nuclear reactors. County supervisors planned to measure public support for the preservation scheme by placing the issue on the electoral ballot in March 2000.[53]

Elements of the nuclear landscape meanwhile emerged as beneficial to local wildlife. In the December 1987 edition of *PG&E Progress* an article entitled "Protecting Wildlife near Diablo Canyon" promoted the creation of "one of the most productive man-made reefs in the world" off the Pecho Coast. Pacific Gas employees had used rubble from the storm-damaged breakwater in 1982 to construct an artificial reef in 1985. A kelp forest swiftly grew over the reef, while snails, crabs, and starfish sheltered among the man-made rocks. In a case of green economics, PG&E saved half a million dollars by creating a haven for marine life rather than hauling the broken concrete and stone off-site. Biologist Dave Behrens explained, "Our main mission is to help the company operate the Diablo Canyon plant safely and efficiently. But each and every one of us here is an environmentalist at heart, and we're also here because PG&E cares about the California environment." In 1990 PG&E established a Land Stewardship Program, designed to identify rare wildlife species on the Pecho Coast, protect or restore crucial wild habitats (exempting the area used by the Diablo plant), and promote better grazing practices on the two ranches. The plan declared PG&E the "caretaker of these irreplaceable natural and cultural resources." Proclamations of environmental stewardship in the 1990s bespoke a different relationship between PG&E and the Pecho Coast from that of the late 1960s, when corporate propaganda portrayed Diablo as a unremarkable and worthless stretch of typical California coastline, ideal for building on rather than protecting.[54]

In 1981 fledgling peregrine falcons visited the rugged slopes of Diablo Rock. Falcon numbers had been decimated by intense use of DDT in the post-1945 period. A buildup of pesticides in the fat reserves of the falcons manifested itself in eggshell thinning, leading to many broken clutches and increased embryo deaths. By 1970 the number of California peregrines had fallen from over two hundred pairs to just two known couples, and the bird was classified as a state and federal endangered species. Falcons gradually recovered during the 1980s and 1990s, thanks to a comprehensive captive-breeding program. Recovery occurred at some of the most unlikely sites. The Santa Cruz Predatory Bird Research Group (SCPBRG), responsible for bird monitoring, announced an unexpected finding: "Because of their refuge-like nature, military and corporate lands such as Vandenberg Air Force Base and Diablo Canyon can be important sources of protected habitat for wildlife." Following the discovery of the Diablo Rock roost in 1981, the SCPBRG liaised with PG&E to initiate a monitoring and egg incubation program for the peregrines. The SCPBRG noted how "PG&E created a refuge-like situation which preserved ideal peregrine habitat." The local peregrines proved "remarkably tolerant of human activity close to the Diablo Rock nest site," skimming between the two reactor domes on foraging flights. From 1982 onward, falcons nested at Diablo Rock every season except 1985, when a nest was instead located at the base of a meteorological tower. SCPBRG project leader Brian Walton noted that such an "unusual site" entailed few unexpected problems. Results for breeding at Diablo proved "typical" for the recovery program, while PG&E's generous financing helped the SCPBRG project survive. Between 1984 and 1992, falcons successfully raised fifteen fledglings on the Diablo site, while the SCPBRG hatched a further thirty-four eggs in captivity. Wildlife biologists released birds of Pecho origin at the Channel Islands, Muir Beach, and El Capitan (in Yosemite National Park), as well as at Diablo Canyon. DDT had nearly killed off California peregrines in the 1960s. With similar postwar origins and insidious dangers, the nuclear landscape had nonetheless helped secure the return of the species.[55]

Sea mammals also prospered on the Diablo headland. California sea otters, mammals close to extinction in the late nineteenth century, relished the protection afforded them by the nuclear exclusion zone, taking advantage of kelp forests, the artificial breakwater, and calm waters. California gray whales journeying past Diablo Canyon seemed untroubled by the giant nuclear plant on the cliffs. Individual animals traveled freely through the edges of the warm-water plume leaking out from Diablo Cove. During his voyage to Alaska in 1879, John Muir witnessed a comparable scene of coastal cordiality. Traveling along the northern shores of California, Muir referred to passing whales as "brave neighbors, fellow-citizens in the commonwealth of the world." He likened the workings of the vessel on which he sailed to the processes of marine biology. While impressed by the "truly noble spectacle" of the ship, with its "great iron heart," Muir implored his readers to consider "the hearts of these whales beating warm against the sea, day and night, through dark and night, on and on for centuries." The enduring presence of whales, porpoises, and other marine creatures afforded Muir a "striking revelation of warm life in the so-called howling waste." A century later, whales continued to migrate along the California coast, passing by the "iron heart" of Diablo Canyon.[56]

The audience of peregrines, pelicans, otters, and whales off the Pecho Coast challenged traditional notions of a nuclear landscape as a dangerous industrial wasteland. Visits by endangered species countered perceptions of an atomic tract as fundamentally devoid of natural life. That animals freely chose to live alongside two nuclear reactors intimated that environmentalists had exaggerated the alien and uninviting qualities of atomic energy sites and production. Wildlife favored the Pecho Coast because, at some level, they recognized a lack of immediate danger at the Diablo plant. The preservation of resident species depended on PG&E's adherence to nuclear safety protocol. An accident at Diablo, however unlikely, presented a risk to animals yet to fully recover from prior decades marked by hunting and chemical industries. Rare falcons and pelicans had, without realizing, chosen an endangered environment as their home. Questions remained over the ethics of celebrating the return of threatened species to such terrain.

SIX *Reconnecting the Headland*

Whether out of an ingrained desire for order, control, or property, we, as a people, love to parcel up territory, compartmentalize the natural, and carve out boundaries in the land. Recall the great stampede westward in the nineteenth century, where thousands of emigrants rushed to stake their claim to 160-acre plots; the orderly grid design of modern cities replete with commercial, residential, and industrial zones; or the straight-line boundaries of Yellowstone National Park, Wyoming, that divide sacred wilderness from economic ranchland. Map borders, invisible lines, tall fences all contribute to our framing, and our understanding, of the great expanse of U.S. territory. Boundaries overlaid the land, creating divisions between soil and sand of equal ecological stature. These imposed lines help foster distinct identities for the spaces they enclose—the painted fence around the family farm, the manicured suburban lawn edges of the township, the signposts of the national park, the barbed wire and Keep Out signs of the nuclear installation. In the process, assigned borders create a semblance of protection: they keep the character of the region intact, preserving the military site, the industrial warehouse, or the wilderness enclave from encroachment.

These boundary ideas played out on the California coast. Twentieth-century Californians divided up the coastline, creating scenic seashore recreational areas, private residential estates, the Santa Cruz boardwalk, the Moss Landing power plant. The process included the Diablo Coast, first set aside for ranching and agriculture, then briefly assigned to military exercises, then, in the mid-1960s, sliced into two distinct territories, one nuclear, one natural. PG&E established a nuclear plant and buffer zone on land south of Point Buchon. Meanwhile, state officials from the Department of Parks and Recreation purchased land to the north. The old Spooner house and Hazard ranch, along with the Morro Bay sandspit, became Montana de Oro State Park. It seemed as though the northern and southern stretches of the Pecho Coast had parted company, that the headland had somehow been cracked apart at Point Buchon. The Coon Creek inlet immediately north of Buchon suggested just that, its meandering stream and sandy shore marking a geographical rift between the rugged cliffs on either side. As this book has documented, two very different perceptions grew up around Montana de Oro and Diablo during the 1970s and 1980s. Obispans interpreted the northern Pecho coastline as a place of recreation, natural wonder, and refuge. Diablo instead embodied an off-limits, industrial, and dangerous territory. A high barbed-wire fence marked the official dividing line between the two properties. By the 1990s, few citizens dared to cross the boundary dividing the nature park from the nuclear site.

As a much-loved recreational landscape, Montana de Oro State Park seemed to share little in common with the pariah nuclear facility to its south. The coastal park encapsulated conservation and leisure pursuits. Enrico P. Bongio from San Luis Obispo declared Montana de Oro to be "a real jewel in the state park system" in a 1991 letter to park authorities. Montana Park fast became a celebrated landscape of San Luis County, a bona fide local treasure. The worth of the northern Pecho Coast was measured according to its high recreational value, landscape aesthetics, and ecological diversity. It represented perfect nature. Bongio deemed Montana de Oro a wonderful jewel because of "the wide variety of still unspoiled flora and fauna" on offer there. The wild coastal landscape imparted a sense of vibrant natural history, with humans as occasional visitors to a greater, flourishing scene. Like many other American parks, Montana was lauded for its "primitiveness." Vacationers adjusted to its sparse facilities, the wooden pit toilets and unpaved parking lots, as part of the wilderness experience. As PG&E *Progress* magazine commented in 1973: "Relatively undeveloped, with primitive campsites, Montana de Oro has been little changed by time. The grizzlies are gone, but deer and other wildlife abound. On the remote and rugged coast, one can visualize the days when settlers smuggled hides to waiting Yankee ships in defiance of Mexican laws."[1]

To the south, despite sharing a common natural and human heritage with Montana de Oro, Diablo was assessed in terms of what it could offer the future of San Luis Obispo County, rather than serving as a testament to times past. Economic values and atomic prospects governed popular evaluations. While PG&E lauded Montana as a fine California park, the corporation interpreted Diablo lands as industrial in purpose. Diablo bespoke atomic utopianism and technological progress. Back in the late 1960s Pacific Gas officials and Nipomo aficionados alike had encouraged citizens to dismiss the southern coastline as worthless on biological and recreational grounds. Attention instead focused on the nuclear pantheon as the centerpiece of the shoreline. Coastal valuations derived from a different set of cultural criteria. The nuclear landscape conjured vivid images of social and economic advance, in contrast to Montana's promise of reconnecting people with primeval wilderness and a simpler existence. One timely commercial advertisement for nuclear fusion presented a picture of hunter-gatherers in the wilds as living a deplorable existence styled by the absence, rather than the presence, of atomic power. Applying organic adjectives to a nuclear landscape seemed irrational or beside the point. Throughout the ensuing decades, Californians rarely connected Diablo with Montana de Oro, the nuclear park with the state park.[2]

However, this demarcated boundary between the landscapes of preservation and electrical generation was, in fact, far from impervious. For some species the border proved amorphous. Faunal residents failed to differentiate the "natural" Montana from the "nuclear" Diablo. On the ground itself, coyotes and king snakes failed to recognize the Keep Out signs at Diablo as any different from the Visitors Welcome boards at Montana de Oro. The dividing fences carried no special messages, and creatures treated them similarly to natural barriers of dense shrubbery or rocky climbs. All kinds of wildlife crossed the border between north and south. Peregrine falcons, brown pelicans, and bald eagles flew freely along the full extent of the Pecho headland. Lizards located basking rocks wherever their instincts took them. Sea otters failed to surmise any decisive marine boundaries. Oaks and shrubbery adorned both lands, emphasizing that the common ecological ground of the California headland survived. To some, the bluffs and crags of Montana de Oro and Diablo were without boundaries and represented one coastal entity.

To others, the nuclear landscape unexpectedly emerged in the late 1990s as a better protector of ecology and nature than its park counterpart. According to some wildlife biologists, with the exception of the core nuclear site itself, most of the southern Pecho Coast offered native flora and fauna a sanctuary on par with, if not better than, the Montana wilds. Biologist Sue Benech, who monitored sea otter movements in the area, referred to the Diablo project as "a blessing in disguise" in 1997. Ten thousand acres of natural habitat had been preserved at a cost of just five hundred or so acres. Brian Walton of the Predatory Bird Research Group likewise interpreted the region as "like a ghost-town in terms of human impacts."[3]

During the 1990s half a million people visited Montana de Oro every year. While a state-commissioned survey indicated that the majority of visitors wanted to keep Montana as a "primitive park," sheer recreational dynamics threatened to overload the natural carrying capacity of the northern Pecho Coast. Parking areas overflowed in peak months, and citizens related desires for additional space for recreational vehicles. Spooner Cove suffered from its own popularity. Visitors raided tide pools for food and souvenirs. Alden Spooner had held impressive picnics at the cove back in 1890, but even his entrepreneurial skills could not have catered for the crowds a century on. The California Department of Parks and Recreation attempted the difficult task of balancing recreational needs with ecological protection. Development projects had to be set against their environmental costs. Educational programs highlighted the natural worth of the region and implored tourists to act with ecological responsibility. A puppet show starring "bucket monster" warned kids of the danger in continually ravaging local sea creatures.[4]

In stark contrast, human activity on the Diablo lands was strictly curtailed. Most of the coastline remained off-limits, with only the small-time rancher and watchful biologist allowed to freely roam the bluffs. The absence of rowdy recreationists translated into unmolested wildlife and undisturbed coves (with the notable exception of Diablo Cove). Attractive blowholes and a coastal "stone circle" of rocks remained hidden features of the landscape, retaining their pristine quality courtesy of infrequent obtrusions by Pacific Gas. Functioning biotic systems seemingly had a better chance of survival on PG&E property.

By deconstructing human expectations we can learn a great deal about both sides of the Pecho Coast. While a nuclear plant was automatically assumed to be detrimental to nature, a state park correspondingly received plaudits as a model of wilderness preservation. However, from a bird's-eye perspective, the two regions appeared remarkably similar by the late 1990s. Both spaces exhibited winding roads leading to concentrations of people. Cars congregated at the parking lots of Diablo and Spooner coves. Diablo and Montana appeared almost symmetrical along a mirror-line drawn at Point Buchon. From high in the air, human activity on the Pecho Coast resembled two distinct anthills, serviced by worker drones on prescribed routes to their mother hives. Similar geographic patterns at the two places suggested a greater idea of convergence. It seems that cultural paradigms masked ecological congruities.

With its technological, atomic patina, Diablo was popularly conceived as anathematic to the quintessential nature park. And yet, alongside all the customary baggage associated with the atomic age, there remains the intriguing concept of preservation in nuclear landscapes. Could Diablo itself, complete with concrete carbuncle, pass itself off as a future park?

Awed at the grand scenery of the Pecho Coast, Steven Marx remarked in the 1990s that "the feeling reminded me of my first view of Yosemite Valley at age twelve." Marx experienced such wonderment on a PG&E tour bus winding its way down to the Diablo plant, rather than during a stroll in Montana de Oro State Park. The journey along PG&E's isolated, weaving road bred anticipation of a grandiose scene lying ahead. The gigantic nuclear plant overlooking the Pacific Ocean resembled the "monumental scenery" found in Yosemite National Park. Marx could have compared his experience on the Diablo drive more directly with the gratification offered by California's Highway 1 or, closer still, the twisty entrance road into Montana de Oro Park. Yet the Yosemite analogy imparted both the scale of the Diablo picture and the irony of situating it alongside one of California's most treasured natural landscapes. Asked for his thoughts on the matter, one PG&E employee enthused that "the scenery at the plant is absolutely stunning! (Yosemite it's not, but stunning it is.) The drive to and from work is very serene and often you will see white-tail deer, coyotes, raccoons, rabbits, hawks . . . and even an occasional roadrunner." It seemed almost heresy to compare a nuclear landscape with Yosemite, and yet Diablo possessed the credentials of a nature park in the making.[5]

Diablo was not the only nuclear landscape to be discussed in parklike terms in the 1990s. In January 1996 the *High Country News* reported that environmentalists and park authorities hoped to turn the Hanford Nuclear Reservation in Washington State into a national wildlife refuge. During the 1940s the tiny settlement of Hanford became a top-secret nuclear research site, while nearby Richland was transformed into an atomic city, serving as a dormitory facility for the nuclear enterprise. Richard White, a historian of the American West, noted the fission-fueled frontier imagery at work in Hanford, with Richland adopting an atomic symbol shining above a covered wagon as its town logo. According to one poster put out in 1948, Richland offered "A New Light on the Old Frontier." Nonetheless, military activity (and resultant contamination) was concentrated on 30 square miles of the Hanford reservation, while 530 square miles remained "as it was in 1942" when the U.S. Army first set aside the area for bomb making. A valuable tract of land had been left to natural processes for fifty years. The *High Country News* duly claimed that the "last substantial stretch of sagebrush-steppe grassland—perhaps anywhere in the world" had been inadvertently protected by military ownership. Mule deer and bald eagles surveyed the landscape of cottonwoods and bunchgrass. With the disbandment of Hanford, the future of the region suddenly seemed more precarious than during the years of military testing. Farmers and developers joined environmentalists in staking claims to postnuclear terrain, hoping to resettle the atomic domain with orchards and farms. Local Yakima Indians asserted their right to use ancestral lands within the Hanford site in accordance with an 1855 treaty. Ideas of property development vied with notions of nature protection. As with Diablo, one possibility for the postnuclear landscape entailed the preservation of extant ecology.[6]

Along with Diablo and Hanford, other atomic sites attracted interest due to their potential as protected spaces. The U.S. Fish and Wildlife Service considered reintroducing the Mexican wolf to the White Sands Missile Range in New Mexico in the mid-1980s. White Sands represented a remote haven where wolves could wander freely without ranchers taking potshots at them. The National Park Service assumed responsibility for the preservation of the Trinity Test Site at White Sands and former Minuteman silos in South Dakota. In 1995 the Rocky Mountain Arsenal (RMA), Colorado, a locale used since the 1940s for the manufacture of deadly chemicals, was dubbed the "Nation's Most Ironic Nature Park." Closed down since 1982, the Denver site was the object of an expensive cleanup operation. The Army Corps of Engineers described the center of the RMA as "the most contaminated square mile on Earth." However, the wider territory boasted a diverse array of wildlife species, including twenty bald eagles. Officials promoted the region as a place of nature tourism.[7]

Traditional notions of atomic sites as despoiled and dangerous nonetheless tempered desires to lavish praise on the new nuclear "parklands." Newspaper articles typically cast Hanford and Rocky Mountain Arsenal as ironic landscapes. The oxymoron of a toxic refuge lingered in popular reportage. Such terrains were taken as exceptional and hard-to-accept places. The combination of healthy natural wonder enveloping lethal human enterprise tested modern sensibilities. Westerners had become accustomed to segregated landscapes where nature and culture resided side by side, yet rarely did the worst of humanity share space with the best of nature. Used to being the dominant party in every environment, people were forced to adjust psychologically to the idea of Mexican wolves freely wandering White Sands or pelicans roosting at Diablo, territories off-limits to almost every citizen.[8]

The nuclear buffer zones of the twentieth century, originally set aside as "worthless lands" but later recognized for their ecological significance, may hark back to the national park experience a century earlier. Although the plutonium ponds at the RMA hardly rival the Rocky Mountain splendor of Yellowstone's geysers, a parallel denouement took place in America's first national park. In 1872 Yellowstone National Park was established to preserve a core area of geothermal wonders. Only later did administrators recognize the wilderness value of surrounding lands protected "by accident" in the hope of discovering further geological curiosities. Perhaps postnuclear parks represent similar accidents.[9]

▪ NUCLEAR WILDERNESS ▪

The Rocky Mountain Arsenal stands as a poignant illustration of the blurring ground between "natural" and "unnatural" environments. Back in 1995

William Cronon interpreted the toxicity of the RMA as "one of the most important things supporting the wild nature for which the place is now celebrated." He argued that "familiar categories of environmentalist thinking don't seem to work" at places such as the RMA, where "unnatural" human activities enable animals and plants to flourish.[10]

Along with other examples found across America, Rocky Mountain Arsenal, with its blend of poisons and ecological vitality, provided useful ammunition to shoot down traditional notions of nature and humanity as distinct enterprises rather than symbiotic forces. In particular, Cronon targeted the environmentalists' holy grail of wilderness, highlighting the cultural roots of this supposedly nonhuman reality. The term *wilderness* represented a social construction, implicitly ignorant of Native American land uses. Unpeopled landscapes had become falsely idealized. Flooded with tourists and fervently managed by park officials, existing national parks hardly constituted regions of negligible human impact, while "despoiled" places such as RMA could never be accepted as wilderness in a conventional sense. Perhaps the time had come for Americans to value a more inclusive set of cultural landscapes.[11]

The nuclear park fits within this theme of learning to appreciate cultural landscapes and helps pioneer new ways of thinking about society and nature. Territories marked by military exigencies and scientific experiment bear the fruits of myriad plants and animals, challenging us to reconsider our qualms over man-made "nature experiences." The nuclear landscape is a culturally determined space with its own unexpected aesthetic and ecological graces. Nuclear landscapes may even help shift the established paradigms of the wilderness debate that William Cronon speaks of. Traditional discussions on the saliency of the term *wilderness* have usually explored how culture enters, and sullies, the pristine and the natural. Yet the history of American nuclear landscapes provides a worthy example of how culture can (consciously or not) support the natural. Custom dictates that when we think of wilderness, we imagine a return to Arcadia, a time capsule, a place untouched by progress, and an outdoor museum. Meaningful consideration of nuclear landscapes may help us carve out a definition of wilderness not solely dependent on primordial, romantic notions of prelapsarian bounty. Postnuclear lands might be used to expand and chronologically update the concept of wilderness. Species-rich places such as Diablo and Trinity, zones determined by human mandate, might yet join the traditional park fraternity, and they illustrate that wildernesses can emerge in unexpected locales. Already a number of former nuclear sites have become parks, from Hanford Reach National Monument on the Columbia River to a recreational park at the decommissioned Trojan nuclear power plant in Oregon. After all, today's national parks were once the homes of Native Americans. Tomorrow's parks may betray recent American land uses. Modern culture hence appears capable of creating wilderness not only in the mind, but also in material reality.

Yet the notion of a postnuclear landscape, bizarrely beautiful as a cultural paradox, is not without significant flaws. On a practical level, human absence, rather than presence, is arguably the key factor that has ensured the ecological productivity of places such as Diablo and White Sands. The lingering presence of toxins passes unnoticed by wildlife, who visit testing grounds because what matters most for them is the lack of more-obvious forms of human artifice. The 1964 Wilderness Act defined *wilderness* as "an area where the earth and its community of life are untrammeled by man, where man himself is a visitor who does not remain . . . an area of undeveloped Federal land retaining its primeval character and influence without permanent improvements or human habitation." Designated nuclear landscapes feature vast reserves off-limits to American settlers and are pregnant with primeval character. Surveillance patrols guard land perimeters, blocking civilian incursions into nuclear terrain. Nature flourishes in such areas precisely due to forced separation from people and their projects; resident flora and fauna are insulated *from*, rather than immersed *in*, civilization.[12]

There is also the question of whether atomic culture can take the credit for the beauty of such places. It may be wrong to overlook the militaristic designs that played out at Hanford and Alamogordo, landscapes appropriated for destruction, not creation. Atomic culture is traditionally looked on as, at best, uninterested in the natural environment and, at worst, highly destructive of it. In the late 1990s Valerie Kuletz explored the differences between Native American and U.S. military conceptions of Yucca Mountain, adjoining the Nevada Test Site. While Native Americans considered the desert sacred and alive, modern "scientific discourses and representations" legitimated "the designation of areas . . . as toxic and nuclear waste dumping grounds—a particularly brutal objectification of the non-human world." Modern culture, with all its antinature epistemology, hardly seems likely to foster fresh and uncomplicated wildernesses. The mindset that led to the Diablo plant and Yucca nuclear waste depository may even reflect a deeper Western tendency to denigrate the natural world as an object, intrinsically inferior, a sacrifice zone. According to the environmental historian Carolyn Merchant, the separation of the human being from the rest of the natural world, the idealization of science and the machine, and the turn against spiritualism within nature all date back to popular Enlightenment dogma. The motivations behind the creation of atomic landscapes seem more appropriate to the park in Francis Bacon's *New Atlantis*—a place of scientific experiment—rather than John Muir's Yosemite.[13]

If social forces cannot explain the coyotes hanging out at ground zero, then what can? Perhaps the idea of a divide between culture and nature can aid our understanding of parklike flora and fauna prospering at military sites. Historically, as scientists and army personnel have focused their experiments on core land sites, distant reaches of nuclear reservations have been ignored or simply left alone. Nature has recovered more quickly than expected at the testing grounds of the nuclear age, plants and coyotes reclaiming the bombed-out craters and polluted soils of ground zero. The military-industrial mindset governing activities inside the concrete domes and army warehouses has failed to dominate the surrounding landscape. Despite occasional military infractions, prairie dogs and eagles claim the sacrifice zone as their own. Trips to the deserted coastal reaches around the Diablo plant and the acres of sagebrush at Trinity thus recall ex–Earth First!er Dave Foreman's definition of wilderness as a "land beyond human control." While the atom manifests an extraordinary human power over nature, the thriving of biological agents at nuclear installations might also be taken as a somewhat paradoxical "affront to the arrogance of humanism" promoted by Foreman. At specific locales across Diablo and Trinity the impression is one of natural dominion, wilderness rebirth, and human desertion.[14]

Whether emblematic of a convergence between nature and culture or of a divide separating us from the rest of the natural world, nuclear landscapes today demonstrate the complexity of human-nature relations. Ideas of valuing cultural landscapes question the efficacy of a polarized view of civilization and wild nature as two forces moving in opposite directions. To unquestioningly accept claims by PG&E officials that wilderness derives from good industrial stewardship misses the underlying role played by ecological agency. Claiming that nuclear landscapes bear no human imprint and thus equate to wilderness ignores seasonal testing forays and lingering radioactivity. Perhaps the best starting point in any discussion of landscape dynamics would be to acknowledge the contributions of both culture and nature, to try to avoid setting one against the other as if diametrically opposed. In places such as Diablo and Trinity, William Cronon's constructed, anthropomorphic landscape and Dave Foreman's untouched nature refuge represent, by themselves, insufficient explanations of an environmental history. By recognizing both perspectives, the importance of cultural *and* natural agencies, we can better understand the evolution of nuclear, and wilderness, territories. Moving beyond cold war propaganda as well as protest narratives, former nuclear test sites can be seen to feature pockets of industrial contamination, tacit signs of stewardship, and active floral and faunal agents. The ecological reality is instructive. American nuclear landscapes ably reveal the importance of deconstructing the absolutes of "nature" and "culture" because neither term alone can explain ravens nesting in the plugs of atomic craters. Biotic agents recolonize, thrive, and coexist with us in urban, manmade and supposedly artificial landscapes. The garden can enter the machine as well as the machine entering the garden. Diablo and Trinity thereby provide unconventional pointers toward a common grounding for wilderness that relates both cultural and ecological dynamics.

▪ THE SPECIFICS OF RECONNECTING ▪

What of wilderness, restoration, and environmental practice on the Diablo Coast? In the 1990s PG&E moved to restore and protect wild flora and fauna on the southern Pecho Coast by instigating an environmental stewardship program. In the hope of naturally limiting summer bush fires, the corporation annually hired a herd of goats. In contrast to Park Service protocols, ranching and agriculture continued unabated on the Diablo lands. While in keeping with the cultural history of the Pecho Coast, ranching compromised the restoration of a "pristine" ecosystem. Land-use practices proved complex at Diablo nuclear facility, just as they did at any state or national park. At Montana de Oro officials grappled with an inherited legacy of former inhabitants, notably a giant eucalyptus grove in the old Hazard ranch region of the park. The 1988 park plan detailed aims to replace the eucalyptus with native plant species. A number of citizens nevertheless articulated an appreciation for the grove, raising concerns for the endangered monarch butterfly that utilized the exotic tree.[15] Restoring the native landscape, re-creating "wilderness," necessitated difficult choices on both stretches of the Pecho Coast. However, the Parks Department remained the more coherent and determined of the two parties. After all, restoring Diablo lands to a pristine state clearly stopped short of ripping out the two nuclear plants embedded in the coastal bluffs.[16]

Conservation efforts in the 1990s also revealed fresh aspirations to reconnect the two halves of the Pecho coastline. In 1993 a collection of government officials, corporate conservationists, and dedicated environmentalists officially opened the Pecho Coast Trail, a seven-mile loop across the Diablo lands. The outcome of a joint operation, or "path of cooperation," between the California Coastal Commission, PG&E, and the Nature Conservancy, the project had taken ten years to reach fruition. Built by the California Conservation Corps, it cost PG&E $300,000. "Never have I walked a more expensive trail," noted hiker John McKinney, who attended the opening ceremony. He also joked of the similar cost overruns at the nearby Diablo plant. The route began at the entrance gates of PG&E property, hugging the southern arch of the headland overlooking Avila Port. The restored Pecho Coast lighthouse provided an attractive stopping point on the trail. The journey offered Californians the chance to discover for themselves the natural riches of the southern Pecho landscape, the intricate intertwining of coastal oak branches, the superb ocean views, and even the occasional rattler. The wilderness had been opened up for the first time in many years. As McKinney pointed out: "Hiking here is a rare treat. The land between Avila Beach and Montana de Oro State Park is ten miles of coast that nobody knows, where nobody goes." Both McKinney and PG&E highlighted the land's obscurity and privacy since Spanish times. That the Pecho Trail bore local significance was graphically demonstrated on the cover of the 1994 San Luis Obispo visitors' guide, which featured a panoramic picture of the "Victorian Lady" lighthouse nestled between wild shrubs and crashing Pacific waves. The Pecho Coast trail booklet advertised the southerly lands as "some of the most pristine in the state." It painted life on the headland as "Living on the Edge," extolling the region as a dynamic place of passing whales, ancient volcanic flows, and earthquakes—without mention of the Diablo nuclear plant.[17]

The presence of the atomic project ultimately complicated visions of extending the trail northward to Montana de Oro. The 1988 Montana de Oro Park plan stated a desire to reunite the Pecho Coast as part of the California Coastal Trail, a state-long 1,300-mile walking route. Progress nevertheless stalled. The stumbling block, the crack in a complete Pecho Coast, remained the still-operational nuclear facility. Safety and security considerations preempted any serious thoughts of the public sauntering between nuclear edifice and Pacific Ocean. An extant atomic boundary had to be removed before reuniting the headland. Significantly, Point Buchon did not mark the critical line dividing north from south. Instead, the atomic project thwarted coastal reconnection.[18]

In November 1994 PG&E successfully extended the license of the Diablo project into the twenty-first century. Unit 1 reactor is expected to shut down in 2021, with Unit 2 following four years later. Obispans began to consider the long-term prospects for the southern Pecho Coast past 2025. Moves by the California Regional Water Quality Control Board to protect Diablo as parkland, rather than losing it to housing estates or industry, reflected a resurgent conservation interest in the region. Ideas of setting aside the Diablo lands for park status dated back to 1959, when the National Park Service earmarked the whole of the Pecho Coast for protection. In the 1960s local conservationists entertained the notion of extending Montana de Oro southward. At a park advisory committee meeting held in 1966, one person "commented that we should never disregard moving into the Rancho Pecho owned by O. C. Field, for future park acquisition when the time is right." The 1988 Montana de Oro General Plan noted similar intentions.[19]

The viability of a state park at Diablo Canyon rests largely on the successful decommissioning of PG&E's nuclear project. In the late 1990s PG&E officials considered how best to store a growing number of spent fuel rods at Diablo, following delays in the opening of a national repository for nuclear waste at Yucca Mountain, Nevada. Wary over the transportation of high-level waste along highways and past urban dwellings, environmentalists motioned for the radioactive artifacts to stay on the headland indefinitely. Ideas of permanent on-site storage nonetheless threatened to jeopardize moves to protect the Pecho coastline. The concept of a nature preserve at Diablo may depend on the removal of all traces of the nuclear artifice. Alternatively, atomic plants might be deemed appropriate features for a twenty-first-century state park. As most parks today offer glimpses into their environmental history, an interpretative program at Diablo might explain how a nuclear sarcophagus had come to rest alongside ancient Indian graves. On a tour of the restored Pecho lighthouse in 1993, John McKinney pondered how tourists of the future might view "a moth-balled nuclear plant turned museum" at Diablo Canyon. The nature lover contemplated: "Will such visitors be amused at this quaint artifact from the late industrial age? Or will they be a little horrified, the way we modern museum-goers regard the Civil War surgeon's medical bag with its knives and saws?" How to commemorate the nuclear age is a question to be answered at every mothballed atomic site across America. The National Park Service, having already dealt with the contested battlefields of Wounded Knee and Gettysburg, may face yet another interpretative challenge if given stewardship of America's postnuclear landscape.[20]

▪ REVISING THE NUCLEAR AGE: ▪
PUTTING THE ATOM BACK INTO NATURE

In June 1995 the *Telegram-Tribune* reported an accident at Montana de Oro involving a mountain biker and a rattlesnake on a backcountry trail. The *Tribune* described how, "after a few warning shakes of its tail, the serpent struck at the mechanical monster that had disturbed it." Unfortunately, the snake got caught in the spokes, and the cyclist killed the rattled reptile. The confrontation had been short and deadly, with the rattlesnake the victim of circumstance. The story seemed unrepresentative of life at Montana de Oro, a park celebrated as a place of peaceful coexistence between humans and nature. Instead, images of devilish rattlers and mechanical monsters edged it closer to the folklore of Diablo Canyon. The "warning shakes" of the rattler harked back to a distant time when Chumash Indians interpreted earthquakes as signs of restless underground serpents, while the cyclist's encounter resembled explorer J. Smeaton Chase's chance meeting with a canyon snake in 1911. Protest images of an industrial monster wreaking havoc on the central coast also seemed apposite. Atomic opponents had expected nature to die at Diablo under the weight of the nuclear juggernaut, like the rattlesnake under the wheels of the bicycle.[21]

Vivid protest visions of Armageddon seemed at best premature, at worst delusional, when nuclear technology in the twentieth century failed to bring about the end of nature. As already stated, environmentalists constructed the atom (and with it, Diablo) as the harbinger of the unnatural, the archenemy of ecology. With the unspectacular demise of the U.S. nuclear industry in the 1980s primarily understood in terms of economic rather than environmental costs, it was the atom itself that decayed, rather than nature.

Such a simple fact may lead us to ignore environmental issues in understanding nuclear history. Was the atomic age really about human-nature relations, or was it simply a matter of economics and cold war rivalry? Did nature factor highly in the military narrative? Certainly many Americans recognized in the atom first and foremost a threat to humanity, above and beyond any ecological fretting. In both corporate and protester visions of Diablo Canyon, the human (rather than the broadly natural) dimension remained significant. PG&E officials highlighted what the nuclear plant could bring to the San Luis region in terms of taxes, jobs, and economic vitality, while the Mothers for Peace prioritized the threat of atomic energy to human life. When compared with how visitors in the distant past conceived the same coastal landscape, modern interpretations are perhaps notable for their passing reference to the natural. Native American stories embodied a reciprocal, sometimes amorphous, dialogue between people and their environs. Chumash belief systems and cultural traditions revolved around ecological interaction. Experiences of collecting shellfish, wandering in the woods, and watching coyotes were passed on in stories, with wild animals and physical landscapes reemerging in the guise of oral testimony. In comparison, modern visitors to the Pecho Coast often seemed ignorant of the landscape beneath their feet. "I am alarmed when it happens that I have walked a mile into the woods bodily, without getting there in spirit. . . . What business have I in the woods, if I am thinking of something out of the woods?" wondered Henry David Thoreau in *Walking* (1862). Protesters and industrialists alike felt little obligation to immerse themselves in the coastal oaks of the Pecho Coast and put to one side their thoughts of outside life. "Diablo Canyon" became the nomenclature of atomic discourse, the living coastal environment subsumed beneath an atomic metanarrative. Stories dealt with the specific wonders or dangers of nuclear energy in terms of social and economic dynamics. Financial sections in San Francisco tabloids interpreted the troubled fortunes of Pacific Gas on the Pecho Coast as symptomatic of the American nuclear industry in its death throes. While Chumash tales embodied a culture of nature, modern stories of Diablo tended to convey only a culture of humanity.[22]

And yet, the nuclear age cannot be understood without some reference to relations between humans and nature. As this and prior chapters show, we all interpret and construct the natural through the framework of human reference—in Diablo's case, the splitting of the atom. We always interpret landscapes through our own cultural filters. Superficially, the pervasiveness of the atomic discourse made it seem as though material nature did indeed succumb at Diablo with the advent of the nuclear construction, just as Martin Litton and like-minded Sierra Club members had feared. The snake had apparently lost out to the bicycle. However, in a broader sense, ideas about ecology and nature influenced much of the imagery surrounding Diablo Canyon in the post-1945 period. While rarely immersing themselves in the natural world to the same degree as their Native American predecessors, modern Californians continued a conversation between people and place that started in Chumash times. Recall how in the 1960s Sierra Club preservationists Frederick Eissler and Litton wrote of the entangled coastal oaks and wild canyons in carefully crafted letters. PG&E officials surveyed the land in terms of what it could offer them, and workers soon grew to admire the road as an ironic wilderness as part of their daily routine. Competing social constructions of nature readily informed on two intriguing perspectives of life. Terra firma drifted in and out of Diablo narratives, scenic shorelines clouded and exposed by social mores. At base, the controversy over Diablo Canyon illuminated a continual exchange of ideas over how to use and treat the land.

As this chapter demonstrates, ecological issues remain important in narratives of sapient progress. Our value systems are informed by verdicts on the natural and the unnatural, the appropriate and the aberrant. The recent history of Diablo Canyon firmly indicates the importance of locating the nuclear age within a broader environmental context, of relating atomic issues to a greater cultural paradigm concerning our rightful place in nature. By conceptualizing the nuclear age as solely about technology run amok or as a scientific manifestation of superpower enmity, we have overlooked underlying human/nature rivalries and the degree to which atomic machinations reflect our relationship with the material world. Put simply, atoms are at the root of it all.

The modern age of ecology began with the bomb at Alamogordo in 1945. This is no coincidence, no chance circumstance. And yet Americans have consistently failed to recognize the extent to which nuclear developments reflect our struggles to locate humanity within (or outside) the natural world. Our preconceived cultural boundaries restrict a nuanced viewpoint on the nuclear age. But much can be read into the genesis of the A-bomb. The bomb embodied an attempt to rival the ultimate natural power source, the blast compared to a "thousand suns," emblematic of our rise toward dominion and unrivaled power. Yet it also represented the perfect expression of humanity's fall from grace, a stark and explosive indicator of our antinature, apocalyptic, and ecocidal tendencies. Commonly viewed as an artificial experiment and essentialized as not "of nature," the making of the bomb in fact centered upon the transmutation of rare and enigmatic raw materials. A decade after Hiroshima, the idea of peaceful atomic energy became so popular because it tapped deep-rooted desires to break free from finite global resources, to transcend nature's ties, to live beyond ecological limits—this facet ideally suited Californian optimism over growth potential. The dream, however, failed to acknowledge that boundaries still existed, that environmental ties remained. For concerned citizens, the atom ushered in the concept of the modern environmental doomsday inaugurated by human folly, pictures of nuclear devastation conjuring subsequent visions of the population bomb and acid rain fallout. For the environmentally inclined, the atom became a potent symbol of pollution, a salient indicator of destitute human/nature relations and questionable land stewardship. Its apparent "unnaturalness" encouraged a reconsideration of the magnetic hold of technology and industry on modern society. Promotional attempts by the nuclear industry to reassert the atom as elemental nature, the building blocks of life, or to picture the sun as one giant nuclear reactor fell short because the atomic age had become, in the public mind, an icon of the separation of humanity from nature. Many citizens envisaged ground zero as a place where humans perfected the technological art of ecological destruction. From the radioactive sands of Alamogordo emerged deep-seated anxieties over the deviation of modern society from the natural order, the harnessing of nuclear energy testifying to humanity's estrangement from the rest of nature. In terms of popular imagery, the rising mushroom cloud narrated the spiraling arrogance of *Homo sapiens* and its quest to dominate biotic systems. The nuclear age came to embody a culture of (anti)nature more than a cult of technology.[23]

Thus it is erroneous to focus entirely on the mushroom cloud and ignore the surrounding sky and desert. They are connected. It is our ingrained cultural values (based around political, scientific, military, and environmental exigencies) that prevent us from realizing an obvious organic connection between the atom and nature—the magnificent, pluming cloud itself is mainly dust and soil. Out at Diablo Canyon we should not view the nuclear plant in isolation from its surroundings. Without the input of resident flora and fauna, Diablo's environmental history would be incomplete, a dislocated tale of one species in artificial isolation rather than a holistic story of the evolution of a greater community. Valuing his communion with nonhuman brethren, John Muir received his "most impressive sermon" from a "cheerful confiding bird" by a stream in Tennessee. Pelicans and peregrines, and rattlers for that matter, have added something to the story of Diablo Canyon, as this final chapter indicates. Ecological realities are important. Despite powerful social constructions of nature, the development of Diablo relates the primacy of the biologic and the organic. Lacking suburban gardens or cityscapes, the Diablo lands today retain a semblance of their primeval wildness, their ranchero past, even after years of nuclear controversy. Nature never really died at Diablo. At the dawning of a new century, wild nature appeared eminently capable of outlasting culture on the Pecho Coast, with native grasses growing over Chumash tombs, ranch-house relics, and, given time, elements of the atomic landscape. Nuclear themes invariably dominate the post-1945 period, but when set against a geological time frame, natural evolution, or nine thousand years of Native American occupancy, the atom can seem but a fleeting phase in the history of the Pecho Coast.[24]

Conclusion

THE ENERGY BOMB AND CONSERVATION FALLOUT

Once described by the Sierra Club as both "a treeless slot" and "the last example of pastoral California coast," Diablo Canyon shows how far conservationists can disagree over environmental issues. Club directors locked horns over coastal wilderness and atomic development. But contrasting takes on the worth of Diablo were hardly confined to the boardrooms of the Sierra Club. The history of Diablo has been shaped by a multitude of agencies and players, all with their own distinct views of nature, energy, and nuclear power.

From the 1960s onward, a series of California-based organizations apprehended the Diablo landscape with a mixture of capitalist, scientific, ecological, and protest-oriented rationales. This resulted in an array of fears and desires being overlaid across the material landscape. In the process, futuristic engineering structures and ancient trees alike were disassembled and reassembled according to collective human imaginings. The Diablo Canyon controversy ably illuminated how the California coastline could serve as a battleground between opposing groups in America. At Diablo itself, two competing visions gained ascendancy. They reflected struggles occurring elsewhere across the state and national landscape. Propagated by corporate and scientific America, the first vision asserted reassuring narratives of progress, development and opportunity. Championed by modern environmentalists, the second vision proclaimed images of decay and decline so abject that only radical solutions could vanquish them. Diablo represented the flashpoint where these two competing visions of America and California collided.

Within each vision, the landscape of Diablo, its nature, proved a malleable resource open to wide interpretation and political meaning. PG&E, like any other developer, interpreted the Pecho Coast as a canvas of convenience, a venue for economic growth and technological prosperity. Put simply, Diablo proffered a gateway to a new scientific era. Nature and land represented simple economic resources, neutral backdrops for progressive engineering projects. The concept of nature as beauty, as an aesthetic resource, was only raised in the arena of public relations, as a tool to gain public acceptance for industrial projects. Mindful of lingering popular wariness over California entering the nuclear age, PG&E, as an atomic booster, shrewdly emphasized the naturalness of its energy projects in the hope of reducing anxieties over new and alien power sources. Forging bucolic images of nature undisturbed by industry—such as the ducks swimming happily in the pond next to the Vallecitos reactor—suggested nothing untoward in nuclear development, the message being that atomic projects posed no fundamental risk to the natural world. Corporations also touted the idea of improving unremarkable landscapes by their benign and sensitive interventions. In the case of PG&E, energy production promised special results—the coastline would be enriched by uranium, and Diablo would fuel state progress.

With the advent of the environmental era, cynicism spread like wildfire over the images of industrial nirvana projected by corporate America. Environmentalists highlighted the dangers posed by large-scale development projects, poking holes in the ecofriendly cellophane wrapped around a multitude of industrial schemes. In California both nuclear power and PG&E came under attack. A cadre of vociferous critics situated Pacific Gas as a polluter that covered its tracks by ecologically framed hyperbole, disingenuously using public relations to fabricate alluring images of ecological management. The Abalone Alliance consistently presented PG&E's environmental claims as hogwash, baloney, and corporate propaganda.[1]

Environmentalist arguments reflected national unease with big business and government power in the aftermath of the Watergate scandal. The corporate view of Diablo was also labeled fake because those who criticized PG&E saw the California landscape very differently. Backcountry protesters linked the landmarks of Diablo with societal ills and political idealism. Abalone activists associated the nuclear plant with the decay of social values, consciously establishing their own alternative community in nearby Los Osos Valley during protests in 1981. For the environmental generation, nature symbolized a perfect state uncluttered by human artifice, a pure realm of nonhuman activity. While reflective of new anxieties concerning environmental doomsday scenarios, such activist ideas mimicked nineteenth-century nature transcendentalists such as Henry David Thoreau and Scottish Californian John Muir in their ardent veneration of nature. In their criticisms of PG&E, environmentalists affirmed an image of industry as anathematic to wilderness survival. The "nature" envisaged by American environmentalists proved very different from the "nature" presented by corporate America.

What drew these disparate visions of nature together was their predilection for drawing on older images of the coastline. Historic attitudes toward the California coast filtered into both corporate and environmentalist viewpoints. However flawed, PG&E's conception of Diablo Canyon as an energy landscape was not with precedent. Generations of indigenous groups in the region had converted animal and fuel resources into valuable energy by their own labor. During the early 1900s the southern California coast earned particular renown for its oil-drilling and export operations. In 1906 Union Oil completed a pipeline at Port San Luis, just south of Diablo Canyon, to carry "black gold" from the Santa Maria basin. As well as invoking the historic energy yield of the California coastline, both PG&E and environmental groups reflected on Diablo's unique reputation as a pariah landscape. While Diablo represented a thriving center in Chumash times—Roberta Greenwood labeled it "the largest, deepest, and oldest community known in this region of Central California"—by the time of Spanish colonization the Pecho Coast resembled an isolated area marked by scant human presence. Diablo remained on the periphery of unbridled ecological, economic, and political changes brought to California by European conquest. Throughout the 1800s bovines proved more numerous on the headland than humans. The Pecho Coast remained largely unsettled, wild, and remote terrain.[2]

For PG&E an anonymous landscape made a good nuclear site. Nuclear plans forwarded by the corporation signified the most concentrated use of the coastline in the region's history. Security fences nonetheless reaffirmed the status of the southern Pecho Coast as an isolated land off-limits to visitors, in stark contrast to the hordes of vacationers gathering at nearby Montana de Oro State Park. At Diablo Canyon, PG&E workers traveled daily to the Pecho Coast but returned home after their shifts. Generations of modern Americans had used, exploited, and valued the California headland, yet the promontory had never been settled in any meaningful way. The lack of sandy beaches at Diablo or of easy routes through the Irish Hills served as geographical impediments to human encroachment. The nuclear project went with tradition, keeping Diablo pariah and secret.

For a minority of Sierra Club conservationists in the 1960s, the reputation of Diablo as a pariah landscape had ensured the protection of its native condition. While Californians had colonized Morro Bay and Pismo Beach, the Pecho Coast remained largely unsettled due to its inaccessibility, rocky demeanor, and sequestered identity. The lack of dwellings on the coastline benefitted the nonhuman residents of the region, biotic communities flourishing without significant human interference. It signified ideal park country. For later environmentalists such as the Abalone Alliance, the exiled landscape took on a specifically nuclear dimension. Diablo became an outpost on the edge of acceptable scientific, social, and political boundaries. Geographical remoteness exaggerated the atomic threat.

Aside from lingering historical and geological influences, both corporate and environmentalist views bespoke the social and political preferences of their chief orators. The dual vision of Diablo that dominated the latter decades of the twentieth century reflected salient debates of the time over the safety of nuclear power, the 1970s energy crisis, and the broader course of state development. This dual vision was very much the product of the competing narratives offered by environmentalists and corporations in postwar America. To a degree, environmentalists proved themselves just as prone to construct "nature" as corporations in order to justify their conservation-minded attitudes toward energy and economic growth. At Diablo Canyon consecutive environmental groups and corporate figures forged their own versions of what the headland amounted to. By chance, history and topography suited their agendas. Both sides framed the landscape according to their personal preferences and political agendas. Diablo was split into two ideological landscapes: one for ecoprotesters, another for energy capitalists. A clash was inevitable.

Everyone sees nature differently. However, at Diablo, social agendas pre-cluded the chance of taking in the real landscape. Both environmentalists and corporate officials proved guilty of ignoring the ecological reality in prefer-ence for keeping their ideologically fueled alternatives alive. For environ-mentalists Diablo represented perfect nature without nuclear power and was rendered dead and lifeless when PG&E set up its reactor site. For PG&E Diablo was dead and lifeless before the utility moved in—and then it exuded perfect nature along with energy production, as local sea otter families testified. The crucial point here is that the material landscape was too often subsumed by greater human imaginings. Using Diablo Canyon as a case in point, this book shows how human attitudes toward the land often operate outside ecologi-cal realities or, at the very least, prove highly selective in determining what environmental information is presented.

Ultimately, did such inaccuracies matter in the fate of Diablo Canyon? Arguably, nature played second fiddle to the atom in most of the key debates that influenced the future of the headland. Radiation was routinely conceptu-alized as first and foremost a human health issue. Opportunities for fair and balanced negotiation based on accurate ecological information were consis-tently missed. At the initial Sierra Club boardroom meeting in 1966 Diablo was labeled a "treeless slot" through ignorance and misinformation. The environmental lobby also proved errant in deeming "nature" a lost cause as soon as PG&E bulldozers went in. Moreover, the hard-line stance of the radi-cal environmental fraternity perhaps failed to reflect on the mixed ecological worth of Diablo itself. Meanwhile, the steadfast line of PG&E that the nuclear plant perfectly fitted in with the natural landscape alienated many Califor-nians, especially when the Hosgri Fault strongly suggested otherwise. Even if some of its land management plans for Diablo in the 1990s seemed genuine, the corporation had by that time little cachet with state environmentalists. The California public increasingly viewed PG&E with suspicion.

Such social constructions matter when they fall outside ecological frames of reference. The discovery of the Hosgri Fault highlighted severe fault lines in the corporate vision of Diablo. At the same time, the safe operation of the Diablo plant from 1985 onward questioned the image of combined nuclear and natural disaster proffered by Abalone activists. Perhaps if both visions had taken a more relativist perspective reflective of biotic conditions, there would have been more room for negotiation, more common ground. As it is, Diablo proved a fundamentally different experience for corporate and environmental America. For environmentalists such as the Abalone Alliance, the natural became solely understood as the nuclear-free; for Pacific Gas and Electric, the Diablo landscape singularly stood as a natural platform for nuclear energy production. Nothing else mattered.

▪ DIABLO AND THE CALIFORNIA ENERGY CRISIS ▪

"Another landmark in the economical generation of electric energy"

—PG&E

As this work has previously argued, both pro and antinuclear forces constructed images of Diablo Canyon that had more to do with hopes and fears about energy use in California than with ecological reality. The lack of material nature in common visions of Diablo reflected the primacy of debates over what form of energy production should occur on the headland. A broader discourse over California's favored energy path took precedence. For PG&E, a nuclearized Diablo embodied an atomic cash cow capable of delivering energy aplenty. The higher the energy consumption, the better the quality of life. When in the 1970s OPEC precipitated a crisis in oil supplies, Diablo seemed poised to deliver cheap and abundant energy to the power-hungry state. PG&E presented atomic power as a clean, renewable, and domestically controlled energy source central to meeting the demands of a growing California. For environmentalists a nuclear plant at Diablo underscored the dangers ahead for California if growth continued unchecked. The nuclear carbuncle taking form on the headland testified to all that was wrong with the Golden State, a region increasingly marked by conspicuous consumption and narcissistic excess. The nonprofit organization California Tomorrow, publisher of *Cry California* magazine, articulated a need for careful state planning, conservation, and energy efficiency in the face of environmental degradation. The clash between the two visions proved fierce and consequential.

Activists from across California congregated at the Diablo site to swear allegiance to the alternative energy path. Headlines ran in both the *San Francisco Chronicle* and the *Los Angeles Times*. Rather than playing itself out in a social and political vacuum, the Diablo controversy impacted on state regulatory practice, environmental mandates, energy regulation, and energy policy. A groundswell of antinuclear feeling fed Proposition 15, the Nuclear Power Plants Initiative of 1976, a state referendum on nuclear power that ultimately failed to win the voters' approval. Reservations nonetheless found outlet in a number of successful state bills in the mid-1970s designed to limit nuclear development. Environmental concern filtered through state government offices, with the California Energy Commission in 1978 vetoing a plan by San Diego Gas & Electric for its proposed Sundesert nuclear facility in Riverside County, the commission pushing instead for conservation and energy diversification on the basis of conservative energy-demand projections. Although most considered the Diablo Canyon controversy over by 1985, its fallout lasted much longer—with the California energy crisis of the twenty-first century arguably one of its by-products.

In summer 2000, enforced power outages hit the Golden State. The lights went out in San Francisco on June 14. The crisis escalated in subsequent months, leaving thousands of Californians facing rolling blackouts during winter 2000–2001. State operating reserves dipped below 5 percent. Governor Gray Davis pulled the plug from the Capitol Christmas Tree soon after he ceremoniously turned on the festive lights to welcome the holiday season. Of the first forty-five days of 2001, thirty-six were listed as "power emergencies." Blackouts threatened Silicon Valley, forcing computer chip manufacturer Intel to scale down operations at its Folsom plant. The glitz even went out of Tinseltown as Jay Leno hosted *The Tonight Show* in murky darkness as impromptu homage to the unfolding crisis. In April 2001 PG&E filed for bankruptcy to the tune of $8.9 billion. As the state felt the squeeze, authorities pleaded with consumers to cut back on their electrical usage while representatives talked with out-of-state suppliers, government agencies, and corporate utilities about how to solve the immediate shortfall. The governors of Oregon, Washington, and California met to address power shortages wracking the West Coast. California no longer symbolized America's bright future—its beleaguered electrical grid and bureaucratic inertia instead suggestive of a third-world country.

The immediate question was what had caused the crisis. The obvious answer came in the form of moves in the late 1990s to restructure statewide energy provision. Following legislation passed in 1996 to deregulate the California electrical industry, officials oversaw the reintroduction of a competitive electricity market in April 1998. By ending the monopoly held by PG&E, San Diego Gas & Electric, and Southern California Edison over state energy supply, officials anticipated a dynamic energy marketplace marked by lower consumer prices and greater corporate efficiency. The enforced sale of generating sources owned by the three major utilities implied an opening up of energy provision and new choices of provider. However, from the summer of 2000 onward, wholesale electric prices increased dramatically as a result of a surge in natural gas prices, a spate of maintenance problems, temperature extremes, storm damage to plants, and out-of-state supply issues. Unable to pass on to their customers the additional costs incurred due to state-enforced price capping (designed to limit profiteering), PG&E and Edison edged toward bankruptcy. San Diego Gas & Electric, having already met deregulation requirements, responded by hiking customer bills threefold. Deregulation was allied with wholesale energy meltdown. Critics argued that the former policy of energy regulation introduced in the early twentieth century had been put there for good reason: to give stability and structure to the state energy system and take advantage of economies of scale.

While deregulatory chaos intersected with political chicanery and scapegoat searching, more-fundamental reasons for blackouts lay in the background. Arguably, the growing divide between supply and demand in energy provision had crippled the state. A lack of new power plants in the 1990s contrasted with rising electricity demand linked to economic and demographic growth. With 40 percent of existing plants over thirty years old, maintenance outages proved critical. Media commentators directed blame toward the individual parties involved in the energy crisis, especially Governor Davis, the Public Utilities Commission, and PG&E. Strict emissions laws and conservation measures came under fire, with the implication being that Californians had been too environmentally friendly. Consumer advocates highlighted the role of independent, out-of-state power producers. Pointing to a very gradual increase in state energy usage (an average 2 percent rise in electricity use per annum in the 1990s), critics argued that the energy crisis was orchestrated by national power producers rather than stemming from any homegrown shortage. By withholding supply and fixing prices, independent producers such as Duke Energy and Enron cashed in on the situation. Enron's chief executive, Ken Lay, responded to attempts by California's state government to intervene: "In the final analysis, it doesn't matter what you crazy people in California do, because I got smart guys who can always figure out how to make money." The media attention given to the crisis further strengthened the hand of the Bush administration, eager to pass a pro-oil, pronuclear energy plan for the nation. As blame for the California energy crisis spread, the specter of Diablo Canyon was raised once more.

The unfolding energy debacle implicated environmentalists and corporations alike for their erroneous attitudes toward state energy regulation. The controversy over Diablo best illuminated the mistaken agendas of both sides. For ardent liberals the energy crisis evinced corporate irresponsibility and poor supply choices. PG&E, Southern California Edison, and San Diego Gas & Electric had caused the crisis by their reckless pursuit of profit, their backroom deals, and their overambitious nuclear schemes. Energy analyst Harvey Wasserman summed up this viewpoint: "The roots of this unnatural disaster lie in the corporate boardrooms of the utility companies now on the brink of bankruptcy." The huge cost of Diablo signified one of the early motivations for state deregulation and consequently helped forge the energy crisis. The nuclear plant represented one of PG&E's most notorious white elephants. At a cost of $5.5 billion, Diablo had become the economic boondoggle that Abalone Alliance members had all along feared. Deemed uncompetitive and uneconomical at 1996 hearings over deregulation, Diablo, together with the San Onofre nuclear plant, represented bad investments that utilities no longer wanted to pay for. As part of the deregulation process, Pacific Gas and Electric along with Southern California Edison received $20 billion in "stranded cost" bailouts for their over-budget nuclear investments—in short, the public compensated corporations for their errors in energy policy by paying surcharges on utility bills. With this payout in mind, California utilities invited deregulation but failed to anticipate losing control of their market to out-of-state suppliers. After championing deregulation, PG&E then became the victim of it as companies such as Enron spiked supply prices when demand rose. In an article entitled "San Francisco: California Energy Crisis Fallout Continues," the left-wing Internet site TomPaine.com highlighted the never-ending spiral of corporate abuse. State approval of hikes in payments to PG&E and SoCal Edison to prevent bankruptcy would not solve anything, the organization argued. PG&E seemed attuned to protecting its own assets, rather than looking out for the people of California. The real victims of the energy crisis were everyday Californians, not California corporations.[3]

Moreover, environmental commentators warned against presenting large utilities with the finance to build new fossil fuel and nuclear plants, especially given the existence of reliable power options such as solar and wind along with prospering publicly owned utilities in Los Angeles and Sacramento. The Diablo plant, they argued, while important to the energy grid, actively contributed to the crisis. When operational, the nuclear installation delivered the most generating capacity of any plant in the state, but the necessity of regular refueling exercises, along with a susceptibility to storm damage to its marine coolant water system, rendered Diablo an unreliable option. Rising sea swells and drifting kelp left Diablo running at 20 percent capacity in January 2001. The net result: a reduced supply at a time of emergency. To environmentalists, such incidents bespoke the dangers of depending on nuclear power as an answer to crisis.

Critics from the right argued that the energy crisis derived from California authorities pandering to environmental radicals. They looked to the Diablo hullabaloo as a supreme example of the way in which environmentalists curtailed California's energy future by a process of dogged determination and media savvy. One conservative forum speaking out on the unfolding energy crisis began simply with the line "Remember the Abalone Alliance." The Ayn Rand Institute, a tireless promoter of free-market capitalism, vociferated that "the origins of today's energy crisis can be traced back to the 1970s . . . when environmental groups committed to stop the construction of Diablo Canyon nuclear plant." From this perspective, environmental campaigning against nuclear sites had, ipso facto, led to the energy crisis. Corporate latitude, technological innovation, and the state's energy grid were scuttled in the process. A radical ecological agenda prevented state officials from backing appropriate energy development schemes. Miro Todorovich, executive director of Scientists and Engineers for Secure Energy in the 1970s, explained: "After the experience with Diablo Canyon no utility in its right mind would build a power plant in California." The experience of Diablo sanctified a mindset of vacillation while encouraging only small-scale, renewable projects incapable of meeting corporate-authored energy forecasts. Put simply, the California energy crisis was rooted in a lack of large-scale, supply-driven projects and a corresponding desertion of confidence in electrical providers. Arguments emphasizing the inadequacy of state electrical supplies in turn showed the merits of massive energy projects such as Diablo Canyon. Stigmatized by environmentalists, PG&E's nuclear plant was in fact a lost harbinger of a better future for California. The energy crisis highlighted how much California had come to depend on the plant for electricity, how important it was in keeping the air-conditioning running and the refrigerators cool. Diablo emerged as a role model for others to emulate, an advertisement for new nuclear plants to be built.[4]

For the dispassionate observer, how could both interpretations be credible? In a sense, the California energy crisis reanimated the dual visions that hung over Diablo in the 1970s and 1980s. Unfortunately, the flaws reappeared with them. The environmentalist vision required fundamental changes in California society in order for it to be tenable. Although partial victories in matters such as renewable energy and air-quality standards showed the potential for change, for the vision to truly prosper necessitated seismic shifts in California away from consumption, away from unchecked development. The vision remained unrealistic without extensive public control over social and industrial forces or, even more desirable, workable environmental stewardship on individual, corporate, and state levels. The corporate vision, meanwhile, ostensibly promoted long-term planning, accountability, and public philanthropy but, at root, championed short-term profits, shareholder returns, and the primacy of business culture. Free-market boosters fell back on antigreen polemics that related little to the realities of the energy crisis—the Ayn Rand Institute, for example, hyperbolized: "The recent blackouts are evidence that their goal is to protect fish, trees, water, and air at the expense of man. . . . The blackouts are an early warning sign of the dangers to human life coming from environmental activism." Neither vision offered a pragmatic, immediate solution for California. Environmentalists and corporate figures alike seemed trapped by their ideological frameworks. Both fitted the history of Diablo into their broader energy treatises. Environmentalists used Diablo as a bludgeon to beat PG&E with. Conservatives, in lionizing the Diablo plant, brushed aside legitimate concerns over the plant's proximity to an earthquake fault line and in light of nuclear dangers underscored by the accident at Three Mile Island. In the case of Diablo, it was painfully unclear what useful lessons could be taken and applied to the energy crisis when presented with two competing and contradictory visions. However, one thing was patently transparent: As one of California's premier energy landscapes, Diablo Canyon could hardly be disconnected from the escalating failures in the state electrical grid.[5]

Perhaps the specific trajectory of Diablo's energy path is of relevance here. To help understand the twenty-first-century energy crisis in California, we need to look to the historic energy path taken by people at Diablo and relate it to the energy path of the Golden State as a whole. As this work shows, Diablo proved itself a capable energy landscape long before the onset of the nuclear age or the advent of twenty-first-century supply problems. Rather than a land set aside for mass settlement, the Pecho Coast provided generations of Americans with malleable forms of energy to exploit. At the beginning of the energy chain, indigenous peoples gathered and expended energy in a direct relationship with the coastal landscape, using hunting, fishing, and burning practices to transform energy resources. During the nineteenth century Euro-Americans utilized the Pecho Coast for raising crops and cattle. Coastal residents focused on exporting energy—as meat and dairy products—to outside markets. Energy production for the first time became an exploitative and commercial venture. New technologies fueled entrepreneurial ambitions. Gas lanterns replaced open fires. Spooner tapped nature's economy for an ambitious hydropower project. Yet natural forces continued to demarcate human activity. Years of drought compromised ranching success, with dried grasses limiting forage and livestock carrying capacity. In the 1960s PG&E's nuclear transformation of the coastline signified a new link in the energy chain. Promoting Diablo's entry into the nuclear era, the corporation proudly emphasized continuity with the past. In one promotional booklet PG&E explained the links between cattle ranching on the headland and its own taming of the atom: "Since men first harnessed the muscles of the oxen to their own use, energy has been the key to man's progress." However, PG&E also hoped to break free from past traditions. Instead of depending on natural resources for energy production (such as animal power, coal, or oil), the corporation offered nuclear energy as an artificially induced panacea to those fearful of running out of energy supplies. Diablo's energy chain was no longer tied to the land or nature, but to the splitting of the atom. On completion, the Diablo nuclear plant fed electricity into the homes of thousands of Californians. Marching pylons linked Diablo with distant places, plugging the Pecho Coast into a statewide energy network. Diablo Canyon became a prime example of the modern energy landscape. From providing the shellfish on Chumash hunts to producing "2000 megawatts of electricity—enough to serve more than 2 million people," the Pecho headland had proved itself able to meet rising human demands. Diablo's nuclear purpose both expanded on and subtly shifted prior energy mandates.[6]

The latest link in the chain of energy produced at Diablo delivered much. The practical contribution to energy production that the Diablo plant made to California's grid proved significant. But the Diablo plant also showed the extent to which Californians had chosen to ignore ecological limits, not just in the building of cities such as Los Angeles in former deserts, or in the irrigated agribusiness of the Central Valley, but also in their favored twentieth- and twenty-first-century energy paths. In the gradual escalation of energy production out on the Central Coast headland, an important bond between humans and the rest of nature was severed. Thick cement walls divided atomic generation from the outside world. Energy no longer came from the natural landscape. Energy no longer came from the land. It seemed possible to make energy out of nothing, for it to come from nowhere. This promise of man-made, infinite supplies of nuclear energy connected in the 1960s with the fervent drive for expansion and growth in the Golden State. Nuclear energy, the nuclear dream, supported a proexpansion mentality. However, many Californians forgot that expansion occurs in a real environment with real consequences. Nuclear energy promised a way out of environmental realities, but it drastically failed to deliver such a future. Thus state growth had nothing to fuel it, but the growth continued all the same.

Blame for the energy malady, of course, is hardly restricted to nuclear power in general or Diablo Canyon in particular. Myriad power-generation schemes failed to keep pace with state growth in the late twentieth century. Without coal reserves of its own, California had long been dependent on out-of-state supplies, from fossil fuel facilities in the Southwest to hydropower from the Pacific Northwest. When these suppliers faced burgeoning in-state demand, maintenance problems, and adverse weather conditions in 2000, the grid lines to California faltered. Arguably, California had been heading toward crisis for some time. Corporations, government, and citizenry, by ignoring real limits in energy capability and seizing upon false schemes that promised quick fixes (nuclear energy being one of them), failed to assuage the situation. Reality indicated that California's energy landscape was marked by limits, flaws, and vulnerabilities. The energy project at Diablo signified a brave attempt to brush aside restrictions, to provide California's energy landscape with an atomic makeover, a nuclear dose of steroids. Ultimately, Diablo did not provide an appropriate solution to California's energy issues. The right answer instead lay in adopting a perspective of environmental realism, of accepting natural boundaries and limits to growth, and operating pragmatically rather than adhering to utopian visions. Right now, Diablo stands as a testament to ignoring ecological realities, to seeking dead-end energy paths. But what will the next link in the energy chain tell us? When the lights from the nuclear enterprise finally go out, Diablo's new energy landscape, like the nuclear one before it, may give some clue as to the state of California's energy landscape as a whole, its health and its direction.

▪ TRACKING CONSERVATION FALLOUT ▪

In 1957, at the peak of atmospheric weapons testing, the United States military carried out a total of thirty nuclear detonations at Nevada Test Site under the code name Plumbbob. The series of tests included the application of several new weapon designs together with the measuring of fallout for its effect on both civilian and military structures. On June 28, 1957, the seventh testing device, designed by the Lawrence Livermore National Laboratory, misfired at Area 2 of Yucca Flat due to a power circuit breakage. The test was rescheduled for July 11, but technical problems and poor weather delayed it for another four days. On July 15, at 4:30 A.M. Pacific Daylight Time, eight hundred military observers (including one hundred Canadians) gathered to watch a nuclear shot called "Diablo" explode from a five-hundred-foot tower 4,400 yards away. Sixteen officers from the Naval Radiological Defense Laboratory huddled inside a purpose-built shelter just 2,000 yards from the explosion as part of an experiment to measure the psychological impact of fallout. The shot lit up the sky over a large segment of the West. Official reports noted that "the blast from this morning's relatively low yield detonation broke at least one window and cracked others in Carson City, Nevada, about 250 air miles from the Nevada Test Site." The *Washington County News* of St. George, Utah, ran the headline "Blinding Flash Follows Detonation of Diablo at Yucca Flat; Fallout Told."[7]

Along with the first atomic test at Alamogordo and the disasters of Hiroshima and Nagasaki, the series of experiments at the Nevada Test Site ushered in the modern environmental era. While the military carried out psychological tests on its personnel, popular fears were raised by mushroom clouds dispersing into the atmosphere. At one Nevada ranch directly in the line of fallout from the Diablo test, rancher Hubert Welch monitored the radiation with his own Geiger counter. He sent the results to the Nevada Test Organization, where an internal communication noted that "Mr. Welch is not in favor of tests—thinks people are being used as guinea pigs—*very outspoken* about it." Nuclear fear traveled with the fallout, insidious, invisible, and inspiring dissidence. The mushroom cloud became the seminal doomsday image of the post-1945 era. Nothing appeared safe. Everything seemed vulnerable. Whereas the American public had initially welcomed the bomb as a wartime peacemaker, many lost faith in the atom due to the scale of secrecy, experimentation, and danger implicit in postwar nuclear development. By continually tinkering with such a weapon, the government-military-scientific triumvirate responsible for the safety of the nation sacrificed a strong dose of public trust.[8]

American conservationists were, like anyone else, far from immune to the bomb's impact. Environmental warnings in the 1960s traded extensively in nuclear iconography. Rachel Carson's landmark critique of pesticides, *Silent Spring*, began with an opening scene clearly inspired by nuclear fallout, of a poisoned and ominously still town where even the birds remained quiet. In *The Population Bomb*, Paul Ehrlich exploited the image of the A-bomb to warn against global overpopulation. Thanks to a series of chilling end-of-nature scenarios, conservationists were forced to broaden their horizons, to look beyond the preservation of wilderness parks and take on wide-ranging threats to the entire ecosphere. Members of the Sierra Club, the Wilderness Society, and the like felt obliged to challenge the direction that society was heading in, transforming themselves into environmental crusaders in the process.

The Diablo Canyon controversy contributed to this conservation fallout in several meaningful ways. Firstly, one Diablo tied in with another. Californians struggled to separate the nuclear plant being constructed on the headland from what they knew of the nuclear age—the bomb, the mushroom cloud, total destruction, militarization, and chaos. The powerful doomsday bomb image was readily applied to peaceful middle-class suburbs. Rather than a controlled explosion in the remote reaches of the Nevada Test Site, far from civilization, PG&E's Diablo posed a tangible threat to mainstream America. Secondly, the growing distrust of governmental, military, and scientific involvement in nuclear projects extended to corporations by their own willingness to join the atomic age. Diablo highlighted the pledge of corporate America to nuclear development. A fallout of distrust grew to encompass such projects and the companies that built them. Thirdly, Diablo sponsored the shift to modern environmentalism. In the case of the Sierra Club, it made conservationists into environmentalists. Diablo alerted social activists, civil rights protesters, suburban homeowners—Californians en masse—to new forms of ecologically driven protest in the 1970s. As the grassroots variegation of the Abalone Alliance demonstrated, activists hailed from all walks of life. Their multifaceted agendas made environmentalism on the coastline vibrant, socially oriented, and explosively original. Diablo helped make modern environmental protest a far cry from traditional conservation lobbying. Events on the Pecho Coast marked essential signposts in the environmental awakening of San Luis Obispo County and beyond. The sociologist Harvey Molotch described "the impact of this [Diablo] event on San Luis Obispo" as "comparable to that of the Santa Barbara Channel oil spill on the city of Santa Barbara." Like the oil spill, Diablo raised new ecological fears, brought media attention to pollution issues, and in impact reached far beyond its geographical constraints.[9]

Like nuclear fallout, America's conservation fallout lingers. Like nuclear fallout, it carries with it serious problems. In the late 1980s and early 1990s, environmentalism appeared a fractured and ideologically divisive movement. Environmental-justice advocates locked horns with Earth First!ers in their differing priorities, with urban-based minority campaigning set against biocentric wilderness protection. Environmental protesters continued to present myriad end-of-the-world scenarios, with the inevitable impact of mass social numbing. Their warnings calls were ignored and sometimes distrusted. The nuclear age, and the Diablo controversy, contributed to such malaise. For all its cultural energy and innovative theater, the anti-Diablo movement failed to inculcate a sustainable vision of protest or progress in California. Activists argued about tactics, and once the reactors went on-line, many gave up or moved to other issues. The Diablo nuclear plant certainly proved an economic boondoggle, but it failed to live up to its devilish portent by the early years of the twenty-first century. Ultimately, doomsday images and ideological divisions are what interest us most in today's California, a state and mentality where Hollywood reigns triumphant. But are images more important than the ecological realities that increasingly contradict them? As the story of Diablo illustrates, perhaps environmentalists need to move beyond the trappings of nuclear doomsdays,   splitting the atom and splitting themselves, and find some common, earthy ground.

notes

INTRODUCTION

1. Bernard Weinraub, "Jeers and Cheers Greet Mondale at Nuclear Site," *New York Times,* 26 May 1984.

2. Michael Cohen, *The History of the Sierra Club, 1892–1970* (San Francisco: Sierra Club Books, 1988), 395; Tom Turner, *Sierra Club: 100 Years of Protecting Nature* (New York: Harry N. Abrams, 1991), 179. The Sierra Club grew rapidly in the 1960s. At the start of the decade, 16,000 Americans belonged to the organization; by 1970 the number had risen to 114,000 (figures from Turner, 278–79). The prolific expansion of the club is discussed in Ulf Hjelmar, *The Political Practice of Environmental Organizations* (Aldershot, UK: Avebury Studies in Green Research, 1996), 88–97. Diablo Canyon was linked with a number of controversies within Sierra circles, including disputes over the role of executive director David Brower. See Cohen, 395–434, Turner, 179–85, and Susan Schrepfer, "The Nuclear Crucible: Diablo Canyon and the Transformation of the Sierra Club, 1965–1985," *California History* 71, no. 2 (Summer 1992): 212–37. Stephen Fox and Thomas Wellock agree. Fox suggests that "Diablo Canyon marked the end of the honeymoon between conservationists and nuclear power"; Stephen Fox, *The American Conservation Movement: John Muir and His Legacy* (Madison: University of Wisconsin Press, 1981), 328. Wellock similarly interprets the Diablo episode as "a valuable example of the forces that turned environmentalists throughout the country from supporters to enemies of nuclear power"; Thomas Raymond Wellock, *Critical Masses: Opposition to Nuclear Power in California, 1958–1978* (Madison: University of Wisconsin Press, 1998), 68–94, quotation 69.

3. Barbara Epstein, *Political Protest and Cultural Revolution: Nonviolent Direct Action in the 1970s and 1980s* (Berkeley: University of California Press, 1991), 92–124.

Epstein focuses on the 1977–81 period of the Alliance's existence, neglecting sizable Abalone protests during the spring of 1984. A number of ex-Abalone members have written about Diablo Canyon. Marcy Darnovsky authored "Direct Action as Living Theater in the Movement against Nuclear Power," unpublished paper, University of California, Santa Cruz, 1989. Mark Evanoff, regularly at the forefront of Alliance activities, wrote "Memorirs [*sic*] of a Movement: PG&E's Nuclear Power Play," unpublished manuscript, 1984. Roger Herried, who kept the Abalone Alliance's San Francisco office open past the mid-1980s, posted a number of useful pieces concerning the history of Diablo Canyon on the Internet in the late 1990s.

4. Harold Miossi, "Somnolent Cape: The Story of the Pecho Coast," *La Vista* (San Luis Obispo County Historical Society), January 1973, 2.

5. The theory of ecological imperialism is expounded in Alfred W. Crosby's *Ecological Imperialism: The Biological Expansion of Europe, 900–1900* (Cambridge, UK: Cambridge University Press, 1986).

6. Steven Marx, "Priesthoods and Power: Some Thoughts on Diablo Canyon," in *Mapping American Culture*, ed. Wayne Franklin and Michael Steiner (Iowa City: University of Iowa Press, 1992), 291–302; John McKinney, *A Walk along Land's End: Discovering California's Unknown Coast* (New York: HarperCollins, 1995), 130–54. PG&E staff kindly made available all environmental records regarding Diablo Canyon, but business documents were outside the scope of this study.

7. Warren Groshong, "There Would Be No Nuclear Plant on the Dunes," *San Luis Obispo County Telegram-Tribune* (hereafter cited as *Telegram-Tribune*), 7 September 1993. Of great use in comprehending Diablo's nuclear makeup have been macro-based studies of nuclear culture, such as Spencer R. Weart's *Nuclear Fear: A History of Images* (Cambridge, MA: Harvard University Press, 1988). Other treatments of atomic culture include: Paul Boyer, *By the Bomb's Early Light: American Thought and Culture at the Dawn of the Atomic Age* (New York: Pantheon, 1985); Paul Boyer, *Fallout: A Historian Reflects on America's Half-Century Encounter with Nuclear Weapons* (Columbus: Ohio State University Press, 1998); and Meredith Veldman, *Fantasy, the Bomb, and the Greening of Britain: Romantic Protest, 1945–1980* (Cambridge, UK: Cambridge University Press, 1994). Works by Richard Meehan and Langdon Winner afford valuable commentary on the philosophy and politics of nuclear technology. See Richard L. Meehan, *The Atom and the Fault: Experts, Earthquakes, and Nuclear Power* (Cambridge, MA: MIT Press, 1984), and Langdon Winner, *The Whale and the Reactor: A Search for Limits in an Age of High Technology* (Chicago: University of Chicago Press, 1986). Meehan and Winner both mention personal experiences of the Diablo plant. Other worthwhile texts on technology include Mary Douglas and Aaron Wildavsky, *Risk and Culture: An Essay on the Selection of Technological and Environmental Dangers* (Berkeley: University of California Press, 1982) and Leo Marx, *The Machine in the Garden: Technology and the Pastoral Ideal in America* (New York: Oxford University Press, 1964).

8. William Riebsame, ed., *Atlas of the New West: Portrait of a Changing Region* (New York: Norton, 1997), 134; Donald Worster, *Nature's Economy: A History of*

Ecological Ideas, 2d ed. (New York: Cambridge University Press, 1994), 342. Valerie L. Kuletz discusses ideas of sacrificial landscapes in *The Tainted Desert: Environmental and Social Ruin in the American West* (New York: Routledge, 1998). For those interested in making connections between atomic development and the American West, a good starting point is Bruce Hevly and John M. Findlay, eds., *The Atomic West* (Seattle: University of Washington Press, 1998).

9. Raymond Williams, *Keywords: A Vocabulary of Culture and Society* (London: Fontana, 1976), 219.

ONE   ■   DIABLO CANYON WILDS

1. "Hike the Pecho Coast Trail" leaflet, 1997, designed by Pandora & Co., Los Osos. The author participated in a guided tour of the Pecho Coast Trail on 28 August 1997.

2. All quotations from "Hike the Pecho Coast Trail."

3. For a fuller exploration of the region's archaeological past, see Roberta S. Greenwood, *9000 Years of Prehistory at Diablo Canyon, San Luis Obispo County, California* (San Luis Obispo County Archaeological Society Occasional Paper 7, 1972). The archaeological significance of the site is also discussed in PG&E's "Draft Environmental Statement" for the Directorate of Licensing, U.S. Atomic Energy Commission (December 1972), section A2, held in the Nuclear Regulatory Commission Public Document Room, California Polytechnic State University, San Luis Obispo (hereafter cited as NRC Public Document Room).

4. The Chumash label is a technical misnomer. Clearly a singular "Chumash nation" never existed along the California coast prior to and during Spanish rule. Most villages acted autonomously, with differences in dialects between regions. Despite the contrived nature of the Chumash name, most academics still regard it as a useful term to describe California's indigenous coast-dwellers, especially given their shared surroundings, culture, and trade practices. The validity of the Chumash label is briefly discussed by Thomas Blackburn in Thomas C. Blackburn, ed., *December's Child: A Book of Chumash Oral Narratives* (Berkeley: University of California Press, 1975), 8, and by Bruce W. Miller in *Chumash: A Picture of Their World* (Los Osos, CA: Sand River Press, 1988), 10, 105. The label is challenged in Brian D. Haley and Larry R. Wilcoxon, "Anthropology and the Making of Chumash Tradition," *Current Anthropology* 38, no. 5 (December 1997): 761–94, Greenwood, *9000 Years of Prehistory,* 94, and Roberta Greenwood, "Surface Survey and Evaluation Report for PG&E" (1978), Appendix A in PG&E, "Archaeological Resources Management Plan" (April 1980), Environmental Folder, NRC Public Document Room.

5. Greenwood, *9000 Years of Prehistory,* 92.

6. In representing Chumash pronunciation, the apostrophe represents a glottal stop, a quick cutting off of a vowel sound in the throat, as with the first syllable of "uh-oh" in English. The "š" sound resembles the "sh" sound of English. See http://www.chumashlanguage.com/pronun/pronun-03-fr.html.

7. María Solares was a Chumash informant for John Peabody Harrington during his ethnological and linguistic study of the Central Coast Indians in the early twentieth century. Her story, "The Three Worlds," can be found in *December's Child,* ed. Blackburn, 91.

8. Greenwood, "Surface Survey and Evaluation Report," A-10. Local Chumash lacked the necessary equipment to hunt marine mammals farther out to sea. Greenwood discovered turtle and whale remains in local middens, but the creatures most likely died while beached on Indian ground. See Greenwood, *9000 Years of Prehistory,* 41, 51.

9. "Animals," in *December's Child,* ed. Blackburn, 102–3; "Coyote and Bat (I)" ibid., 211. The coyote, archetypal "trickster" (and "cultural hero"), holds a special place in the Chumash psyche, perhaps unexpected given the coastal setting and marine activities of most villagers. Chumash stories bear remarkable similarity to canine tales recanted by Sioux and Blackfeet elders. Lavish reference to the coyote, together with creation stories and religious ceremonies familiar to other nations, situates the Chumash within a broader Native American religious tradition, despite their shoreline environment's setting them apart from Plains tribes.

10. "The Making of Man," in *December's Child,* ed. Blackburn, 95; "The Sky People," ibid., 91.

11. "The Soul's Journey to Similaqsa," in *December's Child,* ed. Blackburn, 98–100; Haley and Wilcoxon, "Anthropology and the Making of Chumash Tradition," 769, 774–75. In this controversial article for *Current Anthropology,* Haley and Wilcoxon cast a doubtful shadow over Native American uses of Point Conception in order to question the validity of the term *Chumash* itself. They argue that a homogeneous Chumash nation never existed and that "only since the 1960s has there been a category of people who both identify themselves and are identified by others as Chumash." Haley and Wilcoxon point the finger of blame at their fellow professionals, highlighting how anthropologists assisted the modern (re)birth of the Chumash nation by idealizing the Native and by practically providing New Agers, dejected divorcees, and avid canoeists with the necessary information with which to "become" Native American.

12. See Thomas C. Blackburn and Kat Anderson, eds., *Before the Wilderness: Environmental Management by Native Californians* (Menlo Park, CA: Ballena Press, 1993), and M. Kat Anderson, Michael G. Barbour, and Valerie Whitworth, "A World of Balance and Plenty: Land, Plants, Animals, and Humans in a Pre-European California," in *Contested Eden: California before the Gold Rush,* ed. Ramon A. Gutierrez and Richard J. Orsi (Berkeley: University of California Press, 1998), 38.

13. Anderson, Barbour, and Whitworth, "World of Balance and Plenty," 14; William Preston, "Serpent in the Garden: Environmental Change in Colonial California," in *Contested Eden,* ed. Gutierrez and Orsi, 264–65, 273–74.

14. "The Origin of Death," in *December's Child,* ed. Blackburn, 96. See also Shephard Krech, *The Ecological Indian: Myth and History* (New York: Norton, 1999).

15. For a reprint of the map by Henry Briggs, see Iris H. W. Engstrand, "Seekers of the 'Northern Mystery': European Exploration of California and the Pacific," in *Contested Eden,* ed. Gutierrez and Orsi, 79.

16. "A Summary Account of Juan Rodríguez Cabrillo's Voyage," in *Spanish Exploration in the Southwest, 1542–1706,* ed. Herbert E. Bolton (New York: Charles Scribner's Sons, 1916), 23. In a late-nineteenth-century history of San Luis Obispo, Myron Angel claimed that Cabrillo entered San Luis Obispo Bay, then, after "sailing northward from Point San Luis [the southerly tip of the Pecho Coast], he discovered a deep indentation, which he placed on his chart as 'Los Esteros,' and in the bay [he indicated] a high conical rock 'El Moro.' There Cabrillo supplied his ships with wood and fresh water." In contrast, Hubert Howe Bancroft, in his *History of California* (1884), suggested a less intimate experience with the San Luis shoreline, positing that after passing Point Conception, Cabrillo traveled "along a wild coast without shelter" up to Point Gorda (south of Big Sur). Local historian Dan Krieger sides with Bancroft, stating that "the storm-tossed seas did not permit safe anchorage along San Luis Obispo County's shores, and the explorer saw little that attracted comment." Myron Angel, *History of San Luis Obispo County, California: With Illustrations and Biographical Sketches of Its Prominent Men and Pioneers* (Oakland: Thompson & West, 1883), 14; Hubert Howe Bancroft, *The Works of Hubert Howe Bancroft, Volume 18: The History of California, Volume 1: 1542–1800* (San Francisco: H. H. Bancroft, 1884), 74; Daniel E. Krieger, *San Luis Obispo County: Looking Backward into the Middle Kingdom,* 2d ed. (San Luis Obispo: EZ Nature Books, 1990), 14–15. For a questioning of Unamuno's landing, see Mike Baird, "Did Pedro de Unamuno Really Land in Morro Bay in 1587? Probably Not!" at http://morro-bay.com/docents/mike-baird/nature-notes/unamuno-1587/index.htm; "quantity of fish" quotation from Engstrand, "Seekers of the 'Northern Mystery,'" 90. During an extended navigation of California shores in 1602–1603, Sebastian Vizcaíno may also have traded goods with the same group of Chumash. Vizcaíno enthused about a great harbor farther north at Monterey and recommended establishing a port there. However, his superior, the Count of Montesclaros, proved less than enamored with the progress of exploration. Having lost a number of Manila galleons along the coast, in return for few noteworthy returns, Spanish officials deemed further ventures too risky. European interest in California ebbed.

17. Fray Juan Crespi, *Missionary Explorer on the Pacific Coast 1769–1774,* ed. Herbert E. Bolton (Berkeley: University of California Press, 1927), 182–85.

18. Harold Miossi, "Somnolent Cape: The Story of the Pecho Coast," *La Vista* (San Luis Obispo County Historical Society), January 1973, 7. Buchon Point on the Pecho Coast similarly bears reference to the Chumash chief according to Crespi, *Missionary Explorer,* 184–85. Quotation from David Lavender, *California: Land of New Beginnings* (1972; reissue ed., Lincoln: University of Nebraska Press, 1987), 46. The first California mission was established at San Diego in 1769.

19. Extracts from Fray Francisco Palóu taken from "A Spaniard Explores the Southern California Landscape, 1774," in *Green versus Gold: Sources in California's*

Environmental History, ed. Carolyn Merchant (Washington, DC: Island Press, 1998), 71, reprinted from Fray Francisco Palóu, *Historical Memoirs of New California,* ed. Herbert E. Bolton (Berkeley: University of California Press, 1926), vol. 3.

20. Charles N. Rudkin, ed., *The First French Expedition to California: Laperouse in 1786* (Los Angeles: Dawson's Book Shop, 1959), 56; Lavender, *California,* 71.

21. Miller, *Chumash: A Picture of Their World,* 31.

22. See Preston, "Serpent in the Garden," 270–89.

23. Description provided on display boards in the Montana de Oro State Park Visitors Center, San Luis Obispo County, during summer 1997. The Los Osos Valley, with land adjoining the northern tip of Rancho Pecho, had originally been granted to Californio Victor Linares in December 1842, but Linares succumbed to the temptation of $1,000 worth of goods and currency.

24. Loren Nicholson, in "Captain John Wilson: Trader of the Pacific," *Pacific Historian* 23, no. 2 (Summer 1979): 70, notes Wilson's trip to Calleo at a young age, followed by regular jaunts along the coasts of South America, Mexico, and Alta California. In 1835 Richard Henry Dana came upon Wilson and the *Ayacucho* along the California coast, noting the ability of the Scot to moor his vessel quickly and efficiently. See Richard Henry Dana Jr., *Two Years before the Mast* (1840; reprint, New York: Penguin, 1981), 100, 111. The description of Wilson as "far and away the wealthiest" is in Montana de Oro Advisory Committee, "Prospectus Montana de Oro State Park" (March 1968), 4, Harold Miossi Collection, Cuesta College (San Luis Obispo) Environmental Archives, box 4, file 001. Mrs. Annie L. Morrison also described Wilson as the wealthiest man in San Luis County in 1850. See Annie L. Morrison and John H. Haydon, *History of San Luis Obispo County and Environs, California, with Biographical Sketches of the Leading Men and Women of the County and Environs* (Los Angeles: Historic Record Co., 1917), 37. Morrison provided a history of San Luis, while Haydon detailed events in the Santa Maria Valley. The county board of supervisors traditionally charged between 50 cents and $1.25 on Rancho property, with the 50 cents figure generally levied upon arid eastern lands. The figure of 28 cents is cited in Miossi, "Somnolent Cape," 13. By contrast, Loren Nicholson documented values on Wilson property ranging from 25 cents to $1.00 per acre, presumably the lower amount relating to Diablo lands: Nicholson, "Captain John Wilson," 85.

25. Information on Wilson's cattle brand from Montana de Oro State Park Visitors Center; theory on "Diablo" name noted on Environmental Tour of Diablo Canyon, 19 August 1997. Captain Wilson's business partner, James Scott, continued trading along the California coast. After several run-ins with American authorities, Scott left for Chile.

26. Hazel Adele Pulling, "A Woman Describes the Decline in Range Forage, 1945," in *Green versus Gold,* ed. Merchant, 189, extracted from Pulling, "Range Forage and the California Range Cattle Industry," *Historian* 7 (Spring 1945): 113–29; Brice M. Henry, under instruction from U.S. surveyor general, "Plot of the Rancho 'Canada de Los Osos' & 'Pecho y Islay,'" confirmed to John Wilson, August and

September 1858. A copy of the land survey is currently held at San Luis Obispo Public Library. In 1846 Edwin Bryant, staying at a ranch close to Mount Diablo, east of San Francisco, remarked: "The horned cattle of California, which I have thus far seen, are the largest and handsomest in shape which I ever saw. There is certainly no breed in the United States equaling them in size. They, as well as the horses, subsist entirely upon the indigenous grasses, at all seasons of the year; and such are the nutritious qualities of the herbage, that the former are always in condition for slaughtering, and the latter have as much flesh upon them as is desirable." Edwin Bryant, *What I Saw in California* (1848; reprint, Lincoln: University of Nebraska Press, 1985), 305.

27. George Vancouver, *A Voyage of Discovery to the North Pacific Ocean and Round the World, 1791–1795,* ed. W. Kaye Lamb (London: Hakluyt Society, 1984), vol. 3, 1088–89. Vancouver also related rumors of an island lying eight leagues off the headland, although coastal fog limited his view to "two to four leagues in any direction." A clear day would have revealed no island off the Pecho Coast. Mount El Buchon (today's Saddle Peak, 1,819 ft.), rising up behind Diablo Canyon, often provided seafarers with a familiar beacon, drawing them to nearby San Luis Obispo Bay. The French traveler Duflot de Mofras, on a visit to San Luis Obispo in 1841, noted that "by sea approach, the leading landmark is the mountain of El Buchon. . . . The mountain is cone-shaped and stands sharply from the chain that parallels the coast." Duflot de Mofras, "How to Get to San Luis Obispo," *La Vista,* January 1972, 4.

28. John Woolfenden, *The California Sea Otter: Saved or Doomed?* rev. ed. (Pacific Grove, CA: Boxwood Press, 1985), 89.

29. See "Harpoons and Pens: Melville and Scammon," in Wayne Hanley, *Natural History in America: From Mark Catesby to Rachel Carson* (New York: Quadrangle and New York Times Book Co., 1977), 169.

30. Morrison and Haydon, *History of San Luis Obispo County,* 72. Bodilla, having sold the Pecho grant to Wilson in the 1840s, regularly returned to his old land to deal in stolen cattle. Vigilantes caught and hanged him in 1859. Captain Wilson died in October 1861. According to Harold Miossi, Wilson's daughter probably held "permanent residency" at the Palace Hotel, San Francisco, during the period. She presumably took little interest in her land inheritance. The young John Wilson lived in Europe. Miossi, "Somnolent Cape," 14.

31. The young Italian spent three years at mining camps in Pinetta, Amador County, then turned to storekeeping in Calaveras. With the introduction of Mexican land grants, the farthest southerly tip of the Pecho Coast meanwhile fell under the San Miguelito Rancho, which comprised 6,500 acres of land on the northern edge of San Luis Obispo Bay. Marre wisely purchased the grant in 1882. He bought up the Pecho lease ten years later. Morrison and Haydon, *History of San Luis Obispo County,* 213. The Montana de Oro State Park Prospectus (March 1968), 4, notes a period of "absentee and neglectful management" following the death of John Wilson.

32. In 1902 Spooner bought the lease. The local newspaper reported that a steamer "discharged a consignment of lumber," then "took on board 2500 sacks of beans and

grain by means of a shoot. . . . The Captain and pursuer [*sic*] said they were delighted with the harbor and thought it the prettiest natural one they had ever seen." "Pecho Landing," dated 9 October 1892, found in Wilmar N. Tagnazzini, ed., "*100 Years Ago*": *Excerpts from the "San Luis Obispo Morning Tribune" [1892]*, 120, in San Luis Obispo Public Library.

33. The lighthouse was a prefabricated redwood building transported from Oakland to Point San Luis. It began operation in June 1890. Unfortunately, passing vessels still managed to miss port. In July 1890 the local paper related the "great sadness in scores of drouthy admirers of Weiland's beer . . . for by some blunder the shipment which should have been landed at Port Harford, was carried past, and left this city without its favorite beverage." "Point San Luis," *Morning Tribune*, week beg. 15 July 1890, in Tagnazzini, ed., "*100 Years Ago*": *[1890]*, 146; "A Delegate Speaks," *Morning Tribune*, week beg. 9 February 1892, Tagnazzini, "*100 Years Ago*": *[1892]*, 24. A narrow-gauge railway along the coast connected Port Harford with the local region, but Marre backed a county-funded rail link with the main Southern Pacific line.

34. J. Smeaton Chase, *California Coast Trails: A Horseback Ride from Mexico to Oregon* (Cambridge, MA: Riverside Press, 1913), 2, 140, 142–43, 147, 148, 150–51, 113, 151. Chase felt none of the remorse of his contemporary John Muir, who, on killing a rattler, decried "the killing business" as a "degrading" endeavor that pushed him "farther from heaven." See John Muir, *Our National Parks* (1901; reprint, Madison: University of Wisconsin Press, 1981), 57–58. Chase quoted Muir's testament in *California Coast Trails*, 113.

35. Miossi, "Somnolent Cape," 24.

36. Morrison and Haydon, *History of San Luis Obispo County*, 288–89.

37. Miossi, "Somnolent Cape," 26.

38. Elliot Curry, "Cavalry in the San Luis Range," *Telegram-Tribune*, 7 December 1968, reprinted in *La Vista* 4, no. 2 (1981): 71.

39. Elliot Curry, "How News of Peace Came to SLO Town," *Telegram-Tribune*, 19 July 1978, reprinted ibid. For wider analysis regarding the impact of World War II on the American West, see Gerald Nash, *The American West Transformed: Impact of the Second World War* (Bloomington: Indiana University Press, 1985), and Richard White, "*It's Your Misfortune and None of My Own*": *A New History of the American West* (Norman: University of Oklahoma Press, 1991), 496–533.

TWO   ■   FROM CATTLE RANCH TO ATOMIC HOMESTEAD

1. *Buttonwillow (CA) Times*, 6 October 1966, in the Sierra Club Collection (hereafter cited as SCC), 71/295c, box 18, file 29, Bancroft Library, University of California, Berkeley; "The PG&E Story," on PG&E's Web site, http://www.pge.com (the account is based largely upon Charles Coleman, *P.G.&E. of California: The Centennial Story of Pacific Gas and Electric Company, 1852–1952* [New York: McGraw-Hill, 1952]); "Special Report on Diablo Canyon," *PG&E Life*, June 1967, 2, copy in SCC 71/103c, box 113, file 40.

2. PG&E's description of Vallecitos as a "pioneer plant" is from "Special Report on Diablo Canyon," 12.

3. Taken from Thomas Raymond Wellock, *Critical Masses: Opposition to Nuclear Power in California, 1958–1978* (Madison: University of Wisconsin Press, 1998), 73.

4. "Special Report on Diablo Canyon," 13.

5. *Sierra Club Bulletin,* February 1969, 7, SCC, 71/103c, box 117, file 33; PG&E, "Background Information for the Press" (February 1967), 1, SCC, 71/295c, box 81, file 19; "Special Report on Diablo Canyon," 10; Anon., "Information Sheet on Nuclear Reactors" (March 1963), 1, SCC, 71/103c, box 78, file 13.

6. "Background Information for the Press," 3; Comments by the *San Luis Obispo County Telegram-Tribune* (hereafter cited as *Telegram-Tribune*), 27 January 1963, highlighted in "Information Sheet on Nuclear Reactors," 1.

7. The *Paso Robles Press,* 11 February 1965, predicted a conservation fight ahead. In a letter to David Brower (March 6, 1963), Sierra Club member Frederick Eissler suggested that "there is every reason to believe that the Nipomo Dunes situation is another Bodega Head," SCC, 71/103c, box 78, file 13. Interview with Kathy Goddard-Jones (formerly Jackson), Nipomo, 20 August 1997.

8. PG&E, "Summary Comparison of Sites for Nuclear Power Plant," 11 February 1967, SCC, 71/295c, box 189, file 30; Board of Directors: Minutes of the Annual Organization (7–8 May 1966), 9, SCC, 71/103c, box 4, file 5.

9. Heinz Haber, *The Walt Disney Story of Our Friend the Atom* (New York: Golden Press, 1956), 134, 136, 137–59; "Background Information for the Press," 10; "Special Report on Diablo Canyon," 6, 22; "Groundwork for an Atomic Plant," *PG&E Progress,* January 1967, 4, SCC, 71/295c, box 18, file 29.

10. Board of Directors: Minutes of the Annual Organization (7–8 May 1966), 8; Elizabeth B. Barrett to Dick Sill, 7 June 1967, SCC, 71/289c, box 40, file 15. In response to George Marshall's contention that two directors knew the region, Hugh Nash stated that "*no* Director present at the May 1966 meeting professed *any* familiarity with the Diablo area" (Marshall offered such comments in his rewrite of the *Sierra Club Bulletin,* February 1967, editorial). Hugh Nash to David Brower, 11 March 1967, SCC, 71/289c, box 40, file 15. The lack of firsthand knowledge of Diablo occasionally angered the club's rank and file. Realizing the shortage of club reports on Diablo, one member accused Kathy Jackson and Will Siri of "bulling through a vote before they or the Club has done a comprehensive study on the area." See Mrs. L. E. Fowler, of Santa Barbara, to David Brower, 9 February 1967, SCC, 71/295c, box 18, file 26. Another suggested that the Canyon should not be sacrificed, as members did not know what was at stake: Mrs. Frederick Golding, of Colorado, to Sierra Board, 22 March 1967, SCC, 71/103c, box 113, file 38.

11. A copy of the original letter can be found in a communication between George Marshall and Martin Litton, 25 June 1966, SCC, 71/103c, box 110, file 1. Marshall called the letter "outrageous" and a work that "undermines the Sierra Club." Litton defended his actions in a letter to the board of directors, 9 September 1966, SCC, 71/103c, box 110, file 1. Martin Litton to Shermer Sibley, 13 June 1966, SCC, 71/103c,

box 110, file 1; Litton quoted in *Herald Recorder* (Arroyo Grande), 8 February 1968, SCC, 71/103c, box 117, file 33.

12. "The Diablo Canyon Area: California's Last Unspoiled Pastoral Coastland," signed by David Brower, Polly Dyer, Jules Eichorn, Fred Eissler, Martin Litton, Daniel Luten, David Pesonen, Eliot Porter, and Georg Treichel, *Sierra Club Bulletin,* February 1967, 7, author's personal copy; James W. Clark, of Porterville, to Sierra Club, 15 February 1967, SCC, 71/295c, box 18, file 26; Richard Leonard to Shermer Sibley, president of PG&E, 4 July 1966, SCC, 71/295c, box 81, file 18.

13. William Siri and Ansel Adams, "In Defense of a Victory: The Nipomo Dunes," *Sierra Club Bulletin,* February 1967, 4.

14. Frederick Eissler to George Marshall, David Brower, and Michael McCloskey, 20 June 1966, SCC, 71/103c, box 110, file 1; Martin Litton to Hugh Nash, 25 July 1966, SCC, 71/103c, box 110, file 1; Martin Litton to Stewart Udall, 13 November 1967, SCC, 71/295c, box 87, file 28; Thomas Jukes (untitled, n.d.) in Ansel Adams collection of club items, SCC, 71/295c, box 1, file 13; *Grover City (CA) Press,* 8 February 1968, SCC., 71/103c, box 117, file 33. For the concept of scenic monumentalism, see Alfred Runte, *National Parks: The American Experience* (Lincoln: University of Nebraska Press, 1979). Runte described the "sheer cliffs and waterfalls of Yosemite Valley" as the epitome of "monumentalism," plate following page 16.

15. Harry Purlam, Modesto, to Sierra Club, 10 April 1967, SCC, 71/103c, box 113, file 39; *Pasadena Star-News,* 6 May 1968, SCC, 71/103c, box 117, file 33; "Testimony of Frederick Eissler before the California Public Utility Commission in the Diablo Canyon Case" (May 1967), 8–9, SCC, 71/103c, box 113, file 39. Litton was more reserved over presenting Diablo as pristine wilderness, preferring "wildness" as a description.

16. Doris Leonard to George Marshall, 19 August 1966, SCC, 71/295c, box 81, file 18; Kathy Jackson, "Correction: John Muir Would Vote No," February 1969, SCC, 71/103c, box 123, file 11.

17. Draft [resolution] for Sierra Club, 7 January 1967, SCC, 71/295c, box 18, file 25. "Roadlessness" also jeopardized the fate of Diablo. Litton noted the sad irony in road access promoting public awareness. Without highways passing close to Diablo, nobody managed to see (or care) for the Pecho Coast. Interview with Martin Litton, Portola Valley, 25 July, 1997; "Diablo Canyon Area," signed by Brower et al. The *San Francisco Chronicle,* 12 February 1967, similarly described the Pecho headland as "the last long stretch of the Californian coast—south of Mendocino County— unmarred by highways, railroads, or any other form of development," SCC, 71/289c, box 40, file 16.

18. Vladimir and Nada Kovalik, "Life and Death along the California Coast," *Cry California: The Journal of California Tomorrow* 2, no. 4 (Fall 1967): 16–17; Litton to the Board of Directors, 9 September 1966.

19. Rising Sierra Club concern over coastal damage had translated into a statement against power plants on scenic ocean shorelines in September 1963, as well as an

increasing interest in other plans for coastal development. The National Park Service completed a coastline survey in 1959 identifying the more precious natural areas. There were hopes for a statewide shoreline master plan. The idea of "rationalizing" coastal development before it was too late became a common concern of the period. Proponents argued for planned coexistence between natural, open spaces and less natural, confined areas of development. In the 1960s the fate of Diablo Canyon illustrated exactly what was happening without such a plan. "Diablo Canyon Area," signed by Brower et al.; Board of Directors: Minutes of the Regular Meeting (18 February 1967), 9, SCC, 71/103c, box 4, file 6.

20. Jim Hayes, "Our Nuclear Neighbor—IX: The Fight Goes On against Reactors," *Telegram-Tribune,* 12 September 1973. Oak Ridge atomic enthusiasts indeed planned a "nuclear-powered agro-industrial complex," but for export to the Middle East rather than the American West. Spencer R. Weart, *Nuclear Fear: A History of Images* (Cambridge, MA: Harvard University Press, 1988), 303. Lewis L. Strauss, at his swearing-in ceremony to be chair of the AEC in July 1953, quoted from the Bible (Micah 4:3) regarding swords into plowshares.

21. "Sierra Club Policy on the Proposed Construction of Industrial Facilities in the Santa Maria River Dunes," 24 June 1965, SCC, 71/295c, box 88, file 19; Board of Directors: Minutes of the Annual Organization (7–8 May 1966), 8. *Bonanza,* the Mother Lode Chapter newsletter, March 1967, noted the impression given by Leonard that the Diablo region was "subject to residential encroachment," with no plans for park acquisition, SCC, 71/103c, box 113, file 39. The same chapter claimed: "We have been informed that even if a power plant is not located in Diablo Canyon, the owner of the land plans to develop the area as an exclusive real estate development." See Mother Lode decision to accept Diablo as a suitable reactor site, "Re: Diablo Canyon Nuclear Power Plant Site," 7 July 1966, SCC, 71/295c, box 81, file 18; Mrs. Harold C. Bradley, of Berkeley, to the editor, *San Francisco Chronicle,* 8 January 1969, SCC, 71/103c, box 123, file 11.

22. Eissler to Marshall, Brower, and McCloskey, 20 June 1966; Board of Directors: Minutes of the Annual Organization (7–8 May 1966), 8; National Park Service Pacific Coast Recreation Area Survey (1959), 175, SCC, 71/103c, box 110, file 1.

23. Eissler to Marshall, Brower, and McCloskey, 20 June 1966; "Testimony of Frederick Eissler," 14; Resources Agency of California—Division of Beaches and Parks, "Montana de Oro State Park—General Development Study," 1965, Ian McMillan Collection, Cuesta College (San Luis Obispo) Environmental Archives, II/05, box 15, file 24. Ansel Adams and William Siri offered such an argument in the *Sierra Club Bulletin,* February 1967), 5.

24. Richard M. Leonard, "Richard M. Leonard: Mountaineer, Lawyer, Environmentalist: Oral History Transcript," vol. 2, 404, SCC, 76/194c; Clare Hardham, "Botanical Report on the Flora of Diablo Canyon" (n.d.), 7, SCC, 71/295c, box 190, file 5; Carl W. Sharsmith, "Diablo Canyon: A Botanist's Impressions" (14 February 1967), 1, 2, SCC, 71/103c, box 113, file 38.

25. *Telegram-Tribune*, 1 April 1967; Clare Hardham to Ken Dierks, PG&E, 24 April 1968, SCC, 71/295c, box 189, file 11.

26. Board of Directors: Minutes of the Regular Meeting (18 February 1967), 9, 10.

27. Kathleen Jackson to Martin Litton, 15 June 1966, SCC, 71/103c. box 110, file 1; Kathleen Jackson to William Siri, 14 June 1966, SCC, 71/103c, box 113, file 38; Mother Lode Chapter, "RE: Diablo Canyon Nuclear Power Plant Site," 7 July 1966. Jackson later regretted the final placement of the plant on the coastal bluffs, obvious not only to illegal hikers but to passing ships as well. Interview 20 August 1997.

28. Litton to the Board of Directors, 9 September 1966. For an example of use of Litton's photographs as discussed here, see his construction-site image, and its pertinent placing alongside a picture of Morro Bay power plant, in *This Is the Issue*, a pamphlet sent out by the "Committee to Clarify the Diablo Issues," New York, SCC, 71/103c, box 64, file 13.

29. *Sacramento Bee*, 30 June 1969, SCC, 71/103c, box 123, file 11. The conservation chairman of the Great Lakes Chapter criticized Eissler's "highly emotional involvement with nuclear energy," in a letter to Eissler, 31 January 1967, SCC, 71/295c, box 18, file 25. Betty Hughes also mentioned to Martin Litton that two chairmen she knew considered Eissler a fanatic; Hughes to Litton, 24 February 1967, SCC, 71/295c, box 18, file 26; Litton to Mr. Gros, PG&E, 10 March 1966, SCC, 71/295c, box 88, file 19 ("bogey" quotation). Anxieties over thermal pollution were also raised in the late 1960s yet failed to dampen spirits concerning nuclear development. Similar to other nuclear issues (for example, low-level radiation), thermal pollution had to be decisively proved before momentum toward atomic power could be questioned.

30. Donald W. Aitken, Dept. of Physics, Stanford University, to Hugh Nash, 9 March 1967, SCC, 71/295c, box 18, file 27; Dale R. Jones, of Mills Tower, to Edgar Wayburn (telegram), 18 October 1968, SCC, 71/295c, box 228, file 43.

31. George Marshall to Hugh Nash, "RE: Revisions of February, 1967 Bulletin," 1 March 1967, SCC, 71/295c, box 18, file 27.

32. Nathan Clark to Directors, 29 August 1968, SCC, 71/295c, box 5, file 17; *Condor Call*, Los Padres Chapter newsletter, September 1968, SCC, 71/295c, box 81, file 23; Edgar Wayburn to the Directors of the Sierra Club, 9 July 1968, SCC, 71/295c, box 5, file 17.

33. *Sierra Club Bulletin*, February 1969, 4-7, SCC, 71/103c, box 117, file 33; *Toiyabe Tattler*, Toiyabe Chapter newsletter, March 1967, SCC, 71/295c, box 18, file 27.

34. For details of the club's campaign to save Echo Park, see Mark W. T. Harvey, *A Symbol of Wilderness: Echo Park and the American Conservation Movement* (Albuquerque: University of New Mexico Press, 1994). For commentary on the shift from conservation to environmentalism in the post-1945 period, see Stephen Fox, *The American Conservation Movement: John Muir and His Legacy* (Madison: University of Wisconsin Press, 1981), 291-329; Samuel P. Hays, *Beauty, Health, and Permanence: Environmental Politics in the United States, 1955-1985* (New York: Cambridge University Press, 1987); and Hal K. Rothman, *The Greening of a Nation?*

Environmentalism in the United States since 1945 (Fort Worth: Harcourt Brace, 1998); "To All Grand Canyon Chapter Members," unofficial mailing (n.d.), SCC, 71/295c, box 218, file 70.

35. Philip Hyde, of Taylorsville, to Tom Hoffer, chairman, Toiyabe Chapter, 6 December 1968, SCC, 71/295c, box 228, file 43 (Hyde quoted Brower's exchange with Morris Udall over the Grand Canyon and applied the same principles to the Diablo Canyon issue); *Paso Robles Press,* 18 September 1968, SCC, 71/103c, box 117, file 33; D. H. Kieselhorst, of San Francisco, to Richard Leonard, 30 December 1968, SCC, 71/295c, box 81, file 22.

36. Betty Hughes to William Siri, 20 February 1967, SCC, 71/295c, box 18, file 26; Kieselhorst to Leonard, 30 December 1968; Eliot Porter to William Simmons, Secretary, San Francisco Bay Chapter, 22 July 1968, SCC, 71/295c, box 81, file 21.

37. Fred Eissler to George Marshall, 26 June 1966, SCC, 71/103c, box 110, file 1; North Group Redwood Chapter newsletter, 27 October 1968, SCC, 71/295c, box 87, file 29. Others were less concerned over the atomic threat. Hugh Nash, a clear proponent of saving Diablo, wondered "what difference does it make from the club's viewpoint whether a scenic resource is sacrificed for hydro or nuclear power"; after all, "what difference does it make that Diablo Canyon and its oaks are to be buried under 400 feet of earthfill instead of water?" Hugh Nash to David Brower, 11 March 1967, SCC, 71/289c, box 40, file 15.

38. David Brower to Miss Iva May Warner, of Boonville, 22 October 1968, SCC, 71/103c, box 117, file 33; Scenic Shoreline Preservation Conference, Inc., newsletter, March 1969, SCC, 71/295c, box 90, file 19; Sue Schmitt, of South Penda Island, British Columbia, to George Marshall and David Brower, 2 April 1967, SCC, 71/103c, box 113, file 39; David Brower to the Board, "New Diablo Material," 10 September 1968, SCC, 71/295c, box 81, file 21. For details of the Santa Barbara oil spill, see Robert Easton, *Black Tide: The Santa Barbara Oil Spill and Its Consequences* (New York: Delacorte Press, 1972).

39. Stewart Ogilvy to Martin Litton, 18 January 1968, SCC, 71/295c, box 87, file 29. Philip Hyde, Taylorsville, wrote to George Marshall on 17 March 1967 complaining over the failures of compromise as a conservation tactic. Hyde interpreted Diablo Canyon as symbol with which to fight industrial development. SCC, 71/103c, box 113, file 39. Hasse Bunnelle, in a letter to James McCracken dated 10 October 1968, saw Diablo as a symptom "of the weakness in our method of using conservation as an educational and political tool. We have ignored it for far too long, enjoyed and explored, but forgot to work at the preservation of resources that are dying before our eyes." SCC, 71/295c, box 87, file 29. The Diablo issue invigorated some members to push ahead with conservation, rather than "retreat" into compromise.

40. Martin Litton to David Saxe, Woodland Hills, 26 August 1968, SCC, 71/295c, box 81, file 21; Hugh Nash to David Brower, 4 September 1968, 5, SCC, 71/289c, box 40, file 15.

41. "Viewpoint: What's Eating the Sierra Club?" 26 February 1969, in David Brower's Scrapbook (10 February to–30 June 1969), SCC, 79/9c, box 3; Richard

Leonard, "Mountaineer, Lawyer, Environmentalist," vol. 2, 337; *Sierra Club Bulletin,* February 1969, 6–7; Kathy Jackson, "Correction: John Muir Would Vote No," February 1969, scc, 71/103c, box 123, file 11; "John Muir" to Kathleen Jackson (n.d.), scc, 71/295c, box 18, file 28. If Brower was like Muir, then Diablo signified his Hetch Hetchy. Both campaigns became personal crusades, alienating Muir and Brower from key Sierra Club members and the public. Despite their efforts, Hetch Hetchy was dammed and Diablo used for a nuclear plant site. Although Diablo probably was not as dear to Brower as Hetch Hetchy was to Muir, both Sierrans committed themselves almost sacrificially. Hetch Hetchy split the club between purists and those who felt more comfortable with business and compromise, as did Diablo. Those accepting Hetch Hetchy's demise argued that San Francisco needed the power supplied by the dam, just as pro-dealers at Diablo believed PG&E's projected electricity demands. While Muir was heartbroken by the loss of Hetch Hetchy and died a year later, Brower was turned away from a club he had spent his life building. For discussions of the Hetch Hetchy episode in club history, see Cohen, *History of the Sierra Club,* 22–33; Fox, *American Conservation Movement,* 139–47, and Thomas Turner, *Sierra Club: 100 Years of Protecting Nature* (New York: Harry N. Abrams, 1991), 66–78.

42. David Brower, "Need History Repeat Itself So Soon?" (n.d.), scc, 71/103c, box 113, file 38.

43. Dick Sill to Fred Eissler and Martin Litton, 7 February 1967, scc, 71/289c, box 40, file 15; Harold Bradley Statement (prepared for 18 February 1967 board meeting), scc, 71/295c, box 5, file 17; "A Sierra Club Member" to the Executive Director and Board of Directors, 3 October 1968, scc, 71/295c, box 1, file 13; *Condor Call,* Los Padres Chapter newsletter, March 1967, scc, 71/103c, box 113, file 39.

44. Ansel Adams to Edgar Wayburn, 18 June 1968, scc, 71/295c, box 171, file 1; *Santa Maria Times,* 25 September 1968, scc, 71/295c, box 1, file 13; *San Francisco Examiner,* 20 December 1968, scc, 71/103c, box 117, file 33.

45. Mother Lode Chapter, "RE: Diablo Canyon Nuclear Power Plant Site," 7 July 1966; *San Francisco Examiner,* 1 July 1966, scc, 71/103c, box 110, file 1; J. G. Gerstley, Sherman Oaks, to Edgar Wayburn, 3 September 1968, scc, 71/295c, box 1, file 13; William Siri to Fred Eissler, 24 January 1965, scc, 71/295c, box 189, file 23.

46. *Sacramento Bee,* 16 September 1968, scc, 71/103c, box 117, file 33; Ansel Adams to Miss Bottemanne, editor, *Toiyabe Tattler* (draft), 13 January 1969, scc, 71/295c, box 1, file 13.

47. William E. Siri, "Reflections on the Sierra Club, the Environment and Mountaineering 1950s–1970s: Oral History Transcript," 118, scc, 80/4c.

48. John L. Harper, of Bakersfield, to William Siri, 25 February 1967, scc, 71/295c, box 189, file 8.

49. David R Brower, "Environmental Activist, Publicist, and Prophet: Oral History Transcript," 141, scc, 80/133c; Dave Van de Mark, of Eureka, to David Brower, n.d. 1967, scc, 71/103c, box 113, file 38; Robert R. Marshall to Editor, *Southern Sierran,* March 1967, scc, 71/295c, box 81, file 20; Elizabeth B. Barrett, Executive Committee member and secretary, Grand Canyon Chapter, to George Marshall, 19

May 1967, scc, 71/289c, box 40, file 15. Martin Litton, in a letter to Congressman Paul McCloskey, also considered the implications of Diablo's loss in the light of the Glen Canyon episode: "At least we can make Californians sorry for what they will have then permitted to happen. As in the case of Glen Canyon, it will be something like a murderer mourning his crime, but it may contain a lesson that will be needed in the future and might help to save what little remains of our shoreline's beauty"; Martin Litton to Paul McCloskey, 17 January 1968, scc, 71/295c, box 87, file 29. Brower's regret over Glen Canyon stayed with him for years. In 1997 Brower offered the idea of re-naturing the region in his article entitled "Let the River Run Through It," *Sierra*, March–April 1997, 42. For further insights into the role of David Brower in the Sierra Club, see Susan Schrepfer, *The Fight to Save the Redwoods: A History of Environmental Reform, 1917–1978* (Madison: University of Wisconsin Press, 1983), 163–85, and Peter Wild, *Pioneer Conservationists of Western America* (Missoula, MT: Mountain Press, 1979), 151–59.

50. Robert P. Hoover, of San Luis Obispo, to George Marshall, 13 March 1967, scc, 71/295c, box 18, file 27; George Marshall to Robert P. Hoover, 18 March 1967, scc, 71/295c, box 18, file 27; Delee S. Marshall, Secretary, Los Padres Chapter to George Marshall, 16 June 1966, scc, 71/103c, box 64, file 13; George Marshall to Delee S. Marshall, 24 June 1966, scc, 71/289c, box 40, file 15. See Norman F. Rohn to George Marshall, 14 July 1966, scc, 71/289c, box 40, file 15 for an insight into the Los Padres Chapter's change of mind. Los Padres was the only chapter in the vicinity of Diablo Canyon in 1966. Another chapter, Santa Lucia, was established along the coast of middle California in October 1968.

51. John Muir Chapter, "Special Bulletin," 9 March 1967, from J. J. Werner, Secretary, scc, 71/289c, box 40, file 15.

52. *Yodeller,* San Francisco Bay Chapter newsletter, October 1968, scc, 71/295c, box 190, file 4; James McCracken to Martin Litton, 12 October 1968, scc, 71/295c, box 87, file 29; River Touring Section, Loma Prieta Chapter to Board of Directors, 13 November 1968 (a petition signed by thirty-seven members), scc, 71/295c, box 87, file 29.

53. Ruth Weiner, Rocky Mountain Chapter, to Editor, *Sierra Club Bulletin,* 22 February 1967, scc, 71/103c, box 113, file 38; Robert Katz, of San Francisco, to Edgar Wayburn, 16 October 1968, scc, 71/295c, box 1, file 13; *San Francisco Examiner,* 20 December 1968, scc, 71/103c, box 117, file 33; James Hupp, of Orinda, to Board of Directors, 13 October 1968, scc, 71/295c, box 1, file 13; John Jencks, of Berkeley, to Bill Simmons, 15 September 1968, scc, 71/291c, box 8, file 28; Mr. Dashiell to Edgar Wayburn, 6 November 1968, scc, 71/295c, box 228, file 43. See Donald McKinley, chairman of Pacific Northwest Chapter, to Members of the Board of the Sierra Club, 18 December 1968, scc, 71/295c, box 1, file 13, for a perceptive analysis of member actions in the 1967 referendum.

54. "David Brower's Statement," board of directors meeting, 3–4 May 1969, scc, 71/103c, box 4, file 8. For details of Brower's exit, see John McPhee, *Encounters with the Archdruid* (New York: Noonday Press, 1971), 208–20.

55. Philip Shabecoff, *A Fierce Green Fire: The American Environmental Movement* (New York: Hill & Wang, 1993), 101.

56. *Daily Commercial News* (San Francisco), 14 February 1969, SCC, 71/103c, box 123, file 11. PG&E displayed some concern for the larger oaks; see C. C. Apra to J. W. Woodward, 4 June 1968, and J. A. Cameron to R.W. O'Neill, 29 May 1968, SCC, 71/295c, box 189, file29. Siri criticized the "functional" approach used in the plans; see William E. Siri to Robert Gerdes, chairman of the board, Pacific Gas and Electric Company, 20 June 1968, SCC, 71/295c, box 189, file 23. PG&E apparently took note of his recommendations; see Robert Gerdes to William Siri, 6 December 1968, SCC, 71/295c, box 189, file 28; PG&E, Environmental Report to the AEC (July 1971), Nuclear Regulatory Commission Public Document Room, California Polytechnic State University, San Luis Obispo, 13; Interview with Martin Litton, 25 July 1997.

THREE ▪ LOCAL MOTHERS, EARTHQUAKE COUNTRY, AND THE "NUCLEAR CENTER OF AMERICA"

1. Quotation from Bruce Deberry, "Diablo Canyon Project History," vol. 1 (March 1987), California Public Utilities Commission—Public Staff Division—Diablo Canyon Rate Case, 12, Abalone Alliance Collection (hereafter cited as AAC), Abalone Alliance Safe-Energy Clearinghouse, San Francisco.

2. PG&E, Environmental Report (July 1971), Nuclear Regulatory Commission Public Document Room, California Polytechnic State University, San Luis Obispo (hereafter cited as NRC Public Document Room), 5

3. PG&E, Environmental Report, 22. For a reference to the discovery by local conservationists of PG&E painting rocky areas with green paint see "Did the Sierra Club Bargain with the Devil at Diablo?" *Big Sur Gazette* (mid-July/mid-August 1979). In a letter to Al Gustus, Gualala, 6 May 1971, Harold Miossi commented: "As for the painting rocks green, that shows the true cosmetic attitude of the operation"; Harold Miossi Collection, Cuesta College (San Luis Obispo) Environmental Archives, 001, box 07, file 04.

4. "Special Report on Diablo Canyon," *PG&E Life,* June 1967, 19, Sierra Club Collection (hereafter cited as SCC), 71/103c, box 113, file 40, Bancroft Library, University of California, Berkeley; PG&E, Environmental Report, 13; Jim Hayes, "Our Nuclear Neighbor—VIII: A Change in Political Climate," *San Luis Obispo County Telegram-Tribune* (hereafter cited as *Telegram-Tribune*), 11 September 1973; "Our Nuclear Neighbor—XI: People Think Plant Is Sure Thing," *Telegram-Tribune,* 14 September 1973.

5. "San Luis Obispo County Eagerly Awaits Nuclear Power Plant," *San Diego Union,* 29 August 1971, Ian McMillan Collection, Cuesta College Environmental Archives, II/07, box 19, file 08.

6. Agreement between Resources Agency, State of California, and Pacific Gas and Electric Company, 6 December 1966, 2, SCC, 71/295c, box 81, file 18; *Santa Lucian,* Santa Lucia Chapter newsletter, April 1971, SCC, 71/295c, box 87, file 30; PG&E

Progress, May 1973, 8, Harold Miossi Collection, Cuesta College Environmental Archives, 001, box 04, file 10.

7. Julie Krejsa, "No Diablo: A First Hand Account of the Evolution of Activism on a Conservative Campus," *Radical Teacher* no. 21 (n.d.): 20, Ian McMillan Collection, Cuesta College Environmental Archives, II/07, box 19; *Telegram-Tribune,* 12 March 1971; Krejsa, "No Diablo," 20.

8. Jim Hayes, "Our Nuclear Neighbor—IX: The Fight Goes On against Reactors," *Telegram-Tribune,* 12 September 1973; Mark Evanoff, "Memorirs [sic] of a Movement: PG&E's Nuclear Power Play," unpublished manuscript, 1984, ch.7, p. 31, author's personal copy.

9. The San Luis Obispo Mothers for Peace are not affiliated with any national women's group. They originally considered serving as a chapter of "Another Mother for Peace," based in Los Angeles, but discovered that the southern group operated without chapters. Interview with Liz Apfelberg, Arroyo Grande, 9 July 1997.

10. Jim Hayes, "Our Nuclear Neighbor—III: A Patient Enters the Nuclear 'Hospital,'" *Telegram-Tribune,* 5 September 1973, and Jim Hayes, "Our Nuclear Neighbor—V: 'Just Don't Call It Disaster . . . ,'" ibid., 7 September 1973.

11. John W. Gofman and Arthur R. Tamplin, *Poisoned Power: The Case against Nuclear Power Plants* (London: Chatto & Windus, 1973), 185, 21, 171–72; Spencer R. Weart, *Nuclear Fear: A History of Images* (Cambridge, MA: Harvard University Press, 1988), 315.

12. "Mothers Plan Verbal Siege of Diablo," *Telegram-Tribune,* 23 March 1974. See "A Partial, Chronological Listing of Projects, Events, and Achievements of the San Luis Obispo Mothers for Peace," Sandy Silver Personal Papers (hereafter cited as SSPP), Santa Cruz, for the leafleting near a naval destroyer stationed at Avila Beach during September 1971.

13. Elizabeth Apfelberg and Sandra Silver to Office of the Secretary of the Commission, U.S. Atomic Energy Commission, Washington, D.C., 15 November 1973, Liz Apfelberg Personal Papers (hereafter cited as LAPP), Arroyo Grande; Robert D. Bullard, *Dumping in Dixie: Race, Class, and Environmental Quality,* 2d ed. (Boulder, CO: Westview Press, 1994), xiii. The work of Lois Gibbs is briefly discussed in Robert Gottlieb, *Forcing the Spring: The Transformation of the American Environmental Movement* (Washington, DC: Island Press, 1993), 167, 186–87, 232.

14. In the Matter of Pacific Gas & Electric Company Units 1 & 2 Diablo Canyon Site, U.S. AEC, Dockets 50–275 and 50–323, "Answer of Pacific Gas & Electric Company to petition for lease to intervene filed by Elizabeth E. Apfelberg & Sandra Silver," LAPP; Sandy Silver quoted in Mark Evanoff, "The 18-Year War against Truth," article featured in "Boondoggle at Diablo," *Not Man Apart* [Friends of the Earth journal], 11 September 1981.

15. Alan Chen, "PG&E's Nuclear Plants: A History of Faults," in "Boondoggle at Diablo"; David Brower, *For Earth's Sake: The Life and Times of David Brower* (Salt Lake City: Gibbs Smith, 1990), 210; Shackleford deposition for the California Public Utilities Commission [CPUC] Rate Case 1984–88 (file: 84-06-014); PG&E,

"Environmental Report" (July 1971), 10. Reference to the Scenic Shoreline Preservation Conference's involvement in seismic issues can be found in a letter from Robert Curry, professor of Environmental Geology at the University of Montana, to Fred Eissler, on January 4, 1974, wherein Curry remembers challenging PG&E on earthquake dangers. A copy of the letter can be found at the Abalone Alliance Clearinghouse, San Francisco, in AAC file: Seismic Retro Documents 1978.

16. Evanoff, "18-Year War against Truth"; Interview with Sandy Silver, Santa Cruz, 23 July 1997. Vrana later commented that the *Bulletin* itself represented a "prestigious geological journal which if PG&E geologists don't read, they ought to go back to grade school." See Ralph Vrana, "Political Facts Concerning Diablo Canyon and the Hosgri Fault," 1, included in Jason Schmitt, "Concerns of the Opposition to the Diablo Canyon Nuclear Power Plant," senior project (History), California Polytechnic State University, San Luis Obispo, focusing on documents and interviews with Vrana. PG&E officials testified that October 1972 was the first time that the company heard of the fault. See PG&E's Executive Summary in CPUC Rate Case, Applications 84-06-014 and 85-08-025, for a valuable summary of the seismic controversy.

17. Earthquakes are traditionally measured using a logarithmic scale devised by U.S. geophysicist Charles Richter in 1935. For each whole number increase on the scale (e.g., 6.0 to 7.0), recorded ground motion is ten times greater, with a total energy release estimated to be thirty-one times greater; Richard L. Meehan, *The Atom and the Fault: Experts, Earthquakes, and Nuclear Power* (Cambridge, MA: MIT Press, 1984), xi.

18. Ibid., 151.

19. Sandy Silver quoted in Evanoff, "18-Year War against Truth."

20. See Ralph Nader and John Abbotts, *The Menace of Atomic Energy* (New York: Norton, 1977), 12–13, and Alexander Wilson, *The Culture of Nature: North American Landscape from Disney to the "Exxon Valdez"* (Cambridge, MA: Blackwell, 1992), 269. Wilson lambasted nuclear fission as "through and through a technology that inhibits human freedom."

21. Testimony of James (Jimmie) Jones before the U.S. Nuclear Regulatory Commission (NRC), dockets 50–275 & 50–323, 25 February 1976 & July 22 1976, LAPP.

22. "Do We Face an Energy Crisis?" *PG&E Progress,* April 1973, 7, AAC file: PG&E; "PG&E News Bureau Release," 7 October 1975, SSPP; "SLO County Residents' Attitudes toward the Energy Situation and the Diablo Canyon Nuclear Power Plant Conducted for PG&E by Field Res. Corp," August 1975, SSPP.

23. Juanita Knapps, of Cayucos, to editor, *Telegram-Tribune,* 8 April 1974.

24. Supervisor Richard Krejsa proved to be the most outspoken critic of nuclear power. Interview with Richard Krejsa, San Luis Obispo, 9 July 1997; "Board to Consider Nuclear Plant Forum," *Telegram-Tribune,* 29 April 1975; "There Won't Be a Nuclear Forum," editorial, *Telegram-Tribune,* 21 May 1975.

25. "The Day the Experts Came to Town," *Central Coast Times,* 23 October 1975; Jane Swanson and Sandy Silver quoted in Evanoff, "18-Year War against Truth."

26. For a more detailed discussion of the Safeguards Initiative, see Thomas Raymond Wellock, *Critical Masses: Opposition to Nuclear Power in California, 1958–1978* (Madison: University of Wisconsin Press, 1998), 147–72; "Jane Fonda Urges Diablo Plant Closure," *Telegram-Tribune,* 9 February 1976.

27. Advertisement can be found in Gofman and Tamplin, *Poisoned Power,* 182–83; "Special Report on Diablo Canyon," 12.

28. John Raymond, "It's Not Their Fault," *Santa Barbara News and Review,* 22 November 1984.

29. Paul Boyer, *By the Bomb's Early Light: American Thought and Culture at the Dawn of the Atomic Age* (New York: Pantheon, 1985), 294 (Lilienthal reference). See also Jane Caputi, "Nuclear Power and the Sacred, or Why a Beautiful Woman Is Like a Nuclear Power Plant," in *Ecofeminism and the Sacred,* ed. Carol J. Adams (New York: Continuum, 1993), 230–33, and Steven Marx, "Priesthoods and Power: Some Thoughts on Diablo Canyon," in *Mapping American Culture,* ed. Wayne Franklin and Michael Steiner (Iowa City: University of Iowa Press, 1992), 293. A reprint of PG&E's "nuclear powered toaster" advertisement can be found in Evanoff, "18-Year War against Truth." With a picture of a stainless-steel, unplugged toaster, the utility commented that "nuclear power has been helping you make your morning toast for the past ten years."

30. Lori McKay designed the poster in June 1975. See "Partial, Chronological Listing of Projects, Events, and Achievements of the San Luis Obispo Mothers for Peace."

31. Interview with Sandy Silver; Interview with Liz Apfelberg. For studies of protest at Greenham Common, see Alice Cook and Gwyn Kirk, *Greenham Women Everywhere: Dreams, Ideas and Actions from the Women's Peace Movement* (London: Pluto Press, 1983); Barbara Harford and Sarah Hopkins, eds., *Greenham Common: Women at the Wire* (London: Women's Press, 1984); and Jill Liddington, *The Long Road to Greenham* (London: Virago, 1989). Meredith Veldman's *Fantasy, the Bomb, and the Greening of Britain: Romantic Protest, 1945–1980* (Cambridge, UK: Cambridge University Press, 1994) is also useful.

32. Greta Gaard, "Living Interconnections with Animals and Nature," in *Ecofeminism: Women, Animals, and Nature,* ed. Greta Gaard (Philadelphia: Temple University Press, 1993), 1. Ecofeminism is also an expression of the age-old relationship between women and the natural world. See Carolyn Merchant, *The Death of Nature: Women, Ecology, and the Scientific Revolution* (San Francisco: Harper & Row, 1980), xix; Interview with Sandy Silver; Jean Beauvais, "Radiation Blues," 20 May 1976, LAPP; Rachel Carson, *Silent Spring* (Boston: Houghton Mifflin, 1962), 2, 3.

33. "San Luis Obispo Mothers for Peace," pamphlet, LAPP; Carson, *Silent Spring,* 100. See Linda Lear, *Rachel Carson: Witness for Nature* (New York: Henry Holt, 1997), 429–35, 462, and, for a broader look at the scientific backlash, Frank Graham Jr., *Since Silent Spring* (Greenwich, CT: Fawcett Crest, 1970), 59–76.

34. Hayes, "Our Nuclear Neighbor—III: A Patient Enters the Nuclear 'Hospital.'"

35. Deberry, "Diablo Canyon Project History," vol.1, 12–13.

36. *Telegram-Tribune*, 13 December 1972, 1 October 1977.

37. AEC, "Discussion and Findings by the Division of Reactor Licensing Relating to Consideration of Suspension Pending NEPA Environmental Review" (29 November 1971); PG&E, "Statement of PG&E" (18 October 1971); AEC, "In the Matter of Pacific Gas and Electric Company," memo and order (7 December 1971); all located in Environmental File #1, NRC Public Document Room.

38. PG&E, "Environmental Report" (July 1971), 42, NRC Public Document Room. See also James Adams et al. (PG&E), "Ecological Investigations Related to Thermal Discharges" (1969), NRC Public Document Room; Bruce Kyse, "Diablo to Benefit Ecology," *Telegram-Tribune*, 18 September 1973; "Abalone Diver Asks AEC for Voice," *Telegram-Tribune*, 1 May 1974. In December 1976 the *Telegram-Tribune* detailed the concerns of the California Department of Fish and Game's director, E. C. Fullerton, over a lack of adequate research into the project's potential environmental effects. See Bob Anderson, "Fish and Game: Diablo Threatens Marine Life," *Telegram-Tribune*, 18 December 1976.

39. Warren Groshong, "Big Abalone Kill at Diablo, Test Shows," *Telegram-Tribune*, 22 January 1975; PG&E, "Supplement 8 to the Environmental Report" (February 1976), with contributions by the California Department of Fish and Game, Environmental Section, NRC Public Document Room; PG&E Department of Engineering Research, "Chemical, Biological, and Corrosion Investigations, Related to the Testing of the Diablo Canyon Unit 1 Cooling Water System," May 1975, Morro Bay Fish and Game Office; "Diablo Cited for Pollution," *Telegram-Tribune*, 10 April 1975; "Diablo to Test New Tubing," *Telegram-Tribune*, 7 November 1975; Bob Anderson, "Abalone: PG&E Gives Funds for Program," *Telegram-Tribune*, 9 December 1976; Bob Anderson, "Abalone Kill: Behind-the-Scenes Actions in Diablo Case," *Telegram-Tribune*, 27 December 1976; Conversations with Sue Benech, biologist, Diablo Canyon, 21 August 1997.

FOUR ▪ THE SHOWDOWN

1. Clamshell Alliance, *Handbook for the Land and Sea Blockade of the Seabrook Reactor Pressure Vessel* (Portsmouth, NH: Clamshell Alliance, n.d.), 2, Abalone Alliance Collection (hereafter cited as AAC), Abalone Alliance Safe-Energy Clearinghouse, San Francisco; Sheryl Crown, *Hell No, We Won't Grow: Seabrook, April 1977— Nonviolent Occupation of a Nuclear Power Site* (London: Housmans, 1979), 23.

2. People Generating Energy, "People Generating Energy" timeline (n.d., ca. July 1977), AAC file: Abalone Alliance Flyers on Diablo; David Hartsough, "Shalan Grant Proposal" (n.d., ca. 1978), American Friends Service Committee (hereafter cited as AFSC), San Francisco office, file: Abalone Alliance; *San Luis Obispo County Telegram-Tribune* (hereafter cited as *Telegram-Tribune*), 25 February 1977.

3. Interview with William Miller, San Luis Obispo, 3 September 1997; Interview with David Hartsough, San Francisco, 18 July 1997; Interview with Barbara Levy,

San Francisco, 29 July 1997. The phrase "Seabrook West" can be found in Harvey Wasserman, "Nuclear Showdown at Diablo Canyon," *Chicago News & Review,* 1 February 1979.

4. George S. Whiting, "Decision at Diablo Canyon," sheriff's report (1978), AAC file: 8/6/78 Diablo Blockade Sheriffs Report; Dorothy Houston, "Nuclear Foes Stage a Protest," *Daily Californian,* 11–12 August 1977; Barbara Evans, "Rally 'Round—Stop the Nukes," *Santa Barbara News and Review,* 5 August 1977.

5. Paul Krassner, "No Nukes Is Good Nukes," *San Francisco Bay Guardian,* 10 August 1978, 6; Susan Stern, "Diablo," *In These Times,* 20–26 September 1978, Mary Moore Personal Papers, Occidental, file: 1981 pre-Diablo; Bill Denneen, "Statement on Diablo," AAC file: Diablo defense '78.

6. Interview with Pam Metcalf, San Luis Obispo, 3 September 1997.

7. Other (less popular) films and novels of the 1970s that served to highlight the dangers of nuclear power include: *The Big Bus* (comedy-disaster movie concerning a nuclear-powered bus), Paramount Pictures, 1976; John G. Fuller, *We Almost Lost Detroit* (novel, based on a true story), New York: Reader's Digest Press, 1975; Alistair MacLean, *Goodbye California* (novel), London: Book Club Associates, 1977; Gordon Pape and Tony Aspler, *Chain Reaction* (novel), London: Barrie & Jenkins, 1979; *Red Alert* (TV movie), Paramount Pictures, 1977; Thomas N. Scortia and Frank M. Robinson, *The Prometheus Crisis* (novel), London: Hodder & Stoughton, 1975. William K. Knoedelseder Jr. and Ellen Farley, "When Fate Follows Fiction—The 'Syndrome' Fallout," *Washington Post,* 30 March 1979.

8. Richard Asinof, "Quake 'n' Bake: The Fight to Stop a Nuclear Reactor Built on a Fault Line," *Village Voice,* 16 April 1979; Burton Wohl, *The China Syndrome* (London: Severn House, 1979), 14, inside cover, 38, 11; Abalone Alliance, "Anti-Nuclear Forces Mobilizing to Stop Diablo Canyon Plant from Opening, Major Legal Rally Scheduled for June 30 in San Luis Obispo," press release, AAC file: SLO Rally June 30 1979; Center for Law in the Public Interest, "Diablo Canyon Threatens Every Californian—My Family as Well as Yours," letter requesting donations, Los Angeles, AAC file: leaflets collection.

9. *It's About Times,* May 1979, 6; Abalone Alliance, "Do You Remember March 28, 1979?" flyer, AAC; Charles Burgess, "Massive S.F. Anti-Nuclear Protest," *Daily Californian,* 9 April 1979; Editorial, "The Nuclear Question and Distorted Values," *Central Coast Sun Bulletin* (San Luis Obispo), 12 April 1979; Editorial, "Three Mile Island and Diablo Canyon," *Telegram-Tribune,* 30 March 1979.

10. David Hartsough, "Staff Report for March–April 1979," AFSC file: (705) Power Literature outside American Friends Service Committee; Interview with Jackie Cabasso, Oakland, 31 July 1997; Abalone Alliance, "Anti-Nuclear Forces Mobilizing to Stop Diablo Canyon . . ."; *Wall Street Journal,* 31 July 1979.

11. Interview with William Miller; Lea Steinberg, "Clear Beginnings," *It's About Times,* September 1979, 2.

12. *Diablo Canyon Blockade-Encampment Handbook,* 1; Elizabeth Whitney, "Diablo Pageant," in *1981 Diablo Canyon Blockade: An Illustrated Anthology of*

Articles, Essays, Poems & Personal Experiences, ed. Diablo Writing Project (Santa Cruz: Diablo Writing Project, 1983), 13–14; Interview with Don Eichelberger, San Francisco, 24 and 26 June 1997.

13. SONOMoreAtomics, "History of Diablo Canyon," Mary Moore Personal Papers, file: Diablo fact sheets. Concern over agricultural contamination was also noted in People against Nuclear Power, "An Open Letter to the Atomic Safety and Licensing Board, Governor Jerry Brown, and the people of California," 15 January 1979, AFSC file: Power literature outside AFSC.

14. SONOMoreAtomics, "History of Diablo Canyon"; *Stockton Record,* 23 January 1984.

15. Citizens' Right to Know and Abalone Alliance, "Everything You Want to Know about Nuclear Power," poster, AFSC; Protester, amateur video of the "Passion Play—Crucifixion Ceremony," Diablo Canyon, 20 April 1984, Don Eichelberger Personal Papers (DEPP), San Francisco; Interview with Don Eichelberger; "Unreddy Killerwatt" can be found in most issues of *It's About Times,* next to the subscription coupon. Reddy Communications objected to the reinterpretation of their trademark: letter reprinted in the Redwood Alliance's quarterly newsletter *Nuclear Free Times,* June 1981, 4, AAC file: Redwood Alliance.

16. Tita Caldwell, "My Mother the Earth," in *1981 Diablo Canyon Blockade,* ed. Diablo Writing Project, 15; Greg Gabby, "Poem for Abalone Alliance (or Nuclear Power Plants Shutdown Poem)," 15 December 1982, AAC file: Interesting Letters.

17. *It's About Times,* June–July 1979, 6.

18. "A License for Diablo Canyon Is a License to Kill," flyer, AAC file: AA flyers on Diablo; Bob Van Scoy, "Are You a Subversive," *It's About Times,* March 1980, 3; Mark Evanoff, "PG&E Buys a 'Grassroots' Group," *It's About Times,* June–July 1981, 7.

19. *It's About Times,* February 1979, 5, mid-December–January 1980, 9.

20. *Diablo Canyon Blockade-Encampment Handbook,* 56; *Nuke Notes* (July–August 1983), 13; Abalone Alliance, "Did You Know," flyer, AAC file: AA flyers on Diablo; *It's About Times,* March–April 1979, 10. Also see Ad Hoc Committee for Socialist Ecosystems, Berkeley, "I'd Rather Be Smashing Capitalism (Than Atoms)" leaflet, AFSC.

21. "Seeing Red: A Forum on Communists in the Peace Movement," *Nuke Notes,* January 1984, 20–28; *It's About Times,* December 1982–January 1983, 4; Interview with Roger Herried, San Francisco, 24 and 25 June 1997.

22. "California A-Plant Targeted for Mass Protests," *Washington Post,* 11 September 1981; *Diablo Canyon Blockade-Encampment Handbook,* 57; Carl Neiburger, "1,000 Protest Diablo, 52 Arrested," *Telegram-Tribune,* 13 February 1984; *Radioactive Times,* Summer 1981, AFSC file: Abalone Alliance; *It's About Times,* September 1979, 2.

23. Burgess, "Massive S.F. Anti-Nuclear Protest"; Susan Mesner, "Which Anti-Nuclear Movement?" *It's About Times,* March 1980, 6; Barbara Levy to Editor, *San Francisco Chronicle,* 11 January 1984, Barbara Levy Personal Papers, San Francisco; Louise Billotte, "Coalitions Reconsidered," *It's About Times,* June–July 1979, 8.

24. Interview with Don Eichelberger; Interview with Mary Moore, Sebastopol, Sonoma County, 24 July 1997.

25. Whitney, "Diablo Pageant," 13; *Diablo Canyon Blockade-Encampment Handbook,* 42–43, 46; Jane Miller, "Diablo as a Feminist Experience," in *1981 Diablo Canyon Blockade,* ed. Diablo Writing Project, 37.

26. Jack Anderson, "The Hosgri Fault," *San Francisco Chronicle,* 27 January 1977.

27. Interview with Jackie Cabasso; Interview with Lauren Alden.

28. Interview with Pam Metcalf; *Santa Rosa Press Democrat,* 13 October 1981.

29. Interview with Peter Lumsdaine, Santa Cruz, 7 July 1997. See also *Telegram-Tribune,* 12 September 1981.

30. "Troubles Keep Delaying California Nuclear Plant," *New York Times,* August 24, 1980; "Diablo Siege: 300 Arrested. Protesters Invade by Land and Sea," *Daily Californian,* 16 September 1981; "Showdown at Diablo Canyon," *Newsweek,* 10 August 1981, 51.

31. *It's About Times,* October–November 1981, 1; David Lazarus, "Diablo Canyon Protesters Failed to Achieve Substantive Victories," *Daily Californian,* 21 September 1981; Interview with Jackie Cabasso; *Telegram-Tribune,* 12 September 1981; *It's About Times,* March–April 1979, 9.

32. Paul Engstrom, "Protesters Play Cat and Mouse with Law in Thick Canyon Brush," *Oakland Tribune,* 16 September 1981; "The Ring of Security around Diablo," *San Francisco Chronicle,* 12 September 1981; Hurst and Sector, "Stage Set at Diablo Canyon"; Marcelo Rodriguez, "Diablo Canyon," *Marin County Pacific Sun,* 18–24 September 1981; "500 Arrested in First Nuclear Protest," *Berkeley Gazette,* 16 September 1981.

33. Jackrabbit interviewed in Barbara Epstein, *Political Protest and Cultural Revolution: Nonviolent Direct Action in the 1970s and 1980s* (Berkeley: University of California Press, 1991), 110; Crystal, "Crystal's Story," in *1981 Diablo Canyon Blockade,* ed. Diablo Writing Project, 62; Interview with Starhawk, Sonoma, 28 July 1997; Abalone Alliance, "The Diablo Canyon Nuclear Power Plant Fact Sheet," Fall 1982, AAC file: AA flyers on Diablo.

34. Interview with Phoebe, Berkeley, 12 August 1997; Krassner, "No Nukes Is Good Nukes"; Interview with Brook.

35. Interview with Barbara Levy; Starhawk, *Dreaming the Dark: Magic, Sex and Politics,* new ed. (Boston: Beacon Press, 1988), 178.

36. Bob Wolf, for People Generating Energy, to editor, *Telegram-Tribune,* 22 September 1977; *It's About Times,* March–April 1979, 2, 3, 8.

37. Interview with Charlotte Davis, San Francisco, 5 August 1997; People Generating Energy, "The Theory and Some Implications of Nonviolence," in George S. Whiting, "Decision at Diablo Canyon," sheriff's report (1978), AAC file: 8/6/78 Diablo Blockade Sheriffs Report.

38. Carl Irving, "Stout-hearted S.F. Group at Diablo Gears Up for Blockade," *San Francisco Examiner,* 15 September 1981; Epstein, *Political Protest and Cultural Revolution,* 116.

39. "Declaration of Nuclear Resistance," in *Diablo Canyon Blockade-Encampment Handbook,* 3; David Hartsough, "Reflections on the Diablo Blockade," AFSC; David Martinez, *Reflections of an Anti-Nuclear Activist* (San Anselmo, CA: San Anselmo Printing, 1981), 55.

40. *Simple Living,* Spring 1976. The Spring 1976 edition similarly highlighted nuclear energy as the antithesis of an ecologically and socially responsible lifestyle.

41. *Diablo Canyon Blockade-Encampment Handbook,* 54.

42. American Friends song-sheet, "Songs," AFSC; *No Nukes* (movie), Castle Hill Productions, 1980.

43. William Moyer, "De-Developing the United States through Nonviolence," 1973, AFSC file: green, campaign building nonviolent action; American Friends Service Committee, "Energy Slideshow Outline," 11 March 1980, AFSC file: 805. Lovins argued his case in Congress, and published numerous books, including *Soft Energy Paths: Towards a Durable Peace* (San Francisco: Friends of the Earth, 1977), *Is Nuclear Power Necessary?* (London: Friends of the Earth, 1979), and *The Energy Controversy: Soft Path Questions and Answers,* ed. Hugh Nash (San Francisco: Friends of the Earth, 1979).

44. Starhawk, *Dreaming the Dark,* 173; Miki Sanders, "The First of Autumn," in *1981 Diablo Canyon Blockade,* 45; *San Francisco Examiner,* 13 September 1981; *San Francisco Chronicle,* 17 September 1981; Whitney, "Diablo Pageant," 13.

45. "Indians Hold Vigil at Diablo Protest," *Los Angeles Times,* 5 October 1981. A year earlier, PG&E noted its intentions to allow Chumash limited access to Diablo due to growing interest in archaeological remains next to the plant. This corresponded with a new land management plan designed to meet National Environmental Protection Act (NEPA) review requirements regarding the disturbance of significant archaeological sites. See PG&E, "Archaeological Resources Management Plan" (April 1980), Environmental Folder, NRC Public Document Room.

46. *New York Times,* 22 November 1981, 5 March 1982; *It's About Times,* April 1982, 1.

47. PG&E Energy Information Center, "Diablo Canyon Nuclear Power Plant," leaflet, May 1984, AAC file: PG&E.

48. As quoted in D'Arcy Fallon, "Bohemian Club's 'Cremation' Draws Fire," *San Francisco Examiner,* 9 July 1987 (Hoover quotation); William Domhoff, "Politics among the Redwoods," article, reprinted in Bohemian Grove Action Network, *Bohemian Digest* (Occidental, CA: Bohemian Grove Action Network, 1982), AAC file: Bohemian Grove. See also John Van der Zee, *The Greatest Men's Party on Earth: Inside the Bohemian Grove* (New York: Harcourt Brace Jovanovich, 1974), and William G. Domhoff, *The Bohemian Grove and Other Retreats: A Study in Ruling-Class Cohesiveness* (New York: Harper & Row, 1974).

49. *It's About Times,* June–July 1983, 12; People against Nuclear Power, "Did You Know," plutonium tour poster, AFSC file: green, anti-nuke local.

50. "Hall of Shame: Nuclear Tour Guide," AAC.

51. Steve Stallone, "So Long, New Deal—Howdy, Raw Deal," *It's About Times,*

March–April 1981, 5; *Nuke Notes,* 15 June 1981, 23; *It's About Times,* May–June 1982, 1.

52. Steve Ladd, "The Nuclear Weapons Freeze," in "Ground Zero Gazette," 4, a supplement to *It's About Times,* August 1981; Marcy Darnovsky, "Smile and Say 'Freeze,'" *It's About Times,* May–June 1982, 5. The Nuclear Weapons Freeze campaign officially began in 1979, although "California Freeze" emerged in early 1981.

53. *Dark Circle* (movie), Independent Documentary Group, 1982 (and revised edition 1991); Telephone interview with Judy Irving, San Francisco, 6 August 1997.

54. Marcy Darnovsky, "Showdown at Diablo Canyon," *Berkeley Barb,* 21 June–4 July 1979, 4; *Nuclear California* also featured a map of California's "Major Radioactive Material Sites and Earthquake Faults," disclosing some dangerous alignments between geology and atomic planning (including Diablo Canyon). See Kaplan, *Nuclear California,* 78, jacket sleeve, 79.

55. *It's About Times,* March–April 1979, 3; ibid., February 1979, 5; *Diablo Canyon Blockade-Encampment Handbook,* 22, 51; Interview with Don Eichelberger. Also see Matthew Glass, "Air Force, Western Shoshone, and Mormon Rhetoric of Place and the MX Conflict," in *The Atomic West,* ed. Bruce Hevly and John M. Findlay (Seattle: University of Washington Press, 1998), 255–75; Valerie L. Kuletz, *The Tainted Desert: Environmental and Social Ruin in the American West* (New York: Routledge, 1998); and Rebecca Solnit, *Savage Dreams: A Journey into the Landscape Wars of the American West* (New York: Vintage, 1994). *It's About Times* also revealed the difficulties involved in forging a mutual alliance between a body of largely white middle-class Americans and a coalition of Native American nations. For example, one letter writer, Jaffery Ryder, felt that the "spiritual guidance and leadership" offered by the American Indian Movement restricted "the anti-nuke and anti-capitalist movement" to an overly rigid structure and antitechnological stance. *It's About Times,* March 1980, 2.

56. Abalone Alliance, *Stop Diablo Canyon: Join the People's Emergency Response Plan,* pamphlet, AFSC file: loose misc; Interview with Jackie Cabasso.

57. *It's About Times,* September 1980, 9; Lawrence Ross, Reason for Blockading, in Richard Frishman, "Defense of Necessity," 15 May 1982, AAC file: Defense of Necessity.

58. Judith Cummings, "Leaders of Nuclear Protests See a Shift in Strategy," *New York Times,* 21 September 1981. The newspaper also noted that by late 1981 "the nature of the movement and the mood of the nation seem to be operating against it," suggesting a transitory element to antinuclearism as the "crucible" of protest.

FIVE   LIVING ALONGSIDE THE MACHINE

1. *The Thing and the Savage She-Hulk: Disaster at Diablo Reactor,* Marvel Comics no. 88 (June 1982), in Sandy Silver Personal Papers (hereafter cited as SSPP), Santa Cruz.

2. "KRON-TV Exclusive: Investigative Unit to Reveal Contents of Confidential Nuclear Regulatory Commission Transcripts," KRON-TV News Release, 10 January 1985, Abalone Alliance Collection (hereafter cited as AAC), Abalone Alliance Safe-Energy Clearinghouse, San Francisco, file: NRC Hearings (leaked); "Discussion of Earthquakes and Emergency Planning for Diablo Canyon and Discussion of Stay Motion," NRC Closed Meeting excerpt, 30 July 1984, 50, AAC file: NRC Hearings (leaked); Nunzio J. Palladino, Chairman (NRC), to Edward Markey, Chairman, Subcommittee on Oversight and Investigations (U.S. House of Representatives), including comment by Commissioner Asseltine, 29 October 1984, 4, AAC file: NRC Hearings (leaked). See "Court Allows Diablo to Skip Quake Plan," *San Francisco Chronicle,* 26 April 1986.

3. See PG&E Rate Case Overview (n.d., ca. mid-1985), 131, in AAC file: Rate case Overview; Michael Robertson, "Living in the Shadow of the Domes," *San Francisco Chronicle,* 2 May 1986.

4. B. Zuanich, "Diablo Canyon in the Wake of the Chernobyl Disaster," senior project (Political Science), 1989, California Polytechnic State University. Zuanich used data collected by David George in 1986. Robertson, "Living in the Shadow of the Domes;" William Loran, San Rafael, to David Hartsough, 6 December 1987, American Friends Service Committee, San Francisco Office, file: Diablo Outside Literature; Iurii Shcherbak, *Chernobyl: A Documentary Story* (Edmonton: Canadian Institute of Ukrainian Studies, 1989), 9.

5. Robertson, "Living in the Shadow of the Domes."

6. Mothers for Peace, Letter Alert, August 1986, SSPP file: Mothers for Peace; Mothers for Peace badge, June von Ruden Personal Papers, San Luis Obispo; William Bennett interviewed in *Who Will Be a Witness? Rancho Seco and the Nuclear Threat to Health and Life* (directed by Jacques Levy, produced by Mary Moore, Jacques Levy, and Al Finn, SONOMOreAtomics, 1986), AAC video collection.

7. Interview with Roger Herried, San Francisco, 24 and 25 June 1997.

8. Interview with former PG&E employee, San Luis Obispo, 21 July 1997.

9. Letter from Nancy Culver, Mothers for Peace, to supporters, 28 May 1986, SSPP file: Mothers for Peace; Editorial, "Hats Off to Sierra Club, Mothers for Peace for Diablo Action," *San Luis Obispo County Telegram-Tribune* (hereafter cited as *Telegram-Tribune*), 9 July 1986.

10. Interview with Rochelle Becker, Grover Beach, 24 August 1997; Edward O'Neill (CPUC), Joseph Malkin (PG&E), and Mark Urban (attorney for John Van de Kamp), "Notice of Settlement Agreement and of Settlement Conference," 27 June 1988 (California Public Utilities Commission, Applications 84-06-014 and 85-08-025), and William M. Bennett, "Request for Examination of Antitrust Factors," 27 September 1988 (ibid.); Editorial, "PG&E and Diablo: A Scandal without End," *San Francisco Bay Guardian,* 19 October 1988.

11. Susan Zakin, *Coyotes and Town Dogs: Earth First! and the Environmental Movement* (New York: Penguin, 1993), 4.

12. *Telegram-Tribune,* 7 December 1982; "Innocent Plea in Diablo Bomb Plot," ibid., 4 January 1983.

13. "Radical Environmentalists Held in Plot against Diablo," ibid., 1 June 1989.

14. Michael A. Lerner, "The FBI vs. the Monkeywrenchers," *Los Angeles Times Magazine,* 15 April 1990; Zakin, *Coyotes and Town Dogs,* 337.

15. "Inside Earth First!" *Arizona Republic,* 6 August 1989; Lerner, "FBI vs. the Monkeywrenchers." The reputation of the FBI was further damaged by Fain's admission of targeting Foreman and by informant Ron Frazier's display of affection for machine tools. Frazier, who helped Davis locate the best cutting torch for sabotaging pylons, chose his secret FBI code names from tool brands, with the Victor label his favorite. See Zakin, *Coyotes and Town Dogs,* 436.

16. Christopher Manes, *Green Rage: Radical Environmentalism and the Unmaking of Civilization* (Boston: Little, Brown, 1990), 175.

17. David Helvarg, "Blowing Up Diablo Canyon," *California,* October 1990, 74–77.

18. Ibid.

19. "Blaze Threatens Diablo Plant," *Telegram-Tribune,* 24 May 1989.

20. "'Kelp Attack' at Diablo," ibid., 27 September 1995; David Sneed, "Diablo Hobbled by Heavy Surf," ibid., 2 December 1998.

21. Lore Lawrence, "El Niño Is Still Warming Up," ibid., 14 November 1997; Matt Lazier, "Ocean Swells Poised to Strike Again," ibid., 20 January 1998; David Sneed, "Avila Preparations Help Minimize Storm Damage," ibid., 3 February 1998.

22. Jan Greene, "Quake at Sea Triggers Diablo Alert," ibid., 7 February 1990; "Quake Felt at Diablo, Los Osos," ibid., 17 January 1992; ibid., 6 February 1995.

23. "Post Quake Rumblings at Nuclear Plant," *Fresno Bee,* 1 April 1990.

24. Mike Davis, "Chaos and California," in *Green versus Gold: Sources in California's Environmental History,* ed. Carolyn Merchant (Washington, DC: Island Press, 1998), 449–50.

25. Stephen Lyons, "Low-tech Ants Give a High-tech Idaho Lab Fits," *High Country News,* 13 June 1994.

26. Neil J. Aiken, "Report of the Diablo Canyon Independent Safety Committee," 5 February 1997, author's personal copy; Daniel Zoll, "Public Power," *San Francisco Bay Guardian,* 14 February 1996. In an article entitled "Yellow Fever," the *Guardian* (29 March 1997) mentioned the American Nuclear Society tour offered to *The Simpsons* crew in 1991. In June 1998 PG&E dismissed Aiken, claiming he suffered mental imbalance, a "paranoid condition" in the atomic workplace. David Sneed, "Veteran Plant Operator Alleges Unsafe Practices at Diablo," *Telegram-Tribune,* 15 February 1997; David Sneed, "Suspended Diablo Worker Files Complaint," *Telegram-Tribune,* 18 November 1998. In October 1999 the NRC upheld the decision of PG&E to relieve Aiken. A month later the U.S. Department of Labor sided against Pacific Gas, ordering the corporation to pay Aiken $116,000 in "lost wages and damages." See David Sneed, "PG&E Upheld on Diablo Firing," *Tribune,* 23 October 1999, and David

Sneed, "Diablo Whistle-blower Wins $116,000 Settlement," *Tribune,* 24 November 1999 (the *San Luis Obispo County Telegram-Tribune* changed its title to the *Tribune* during the summer of 1999).

27. David Sneed, "PG&E Readies for Y2K Woes at Diablo," *Telegram-Tribune,* 22 March 1999. See Patrick Pemberton, "Y2K Arrives Not Like a Lion, but a Pussycat," *Tribune,* 2 January 2000.

28. Interview with PG&E employee, Arroyo Grande, 4 June 1999; David Sneed, "PG&E Readies for Y2K Woes at Diablo," *Telegram-Tribune,* 22 March 1999;

29. Jerry Bunin, "Diablo Reactor Sets 16-Month Milestone," *Telegram-Tribune,* 29 September 1998; David Sneed, "Diablo Canyon Passes Inspection," ibid., 12 September 1997; Jonathan Marshall, "PG&E to Cut Price of Power from Diablo," *San Francisco Chronicle,* 7 December 1994.

30. "Diablo Experts Radiate Confidence in Nuclear Power," *Telegram-Tribune,* 20 May 1995.

31. Interview with Bob Wolf, San Luis Obispo, 21 July 1997; Stephanie A. Penner, "Diablo Canyon: Determining Student Awareness and Attitudes toward Nuclear Power," senior project (Journalism), 1991, California Polytechnic State University; Interview with Richard Krejsa, San Luis Obispo, 9 July 1997.

32. See Paul Chilton, "Nukespeak: Nuclear Language, Culture, and Propaganda," in *Nukespeak: The Media and the Bomb,* ed. Crispin Aubrey (London: Comedia, 1982), 94–112.

33. Silas Lyons, "Keeping Diablo Cost-Competitive," *Telegram-Tribune,* 13 December 1997.

34. Interview with Raye Fleming; Conversation with Geoff Land, San Luis Obispo, 18 August 1997; Interview with activist, San Luis Obispo, 21 July 1997; *Telegram-Tribune,* 9 April 1994; Richard Krejsa, "High Cost of Electricity from Diablo Should Be Everyone's Business," *Telegram-Tribune,* 20 May 1996.

35. Jerry Bunin and Silas Lyons, "Closure Would Send Out Ripples," *Telegram-Tribune,* 1 July 1996, notes the local effects of a possible shutdown. Rancho Seco is mentioned in Silas Lyons, "It's a Lot More Complicated Than Hitting a Switch," ibid., 2 July 1996. For the sale to Duke Power, see Silas Lyons, "PG&E Sells Morro Power Plant," ibid., 19 November 1997; Jonathan Marshall, "A Fiscal Meltdown," *San Francisco Chronicle,* 22 May 1996.

36. Silas Lyons, "Keeping Diablo Cost-Competitive"; David Sneed, "Center Would Reveal Sea's Mystery," *Telegram-Tribune,* 18 April 1998; Silas Lyons, "PG&E Stopping Calendar," ibid., 14 February 1998; Lore Lawrence, "Phone Book Insert Replaces Popular PG&E Calendar," ibid., 18 September 1998.

37. June von Ruden, Mothers for Peace, to supporters, December 1994, SSPP file: Mothers for Peace; Jeff Wheelwright, "Of Man-Rems and Millirems," courtesy of author (retitled "Diablo Canyon: A View from the Inside" in the *Telegram-Tribune,* 18 April 1996); Interview with Rochelle Becker.

38. Chumash narrative "A Pact with the Devil," collected by J. P. Harrington. See Thomas C. Blackburn, ed., *December's Child: A Book of Chumash Oral Narratives*

(Berkeley: University of California Press, 1975), 277; Mike Steere, "San Luis Obispo, California," *Outside,* July 1995.

39. *Telegram-Tribune,* 8 September 1998; Newt Imes, "Avila Shoreline to Become Oilworld USA," *New Times,* 1 April 1999.

40. Interview with Richard Krejsa; David Sneed, "Avila Is Waking Up to Smell the Oil," *Telegram-Tribune,* 27 March 1999.

41. Leonard Nevarez, Harvey Molotch, and William Freudenberg, eds., "San Luis Obispo County: A Major Switching—Final Report," prepared for U.S. Department of the Interior, Minerals Management Service (March 1997), 95; C. Elwoods, "An Ode to Morro Rock," (1800s—specific date unknown), featured in Sharon Lewis Dickerson, *Mountains of Fire: San Luis Obispo County's Nine Sisters—A Chain of Ancient Volcanic Peaks* (San Luis Obispo: EZ Nature Books, 1990), 61; David Sneed, "Hearst Ranch Resort: The Showdown," *Telegram-Tribune,* 3 January 1998.

42. Unocal Corporation, *Yesterday, Today, Tomorrow: A Commitment of the Community* (Santa Maria, CA: Unocal Corporation, 1996), 5; Tom Athanasiou, *Slow Reckoning: The Ecology of a Divided Planet* (London: Secker & Warburg, 1997), 227; Exhibit on radiation at PG&E Community Center, 6588 Ontario Road, San Luis Obispo, during 1997.

43. PG&E, "Diablo Canyon Power Plant," pamphlet (undated, approx. mid-1990s).

44. Mothers for Peace, "Revised Special Edition: What PG&E Can Do to Save the Earth—30 Simple Energy Things You Can Do to Save the Earth" (n.d.), SSPP; "Earth Day Clan Fumes over PG&E's Participation," *Telegram-Tribune,* 13 April 1991; Jack Yorida, "Gag Me with a Green Ad," *Earth Journal,* September 1991, 8.

45. Thomas Turner, "Eco Pornography, or How to Spot an Ecological Phony," in *The Environmental Handbook,* ed. Garrett de Bell (New York: Ballantine/Friends of the Earth, 1970), 263; "Earth Day Clan Fumes." Dow Chemical and Ford Motors both proffered contributions to the Earth Day steering committee at the University of Michigan. See Robert Gottlieb, *Forcing the Spring: The Transformation of the American Environmental Movement* (Washington, DC: Island Press, 1993), 110, 351–52.

46. Abalone Alliance, "What's Wrong with This Picture?" flyer, AAC file: Abalone Alliance flyers on Diablo.

47. George DeBord, "Massive Diablo Plant Hasn't Proven Itself Yet," *Telegram-Tribune,* 18 February 1985; *Sea Changes: A Year at Diablo Canyon* (n.d.), PG&E promotional documentary, filmed by Patrick Mulvey.

48. PG&E, "Ecological Monitoring Program: 1995 Status Report, Summer and Fall Surveys" (February 1996): 1–3/4, held at the Morro Bay U.S. Fish and Game offices.

49. PG&E, "Diablo Canyon Power Plant: Thermal Effects Monitoring Program Analysis Report, Chapter 1—Changes in the Marine Environment Resulting from the Diablo Canyon Power Plant Discharge" (December 1997), author's personal copy, courtesy of California Regional Water Quality Control Board, Central Coast Region. For details of the "unusual community," see summary section, especially S-34; for kelp effects, see 4–36.

50. Conversations with Jim Blecha, Diablo Canyon, 21 August 1997; PG&E, "Thermal Effects Monitoring Program: 1990 Annual Report" (March 1991): 1–5.

51. "PG&E to Pay $14 Million to Settle Diablo Canyon Missing Data Case," California Environmental Protection Agency press release, 27 May 1997, author's personal copy, courtesy of California Regional Water Quality Control Board, Central Coast Region; Glenn Roberts Jr., "Estuary Program in the Right Place at the Right Time," *Telegram-Tribune*, 29 May 1997; Chris Bowman, "Big PG&E Settlement over Nuclear Plant," *Sacramento Bee*, 28 May 1997; David Sneed, "PG&E to Pay $14 Million Fine in Diablo Environmental Case," *Telegram-Tribune*, 24 May 1997; Silas Lyons, "$3.6 Million for Morro Estuary," *Telegram-Tribune*, 28 May 1997.

52. David Sneed, "State Mulls Diablo Impacts," *Telegram-Tribune*, 12 December 1998; "PG&E to Pay $14 million to Settle Diablo Canyon Missing Data Case"; Alex Barnum, "$14 Million Settlement by PG&E to Help Coast," *San Francisco Chronicle*, 28 May 1997.

53. David Sneed, "Water Board Working to Preserve PG&E Land," *Tribune*, 17 August 1999; David Sneed, "PG&E Supports Diablo Preserve," ibid., 3 October 1999; David Sneed, "Board Sends Land-saving Measure to Voters," ibid., 20 October 1999; David Sneed, "PG&E in Hot Water over Discharge," ibid., 19 November 1999; David Sneed, "Water Board Delays Sanctions," ibid., 20 November 1999.

54. "Protecting Wildlife Near Diablo Canyon," *PG&E Progress*, December 1987, 4–5; PG&E, "Diablo Canyon Land Stewardship Program: Toward Conserving Biological Diversity" (n.d., ca. 1993), 1, author's personal copy, courtesy of PG&E. A useful overview of wildlife on the headland prior to the operation of the plant remains the PG&E Department of Engineering Research's "Terrestrial Ecology Study" (July 1971), held at the Diablo plant.

55. Santa Cruz Predatory Bird Research Group (SCPBRG), "Peregrine Falcon Activity at Diablo Canyon, 1981–1994," report held at the SCPBRG, Joseph M. Long Marine Laboratory, University of California, Santa Cruz; SCPBRG, "1994 Activities" report, November 1994, 16; Brian Walton to Ed Coulson, Pacific Gas and Electric Company, 11 March 1981, SCPBRG; Conversations with Brian Walton, SCPBRG, Santa Cruz, 15 August 1997. Loss of baby peregrine noted in *Telegram-Tribune*, 16 May 1987.

56. Conversations with Sue Benech, consultant biologist, Diablo Canyon, 21 August 1997; PG&E, "Environmental Investigations at Diablo Canyon 1986 Volume One—Marine Ecological Studies," December 1987, 9; *Endangered Species Monitoring at Diablo Canyon* (1990), PG&E documentary by Patrick Mulvey, available at Diablo Canyon Community Center; John Muir, *Travels in Alaska* (1915; reprint, Boston: Houghton Mifflin, 1979), 5.

SIX ■ RECONNECTING THE HEADLAND

1. Enrico P. Bongio, San Luis Obispo, to Kenneth Schwartz, 2 July 1991, Harold Miossi Collection, Cuesta College (San Luis Obispo) Environmental Archives, box 001, file 4; "Parks of California—Morro Bay State Park," *PG&E Progress*, May 1973, 8.

2. Advertisement for the magazine of the Fusion Energy Foundation, *Fusion*. With the header "Imagine a world without fusion," the advertisement outlined the dangers implicit in a "world" lacking nuclear energy. Reprinted in *It's About Times*, June–July 1981, 6.

3. Conversations with Sue Benech, consultant biologist, Diablo Canyon, 21 August 1997; Conversations with Brian Walton, Santa Cruz, 15 August 1997.

4. Montana de Oro User Survey, 1986, featured in "Montana de Oro State Park General Plan" (June 1988), 164. To the question "What kind of place should this park be?" notable visitor responses included, "Leave it as it is: primitive, quiet, unspoiled, undeveloped," and "Montana de Oro is special as a primitive park—we need these!" Conversations with Diane McGrath, Department of Parks and Recreation, San Luis Obispo, 29 August 1997.

5. Steven Marx, "Priesthoods and Power: Some Thoughts on Diablo Canyon," in *Mapping American Culture*, ed. Wayne Franklin and Michael Steiner (Iowa City: University of Iowa Press, 1992), 293; Interview with PG&E employee, Arroyo Grande, 11 June 1999.

6. Ken Olsen, "At Hanford, the Real Estate Is Hot," *High Country News*, 22 January 1996; Richard White, "Hanford: Boomtown of the Atomic Frontier," ibid., 22 January 1996. Hanford and Richland are discussed in chapters by Stanley Goldberg, "General Groves and the Atomic West: The Making and the Meaning of Hanford," and Carl Abbott, "Building the Atomic Cities: Richland, Los Alamos, and the American Planning Language," in *The Atomic West*, ed. Bruce Hevly and John M. Findlay (Seattle: University of Washington Press, 1998), 39–89, 90–115.

7. Urban Design Forum (Denver), "The Nation's Most Ironic Nature Park," reprinted in *Uncommon Ground: Toward Reinventing Nature*, ed. William Cronon (New York: W. W. Norton, 1995), 59; Army Corps commentary noted in Alexander Wilson, *The Culture of Nature: North American Landscape from Disney to the "Exxon Valdez"* (Cambridge, MA: Blackwell, 1992), 281.

8. The U.S. military resisted the wolf reintroduction scheme proposed for White Sands. "We do not want wolves on the White Sands Missile Range," declared one army leader in 1987. See Steve Grooms, *The Return of the Wolf* (Minocqua, WI: Northword, 1993), 159. Military intransigence stalled the program until 1990, when a court ruling stipulated that the U.S. Army was legally bound to comply with the recovery project under the terms of the Endangered Species Act of 1973.

9. See chapter 3 of Alfred Runte, *National Parks: The American Experience* (Lincoln: University of Nebraska Press, 1979), for an elaboration on the idea of national parks as "worthless lands." While extolled for their spectacular scenery, early national parks such as Yellowstone (1872) were deemed of little value for resource extraction purposes.

10. Cronon, ed., *Uncommon Ground*, 28.

11. For details of how Euro-American conservationists excluded Native Americans from national park "wilderness" landscapes, see Mark D. Spence, *Dispossessing the Wilderness: Indian Removal and the Making of the National Parks* (New York: Oxford University Press, 1999), and Cronon, ed., *Uncommon Ground*, 27–28.

12. Wilderness Act of 1964, specific extract cited in Ian McTaggart-Cowan, "Wilderness—Concept, Function, and Management," in *Conservators of Hope: The Horace M. Albright Conservation Lectures* (Moscow: University of Idaho Press, 1988), 176.

13. Valerie L. Kuletz, *The Tainted Desert: Environmental and Social Ruin in the American West* (New York: Routledge, 1998), xvii. See also Richard W. Stoffle and Michael J. Evans, "American Indians and Nuclear Waste Storage: The Debate at Yucca Mountain," *Policy Studies Journal* 16, no. 4 (1988): 751–67, and Carolyn Merchant, *The Death of Nature: Women, Ecology, and the Scientific Revolution* (San Francisco: Harper & Row, 1980), 294–95, 86. Merchant viewed the deadly toxicity of the nuclear age, and specifically the accident at Three Mile Island, Pennsylvania, as symptomatic of the "death of nature," precipitated by the male-dominated scientific revolution and its motifs of rationality and technological control of the earth.

14. Dave Foreman, "Around the Campfire," *Wild Earth* 6, no. 4 (Winter 1996–97): 2.

15. "Montana de Oro State Park General Plan," 210, 48.

16. PG&E, "1994 Non-Radiological Environmental Operating Report" (April 1995), 6, Nuclear Regulatory Commission Public Document Room, California Polytechnic State University, San Luis Obispo. Also see Francesca Cline, "Caring for Kids: Diablo Canyon Employees Nurse Traumatized Goats," *San Luis Obispo County Telegram-Tribune* (hereafter cited as *Telegram-Tribune*), 2 March 1996. The goats had been traumatized not by their work at the Diablo plant, but after the trailer transporting them to the headland crashed near Los Angeles.

17. Melvin Lane, speaker at trail opening, cited in John McKinney, *A Walk along Land's End: Discovering California's Unknown Coast* (New York: HarperCollins, 1995), 145, cost noted by McKinney, 132, 133; "San Luis Obispo, California," San Luis Obispo Chamber of Commerce Visitors Guide (1994), front cover (in the same magazine, an advertisement by Pacific Gas proclaimed, "Your neighbors at PG&E are pleased to be a part of the central coast"); "Hike the Pecho Coast Trail," leaflet (n.d.), designed by Pandora & Co., Los Osos.

18. "Montana de Oro State Park General Plan," 146.

19. National Park Service, "Pacific Coast Recreation Area Survey" (1959), Sierra Club Collection, 71/103c, box 110, file 1, Bancroft Library, University of California, Berkeley. In 1977 the California Coastal Commission Survey recommended the terrain between the Diablo nuclear plant and Point Buchon for "designation to protect the view, marine resources, and potential recreational use." It discounted lands from Diablo Cove to the Pecho Lighthouse "largely on the existence of the Diablo Canyon power plant." California Coastal Commission, "Staff Recommendation of Designation of Coastal Areas Where Power Plants Would Be Inconsistent with Coastal Act Objectives" (December 1977), 61, Abalone Alliance Collection (AAC), Abalone Alliance Safe Energy Clearinghouse, San Francisco, file: California Coastal Commission; Notes from the Montana de Oro Advisory Committee meeting, Morro Bay Museum, 6 December

1966, Ian McMillan Collection, Cuesta College Environmental Archives, box 15, file 24.

20. High-level radioactive waste from Diablo Canyon, along with waste from all other U.S. nuclear plants, will eventually be stored at Yucca Mountain repository. Priority will be given to spent fuel from the oldest reactors. PG&E may have to keep waste on-site until past 2020. See David Sneed, "A Place for Nuclear Waste," *Tribune,* 12 December 1999; McKinney, *Walk along Land's End,* 139. Describing Diablo as "a wonderful spot for a public park," Langdon Winner similarly suggested keeping PG&E's project as a poignant "monument to the nuclear age." See Langdon Winner, *The Whale and the Reactor: A Search for Limits in an Age of High Technology* (Chicago: University of Chicago Press, 1986), 177.

21. *Telegram-Tribune,* 29 June 1995.

22. Ralph Waldo Emerson/Henry David Thoreau, *Nature/Walking* ([*Walking,* 1862]; reprint, Boston: Beacon Press, 1991), 78–79.

23. Donald Worster, *Nature's Economy: A History of Ecological Ideas,* 2d ed. (New York: Cambridge University Press, 1994), 342.

24. John Muir to Rachel Trout Beach, 13 September 1870, cited in Stephen Fox, *The American Conservation Movement: John Muir and His Legacy* (Madison: University of Wisconsin Press, 1981), 50. The letter can be found in the John Muir papers, Bancroft Library, University of California, Berkeley.

CONCLUSION ※ THE ENERGY BOMB AND CONSERVATION FALLOUT

1. Tom Athanasiou, *Slow Reckoning: The Ecology of a Divided Planet* (London: Secker & Warburg, 1997), 226; Thomas Turner, "Eco Pornography, or How to Spot an Ecological Phony," in *The Environmental Handbook,* ed. Garrett de Bell (New York: Ballantine/Friends of the Earth, 1970), 263–67.

2. Roberta Greenwood, "Surface Survey and Evaluation Report" (1978), A-10, in Appendix A of PG&E, "Archaeological Resources Management Plan" (April 1980), Environmental Folder, Nuclear Regulatory Commission Public Document Room, California Polytechnic State University, San Luis Obispo.

3. Harvey Wasserman, "California's Deregulation Disaster," *Nation,* February 12, 2001; "San Francisco: California Energy Crisis Fallout Continues," 29 January 2002, TomPaine.com. See also Harvey Wasserman, "Deregulatory Disaster in California," WISE News Communique, 26 January 2001, Nuclear Information and Resource Service (http://www.nirs.org).

4. "The NRDC Blackouts," *Quivis Magazine,* htttp://www.quivis.com/caenergy01.html; David Holcberg, "Why Greens Are to Blame for Blackouts," Ayn Rand Institute, www.aynrand.org/medialink/blackouts.html; David Isaac, "California's Recipe for Energy Crisis: When Demand Booms, Forget Supply," *Investor's Business Daily,* 22 January 22 2001.

5. Holcberg, "Why Greens are to Blame for Blackouts."

6. "Special Report on Diablo Canyon," *PG&E Life,* June 1967, 10, Sierra Club Collection, 71/103c, box 113, file 40, Bancroft Library, University of California, Berkeley; PG&E, scenic postcard of "Diablo Canyon Nuclear Power Plant."

7. Reports on the Diablo test issued 15 July 1957 by the Nevada Test Organization, Office of Test Information, Las Vegas, documents held by Bechtel Nevada; *Washington County News,* St. George, 18 July 1957.

8. Handwritten counter readings and response, Nevada Test Organization, Bechtel Nevada, Docket No. 150813.

9. Leonard Nevarez, Harvey Molotch, and William Freudenburg, eds., "San Luis Obispo County: A Major Switching—Final Report," prepared for the U.S. Department of the Interior, Minerals Management Service (March 1997), 65. Nevarez et al. rated the effect of the Diablo plant on San Luis Obispo County as comparable to that of the Santa Barbara oil spill on Santa Barbara, noting that both "polarized sentiments among county residents, and brought forth a new generation of local activists and government officials."

bibliography

ARCHIVAL SOURCES

Abalone Alliance Safe-Energy Clearinghouse, San Francisco

Abalone Alliance press releases, flyers, posters, letters, handbooks.
Abalone Alliance protest files.
Documents relating to consensus process and nonviolence.
Press stories and newspaper clippings.
California Public Utilities Commission documents.
Nuclear Regulatory Commission documents.
Evanoff, Mark. "Memorirs [sic] of a Movement: PG&E's Nuclear Power Play." Unpublished manuscript, 1984.

Lauren Alden Personal Papers, Berkeley

American Friends Service Committee, San Francisco Office .

Papers of David Hartsough, AFSC staffperson.

Liz Apfelberg Personal Papers, Arroyo Grande

Bancroft Library, University of California, Berkeley

Sierra Club Records, 71/103c.
Sierra Club Members Papers, 71/295c.
Sierra Club National Legislative Office Records, 71/289c.
Oral History Transcripts of interviews with David Brower (80/133c), Richard Leonard (76/194c), Stewart M. Ogilvy (79/10z), William E. Siri (80/4c), and Tom Turner (83/53c).

California Department of Fish and Game, Morro Bay

Various environmental studies, including PG&E's Thermal Effects Monitoring Program reports.

California Polytechnic State University, San Luis Obispo (Cal Poly)

Ian McMillan Collection, temporarily held at Cal Poly "Special Collections," belonging to Cuesta College (San Luis Obispo) Environmental Archives.
Harold Miossi Collection, temporarily held at Cal Poly "Special Collections," belonging to Cuesta College (San Luis Obispo) Environmental Archives.
Chambers, James, Jr. "Population Studies of California Sea Lions near Diablo Canyon, California." M.S. thesis, 1979.
Penner, Stephanie. "Diablo Canyon: Determining Student Awareness and Attitudes toward Nuclear Power." Senior project (Journalism), 1991.
Schmitt, Jason. "Concerns of the Opposition to the Diablo Canyon Nuclear Power Plant." Senior project (History), 1993.
Zuanich, B. "Diablo Canyon in the Wake of the Chernobyl Disaster." Senior project (Political Science), 1989.

California Regional Water Quality Control Board, Central Coast Region, San Luis Obispo

PG&E. Thermal Effects Monitoring Program Analysis Reports.
"Diablo Canyon Power Plant 316(B) Demonstration, Phase 1: Entrainment Study Design," August 1997.
Various reports and minutes, 1997–2000.

Bill Denneen Personal Papers, Nipomo

Department of Planning and Building, County Government Center, San Luis Obispo

PG&E. "Preliminary Safety Analysis, Nuclear Unit 2, Diablo Canyon Site," vol. 1.
Bulge, Richard T., and Steven A. Schultz. "The Marine Environment in the Vicinity of Diablo Cove with Special Reference to Abalone and Bony Fishes." Marine Resources Technical Report 19 (1973).
"Unocal Avila Beach Cleanup Project: Public Draft Environmental Impact Report." Executive Summary (May 1997).

Don Eichelberger Personal Papers, San Francisco

Nuke Notes, newspaper of SONOMOreAtomics.

Barbara Levy Personal Papers, San Francisco

Mary Moore Personal Papers, Occidental

Montana de Oro State Park Visitors Center, Los Osos

Wall exhibits.

Nuclear Regulatory Commission Public Document Room,
California Polytechnic State University, San Luis Obispo

PG&E. "Draft Environmental Statement" for the Directorate of Licensing, U.S. Atomic Energy Commission (December 1972), relating to the continuing construction and proposed issuance of an operating license for Diablo Canyon Units 1 and 2.

PG&E. "Archaeological Resources Management Plan." Diablo Canyon site (April 1980).

PG&E. Annual Non-Radiological Environmental Operating Reports.

PG&E. "Environmental Report: Units 1 and 2 Diablo Canyon Site." San Francisco: PG&E, 1971.

Various documents in environmental folders pertaining to the Diablo plant.

Ocean and Coastal Policy Center, Marine Science Institute,
University of California, Santa Barbara

Nevarez, Leonard, Harvey Molotch, and William Freudenburg, eds. "San Luis Obispo County: A Major Switching—Final Report." Prepared for U.S. Department of the Interior, Minerals Management Service (March 1997).

PG&E Marine Laboratory, Diablo Canyon Power Plant, San Luis Obispo County

PG&E. "Diablo Canyon Land Stewardship Program: Draft Comprehensive Grazing Plan." November 1996.

———. "Diablo Canyon Land Stewardship Program: Toward Conserving Biological Diversity." N.d. (ca. 1993).

———. "A Sensitive Plant and Wildlife Resource Inventory of Diablo Canyon Lands." 1995.

Various ecological reports.

PG&E Community Center, Ontario Road, San Luis Obispo

Endangered Species Monitoring at Diablo Canyon (directed by Patrick Mulvey, 1990).

Inside Diablo Canyon (PG&E, 1989).

The Peregrine Falcon: Recovery on the Horizon (directed by Patrick Mulvey, n.d.).

Sea Changes: A Year at Diablo Canyon (directed by Patrick Mulvey, n.d.).

Resource Center for Nonviolence, Santa Cruz

It's About Times (official newspaper of the Abalone Alliance, published by the American Friends Service Committee).

San Luis Obispo Public Library, San Luis Obispo

Henry, Brice M., under instruction from U.S. surveyor general. "Plot of the Rancho 'Canada de Los Osos' & 'Pecho y Islay,'" confirmed to John Wilson, August and September 1858.

Tagnazzini, William, ed. *"100 Years Ago": Excerpts from the "San Luis Obispo Morning Tribune."*

Santa Cruz Predatory Bird Research Group, Joseph M. Long Marine Laboratory, University of California, Santa Cruz

Correspondence, Brian Walton to Ed Coulson, PG&E, 11 March 1981.
"Diablo Canyon Peregrine Observation" (research proposal).
"Nest Site Information 1989 Diablo Canyon" (map).
SCPBRG. "Peregrine Falcon Activity at Diablo Canyon, 1981–1994."
SCPBRG. "Peregrine Falcon Monitoring, Nest Management, Hack Site, and Cross-Fostering Efforts, 1992."
SCPBRG. "Santa Cruz Predatory Bird Research Group 1994 Activities." November 1995.

Sandy Silver Personal Papers, Santa Cruz

University of California, Santa Cruz

Darnovsky, Marcy. "Direct Action as Living Theater in the Movement against Nuclear Power." Unpublished paper, 1989.

INTERVIEWS AND CONVERSATIONS
Interviews

Lauren Alden, ex-Abalone, Berkeley, 13 August 1997.
Liz Apfelberg, Mothers for Peace, Arroyo Grande, 9 July 1997.
Sanderson Beck (e-mail), ex-Abalone, Ojai, 12 March 1997.
Rochelle Becker, Mothers for Peace, Grover Beach, 24 August 1997.
Brook, ex-Abalone, Berkeley, 12 August 1997.
David Brower, Sierra Club, Berkeley, 16 July 1997.
Jackie Cabasso, ex-Abalone, Oakland, 31 July 1997.
Marcy Darnovsky (e-mail), ex-Abalone, 28 April 2000.
Dennis Davie (e-mail), ex-Abalone, Santa Cruz, 7 and 10 June 1999.
Charlotte Davis, ex-Abalone, San Francisco, 5 August 1997.
Don Eichelberger, Abalone Clearinghouse, San Francisco, 24 and 26 June 1997.
Raye Fleming, ex-Abalone and ex-Mother, San Luis Obispo, 3 September 1997.
Kathleen Goddard-Jones (formerly Jackson), conservationist, Nipomo, 20 August 1997.
Chris Gray (e-mail), ex-Abalone, Montana, 8 and 14 June 1999.
David Hartsough, ex-Abalone, San Francisco, 18 July 1997.
Roger Herried, Abalone Clearinghouse, San Francisco, 24 and 25 June 1997.
Judy Irving (telephone), filmmaker, San Francisco, 6 August 1997.
Richard Krejsa, environmentalist and former county supervisor, San Luis Obispo, 9 July 1997.
Pilulaw Kush, Chumash representative, Morro Bay, 25 August 1997.

Barbara Levy, ex-Abalone, San Francisco, 29 July 1997.

Martin Litton, Sierra Club, Portola Valley, 25 July 1997.

Peter Lumsdaine, ex-Abalone, Santa Cruz, 7 July 1997.

Former PG&E worker, San Luis Obispo, 21 July 1997.

Pam Metcalf, ex-Abalone, San Luis Obispo, 3 September 1997.

William Miller, ex-Abalone, San Luis Obispo, 3 September 1997.

Mary Moore, ex-Abalone, Sebastopol, 24 July 1997.

Willard Osibin, Physicians for Social Responsibility, Templeton, 22 July 1997.

Phoebe, ex-Abalone, Berkeley, 12 August 1997.

PG&E employee, Arroyo Grande, 4 and 11 June 1999.

Sandy Silver, Mothers for Peace, Santa Cruz, 23 July 1997.

Starhawk (telephone), ex-Abalone, Sonoma County, 28 July 1997.

Bob Wolf, ex-Abalone, San Luis Obispo, 21 July 1997.

Local protester, San Luis Obispo, 21 July 1997.

Ward Young (telephone), ex-Abalone, Bolinas, 17 July 1997.

Conversations

Tom Becker, ex-Abalone, Grover Beach, 17 and 19 August 1997.

Sue Benech, biologist, Tenera Environmental Services, Diablo Canyon, 21 August 1997.

Jim Blecha, consultant, Tenera Environmental Services, Diablo Canyon, 21 August 1997.

David Church, county planner, San Luis Obispo, 18 August 1997.

Bill Denneen, environmentalist, Nipomo, 16 August 1997.

Bob Hardy, California Fish and Game, Morro Bay, 20 August 1997.

Geoff Land, EcosLO, San Luis Obispo, 18 August 1997.

Janet Linthicum, Santa Cruz Predatory Bird Research Group, Santa Cruz, 15 August 1997.

Diane McGrath (telephone), Department of Parks and Recreation, San Luis Obispo, 29 August 1997.

Harold Miossi (telephone), conservationist, San Luis Obispo County, 26 August 1997.

Jay Swanson (e-mail), photographer, San Luis Obispo, 9 June 1999.

June von Ruden, Mothers for Peace, Pismo Beach, 8 July 1997.

Brian Walton, Santa Cruz Predatory Bird Research Group, Santa Cruz, 15 August 1997.

Michael Welch (telephone), Redwood Alliance, 17 July 1997.

Karen Wood (telephone), Nature Conservancy, 24 June 1997.

California Newspapers and Periodicals

Berkeley Gazette

Central Coast Sun Bulletin (San Luis Obispo)

Daily Californian (University of California, Berkeley)

Fresno Bee
Herald Recorder (Arroyo Grande)
La Vista (San Luis Obispo)
Los Angeles Times
Marin County Pacific Sun (San Rafael)
Metro Santa Cruz (Santa Cruz)
New Times (San Luis Obispo)
Oakland Tribune
Paso Robles Press (Paso Robles)
Press Democrat (Santa Rosa)
Sacramento Bee
San Francisco Bay Guardian
San Francisco Chronicle
San Francisco Examiner
San Jose Mercury News
Santa Barbara News and Review
Tribune (formerly *San Luis Obispo County Telegram-Tribune*) (San Luis Obispo)

ARTICLES AND ESSAYS

Barkin, Steven E. "Strategic, Tactical, and Organizational Dilemmas of the Protest Movement against Nuclear Power." *Social Problems* 27, no. 1 (October 1979): 19–37.

Boyer, Paul. "From Activism to Apathy: The American People and Nuclear Weapons, 1963–1980." *Journal of American History* 70, no. 4 (March 1984): 821–44.

Caputi, Jane. "Nuclear Power and the Sacred, or Why a Beautiful Woman Is Like a Nuclear Power Plant." In *Ecofeminism and the Sacred,* ed. Carol J. Adams, 229–50. New York: Continuum, 1993.

Darnovsky, Marcy. "Stories Less Told: Histories of U.S. Environmentalism." *Socialist Review* 22, no. 4 (October–December 1992): 11–54.

Davis, Mike. "Dead West: Ecocide in Marlboro Country." In *Over the Edge: Remapping the American West,* ed. Valerie Matsumoto and Blake Allmendinger, 339–69. Berkeley: University of California Press, 1999.

Downey, Gary L. "Ideology and the Clamshell Identity: Organizational Dilemmas in the Anti-Nuclear Power Movement." *Social Problems* 33, no. 5 (June 1986): 357–73.

George, David L., and Priscilla L. Southwell. "Opinion on the Diablo Canyon Nuclear Power Plant: The Effects of Situation and Socialization." *Social Science Quarterly* 67, no. 4 (December 1986): 722–35.

Gottlieb, Robert. "Reconstructing Environmentalism: Complex Movements, Diverse Roots." *Environmental History Review* 17, no. 4 (Winter 1993): 1–19.

Greenwood, Roberta S. *9000 Years of Prehistory at Diablo Canyon, San Luis Obispo County, California.* San Luis Obispo County Archaeological Society Occasional Paper 7, 1972.

Haley, Brian D., and Larry R. Wilcoxon. "Anthropology and the Making of Chumash Tradition." *Current Anthropology* 38, no. 5 (December 1997): 761–94.

Kovalik, Vladimir, and Nada Kovalik. "Life and Death along the California Coast." *Cry California: The Journal of California Tomorrow* 2, no. 4 (Fall 1967): 16–27.

Lutts, Ralph H. "Chemical Fallout: Rachel Carson's *Silent Spring*, Radioactive Fallout, and the Environmental Movement." *Environmental Review* 9 (Fall 1985): 211–25.

Marx, Stephen. "Priesthoods and Power: Some Thoughts on Diablo Canyon." In *Mapping American Culture*, ed. Wayne Franklin and Michael Steiner, 291–302. Iowa City: University of Iowa Press, 1992.

McTaggart-Cowan, Ian. "Wilderness—Concept, Function, and Management." In *Conservators of Hope: The Horace M. Albright Conservation Lectures*, 153–86. Moscow: University of Idaho Press, 1988.

Miossi, Harold. "Somnolent Cape: The Story of the Pecho Coast." *La Vista* (San Luis Obispo County Historical Society), January 1973, 1–31.

Mofras, Duflot de. "How to Get to San Luis Obispo." *La Vista* (San Luis Obispo County Historical Society), January 1972, 4–5.

Nicholson, Loren. "Captain John Wilson: Trader of the Pacific." *Pacific Historian* 23, no. 2 (Summer 1979): 69–90.

Schrepfer, Susan R. "The Nuclear Crucible: Diablo Canyon and the Transformation of the Sierra Club, 1965–1985." *California History* 71, no. 2 (Summer 1992): 212–37.

Stoffle, Richard W., and Michael J. Evans. "American Indians and Nuclear Waste Storage: The Debate at Yucca Mountain." *Policy Studies Journal* 16, no. 4 (1988): 751–67.

Turner, Thomas. "Eco Pornography, or How to Spot an Ecological Phony." In *The Environmental Handbook*, ed. Garrett de Bell, 263–67. New York: Ballantine/Friends of the Earth, 1970.

Walker, J. Samuel. "Nuclear Power and the Environment: The Atomic Energy Commission and Thermal Pollution, 1965–1971." *Technology and Culture* 30, no. 4 (October 1989): 964–92.

Wellock, Thomas R. "The Battle for Bodega Bay: The Sierra Club and Nuclear Power, 1958–1964." *California History* 71, no. 2 (Summer 1992): 192–211.

———. "'Stick It in L.A.!' Community Control and Nuclear Power in California's Central Valley." *Journal of American History* 84, no. 3 (December 1997): 942–78.

White, Lynn, Jr. "The Historical Roots of Our Ecologic Crisis." *Science*, 10 March 1967, 1203–7.

BOOKS

Abbey, Edward. *Desert Solitaire: A Season in the Wilderness*. New York: Ballantine, 1968.

Angel, Myron. *History of San Luis Obispo County, California: With Illustrations and*

Biographical Sketches of its Prominent Men and Pioneers. Oakland: Thompson & West, 1883.

Athanasiou, Tom. *Slow Reckoning: The Ecology of a Divided Planet.* London: Secker & Warburg, 1997.

Aubrey, Crispin, ed. *Nukespeak: The Media and the Bomb.* London: Comedia, 1982.

Bailey, Gilbert E., and Paul S. Thayer. *California's Disappearing Coast: A Legislative Challenge.* Berkeley: Institute of Government Studies, 1971.

Ball, Howard. *Justice Downwind: America's Atomic Testing Program in the 1950s.* New York: Oxford University Press, 1986.

Balogh, Brian. *Chain Reaction: Expert Debate and Public Participation in American Commercial Nuclear Power, 1945–1975.* Cambridge, UK: Cambridge University Press, 1991.

Bancroft, Hubert Howe. *The Works of Hubert Howe Bancroft, Volume 18: The History of California, Volume 1: 1542–1800.* San Francisco: H. H. Bancroft, 1884.

Bedford, Henry F. *Seabrook Station: Citizen Politics and Nuclear Power.* Amherst: University of Massachusetts Press, 1990.

Blackburn, Thomas C., ed. *December's Child: A Book of Chumash Oral Narratives.* Berkeley: University of California Press, 1975.

Blackburn, Thomas C., and Kat Anderson, eds. *Before the Wilderness: Environmental Management by Native Californians.* Menlo Park, CA: Ballena Press, 1993.

Bolton, Herbert, ed. *Spanish Exploration in the Southwest, 1542–1706.* New York: Charles Scribner's Sons, 1916.

Boyer, Paul. *By the Bomb's Early Light: American Thought and Culture at the Dawn of the Atomic Age.* New York: Pantheon, 1985.

———. *Fallout: A Historian Reflects on America's Half-Century Encounter with Nuclear Weapons.* Columbus: Ohio State University Press, 1998.

Brower, David R. *For Earth's Sake: The Life and Times of David Brower.* Salt Lake City: Gibbs Smith, 1990.

Bryant, Edwin. *What I Saw in California.* 1848. Reprint, Lincoln: University of Nebraska Press, 1985.

Bullard, Robert D. *Dumping in Dixie: Race, Class, and Environmental Quality.* 2d ed. Boulder, CO: Westview Press, 1994.

Cabasso, Jackie, and Susan Moon. *Risking Peace: Why We Sat in the Road.* Berkeley: Open Books, 1985.

Carson, Rachel. *Silent Spring.* Boston: Houghton Mifflin, 1962.

Chase, J. Smeaton. *California Coast Trails: A Horseback Ride from Mexico to Oregon.* Cambridge, MA: Riverside Press, 1913.

Clarfield, Gerard H., and William M. Wiecek. *Nuclear America: Military and Civilian Nuclear Power in the United States, 1940–1980.* New York: Harper & Row, 1984.

Cohen, Michael P. *The History of the Sierra Club, 1892–1970.* San Francisco: Sierra Club Books, 1988.

Coleman, Charles. *P.G.&E. of California: The Centennial Story of Pacific Gas and Electric Company, 1852–1952*. New York: McGraw-Hill, 1952.

Commoner, Barry. *The Closing Circle: Confronting the Environmental Crisis*. London: Jonathan Cape, 1971.

Crespi, Fray Juan. *Missionary Explorer on the Pacific Coast, 1769–1774*. Ed. Herbert E. Bolton. Berkeley: University of California Press, 1927.

Cronon, William, ed. *Uncommon Ground: Toward Reinventing Nature*. New York: W. W. Norton, 1995.

Cronon, William, George Miles, and Jay Gitlin, eds. *Under an Open Sky: Rethinking America's Western Past*. New York: W. W. Norton, 1992.

Crosby, Alfred W. *Ecological Imperialism: The Biological Expansion of Europe, 900–1900*. Cambridge, UK: Cambridge University Press, 1986.

Crown, Sheryl. *Hell No, We Won't Grow: Seabrook, April 1977—Nonviolent Occupation of a Nuclear Power Site*. London: Housmans, 1979.

Curtis, Richard, and Elizabeth Hogan. *Nuclear Lessons: An Examination of Nuclear Power's Safety, Economic, and Political Record*. Harrisburg, PA: Stackpole, 1980.

Dana, Richard Henry, Jr. *Two Years before the Mast*. 1840. Reprint, New York: Penguin, 1981.

Darlington, David. *In Condor Country: A Portrait of a Landscape, Its Denizens, and Its Defenders*. New York: Henry Holt, 1987.

Dasmann, Raymond F. *California's Changing Environment*. San Francisco: Boyd & Fraser, 1981.

———. *The Destruction of California*. New York: Collier, 1966.

Dickerson, Carrie Barefoot. *Aunt Carrie's War against Black Fox Nuclear Power Plant*. Tulsa: Council Oak Distribution, 1995.

Dickerson, Sharon Lewis. *Mountains of Fire: San Luis Obispo County's Nine Sisters—A Chain of Ancient Volcanic Peaks*. San Luis Obispo: EZ Nature Books, 1990.

Domhoff, William G. *The Bohemian Grove and Other Retreats: A Study in Ruling-Class Cohesiveness*. New York: Harper & Row, 1974.

Douglas, Mary, and Aaron Wildavsky. *Risk and Culture: An Essay on the Selection of Technological and Environmental Dangers*. Berkeley: University of California Press, 1982.

Dunlap, Thomas R. *DDT: Scientists, Citizens, and Public Policy*. Princeton, NJ: Princeton University Press, 1981.

Easton, Robert. *Black Tide: The Santa Barbara Oil Spill and Its Consequences*. New York: Delacorte Press, 1972.

Emerson, Ralph Waldo/Henry David Thoreau. *Nature/Walking*. (*Walking*, 1862.) Reprint, Boston: Beacon Press, 1991.

Epstein, Barbara. *Political Protest and Cultural Revolution: Nonviolent Direct Action in the 1970s and 1980s*. Berkeley: University of California Press, 1991.

Farber, David, ed. *The Sixties: From Memory to History*. Chapel Hill: University of North Carolina Press, 1994.

Ford, Daniel F. *Three Mile Island: Thirty Minutes to Meltdown.* New York: Viking Press, 1982.

Fox, Stephen. *The American Conservation Movement: John Muir and His Legacy.* Madison: University of Wisconsin Press, 1981.

Fuller, John G. *We Almost Lost Detroit.* New York: Reader's Digest Press, 1975.

Gaard, Greta, ed. *Ecofeminism: Women, Animals, and Nature.* Philadelphia: Temple University Press, 1993.

Gilliam, Ann, ed. *Voices for the Earth: A Treasury of the Sierra Club Bulletin, 1893–1977.* San Francisco: Sierra Club Books, 1979.

Gofman, John W., and Arthur R. Tamplin. *Poisoned Power: The Case against Nuclear Power Plants.* London: Chatto & Windus, 1973.

Gottlieb, Robert. *Forcing the Spring: The Transformation of the American Environmental Movement.* Washington, DC: Island Press, 1993.

Grossman, Karl. *Cover Up: What You Are Not Supposed to Know about Nuclear Power.* Sagaponack, NY: Permanent Press, 1980.

Gutierrez, Ramon A., and Richard J. Orsi, eds. *Contested Eden: California before the Gold Rush.* Berkeley: University of California Press, 1998.

Gyorgy, Anna, and Friends. *No Nukes: Everyone's Guide to Nuclear Power.* Boston: South End Press, 1979.

Haber, Heinz. *The Walt Disney Story of Our Friend the Atom.* New York: Golden Press, 1956.

Hanley, Wayne. *Natural History in America: From Mark Catesby to Rachel Carson.* New York: Quadrangle and New York Times Book Co., 1977.

Harvey, Mark W. T. *A Symbol of Wilderness: Echo Park and the American Conservation Movement.* Albuquerque: University of New Mexico Press, 1994.

Hays, Samuel P. *Beauty, Health, and Permanence: Environmental Politics in the United States, 1955–1985.* New York: Cambridge University Press, 1987.

Hevly, Bruce, and John M. Findlay, eds. *The Atomic West.* Seattle: University of Washington Press, 1998.

Hjelmar, Ulf. *The Political Practice of Environmental Organizations.* Aldershot, UK: Avebury Studies in Green Research, 1996.

Kaplan, David E., ed. *Nuclear California: An Investigative Report.* San Francisco: Greenpeace/Center for Investigative Reporting, 1982.

Krieger, Daniel E. *San Luis Obispo County: Looking Backward into the Middle Kingdom.* 2d ed. San Luis Obispo: EZ Nature Books, 1990.

Kuletz, Valerie L. *The Tainted Desert: Environmental and Social Ruin in the American West.* New York: Routledge, 1998.

Lavender, David. *California: Land of New Beginnings.* 1972. Reissue ed. Lincoln: University of Nebraska Press, 1987.

Lear, Linda. *Rachel Carson: Witness for Nature.* New York: Henry Holt, 1997.

Linden-Ward, Blanche, and Carol Hurd Green. *American Women in the 1960s: Changing the Future.* New York: Twayne, 1993.

Lovins, Amory. *The Energy Controversy: Soft Path Questions and Answers*. Ed. Hugh Nash. San Francisco: Friends of the Earth, 1979.

———. *Soft Energy Paths: Towards a Durable Peace*. San Francisco: Friends of the Earth International, 1977.

MacLean, Alistair. *Goodbye California*. London: Book Club Associates, 1978.

Manes, Christopher. *Green Rage: Radical Environmentalism and the Unmaking of Civilization*. Boston: Little, Brown, 1990.

Marinacci, Barbara, and Rudy Marinacci. *California's Spanish Place Names*. San Rafael, CA: Presidio Press, 1980.

Martinez, David. *Reflections of an Anti-Nuclear Activist*. San Francisco: San Anselmo, 1981.

Marx, Leo. *The Machine in the Garden: Technology and the Pastoral Ideal in America*. New York: Oxford University Press, 1964.

McCracken, Samuel. *The War against the Atom*. New York: Basic, 1982.

McKinney, John. *A Walk along Land's End: Discovering California's Unknown Coast*. New York: HarperCollins, 1995.

McPhee, John. *Encounters with the Archdruid*. New York: Noonday Press, 1971.

Meehan, Richard L. *The Atom and the Fault: Experts, Earthquakes, and Nuclear Power*. Cambridge, Mass.: MIT Press, 1984.

Melville, Herman. *Moby Dick*. 1851. Reprint, Evanston, IL: Northwestern University Press and the Newberry Library, 1988.

Merchant, Carolyn. *The Death of Nature: Women, Ecology, and the Scientific Revolution*. San Francisco: Harper & Row, 1980.

Merchant, Carolyn, ed. *Green versus Gold: Sources in California's Environmental History*. Washington, DC: Island Press, 1998.

Miller, Bruce W. *Chumash: A Picture of Their World*. Los Osos, CA: Sand River Press, 1988.

Morrison, Annie L., and John H. Haydon. *History of San Luis Obispo County and Environs, California, with Biographical Sketches of the Leading Men and Women of the County and Environs*. Los Angeles: Historic Record Co., 1917.

Muir, John. *Our National Parks*. 1901. Reprint, Madison: University of Wisconsin Press, 1981.

———. *Travels in Alaska*. 1915. Reprint, Boston: Houghton Mifflin, 1979.

Nader, Ralph, and John Abbotts. *The Menace of Atomic Energy*. New York: Norton, 1977.

Nash, Roderick. *Wilderness and the American Mind*. 3d ed. New Haven: Yale University Press, 1982.

Novick, Sheldon. *The Careless Atom*. Boston: Houghton Mifflin, 1969.

Pape, Gordon, and Tony Aspler. *Chain Reaction*. London: Barrie & Jenkins, 1979.

Peterson, F. Ross. *The Teton Dam Disaster: Tragedy or Triumph?* Logan: Utah State University Press, 1982.

Rashke, Richard L. *The Killing of Karen Silkwood*. Boston: Houghton Mifflin, 1981.

Reibsame, William, ed. *Atlas of the New West: Portrait of a Changing Region.* New York: Norton, 1997.

Rothman, Hal K. *The Greening of a Nation? Environmentalism in the United States since 1945.* Fort Worth: Harcourt Brace, 1998.

Rudkin, Charles, ed. *The First French Expedition to California: Laperouse in 1786.* Los Angeles: Dawson's Book Shop, 1959.

Runte, Alfred. *National Parks: The American Experience.* Lincoln: University of Nebraska Press, 1979.

Schrepfer, Susan R. *The Fight to Save the Redwoods: A History of Environmental Reform, 1917–1978.* Madison: University of Wisconsin Press, 1983.

Scortia, Thomas N., and Frank M. Robinson. *The Prometheus Crisis.* London: Hodder & Stoughton, 1975.

Shabecoff, Philip. *A Fierce Green Fire: The American Environmental Movement.* New York: Hill & Wang, 1993.

Shcherbak, Iurii. *Chernobyl: A Documentary Story.* Edmonton: Canadian Institute of Ukrainian Studies, 1989.

Shute, Nevil [Nevil Shute Norway]. *On the Beach.* New York: William Morrow, 1957.

Solnit, Rebecca. *Savage Dreams: A Journey into the Landscape Wars of the American West.* New York: Vintage, 1994.

Starhawk. *Dreaming the Dark: Magic, Sex, and Politics.* New ed. Boston: Beacon Press, 1988.

Stephens, Mark. *Three Mile Island.* London: Junction Books, 1980.

Stoler, Peter. *Decline and Fail: The Ailing Nuclear Power Industry.* New York: Dodd, Mead, 1985.

Storke, Yda Addis. *A Memorial and Biographical History of the Counties of Santa Barbara, San Luis Obispo, and Ventura, California.* Chicago: Lewis, 1891.

Thomas, Janet, et al., eds. *That Day in June: Reflections on the Teton Dam Disaster.* Rexburg, ID: Ricks College Press, 1977.

Thoreau, Henry David. *Civil Disobedience and Other Essays. (Civil Disobedience, 1849.)* Reprint, New York: Dover Thrift, 1993.

———. *The Maine Woods.* 1864. Reprinted in *Henry David Thoreau: Three Complete Books.* New York: Gramercy, 1993.

Turner, Tom. *Sierra Club: 100 Years of Protecting Nature.* New York: Harry N. Abrams, 1991.

Vancouver, George. *A Voyage of Discovery to the North Pacific Ocean and Round the World, 1791–1795.* Ed. W. Kaye Lamb. London: Hakluyt Society, 1984.

Van der Zee, John. *The Greatest Men's Party on Earth: Inside the Bohemian Grove.* New York: Harcourt Brace Jovanovich, 1974.

Veldman, Meredith. *Fantasy, the Bomb, and the Greening of Britain: Romantic Protest, 1945–1980.* Cambridge, UK: Cambridge University Press, 1994.

Weart, Spencer R. *Nuclear Fear: A History of Images.* Cambridge, MA: Harvard University Press, 1988.

Wellock, Thomas Raymond. *Critical Masses: Opposition to Nuclear Power in California, 1958–1978.* Madison: University of Wisconsin Press, 1998.

White, Richard. *"It's Your Misfortune and None of My Own": A New History of the American West.* Norman: University of Oklahoma Press, 1991.

Wild, Peter. *Pioneer Conservationists of Western America.* Missoula, MT: Mountain Press, 1979.

Williams, James C. *Energy and the Making of Modern California.* Akron, OH: University of Akron Press, 1997.

Wilson, Alexander. *The Culture of Nature: North American Landscape from Disney to the "Exxon Valdez."* Cambridge, MA: Blackwell, 1992.

Winner, Langdon. *The Whale and the Reactor: A Search for Limits in an Age of High Technology.* Chicago: University of Chicago Press, 1986.

Wohl, Burton. *The China Syndrome.* London: Severn House, 1979.

Woolfenden, John. *The California Sea Otter: Saved or Doomed?* Rev. ed. Pacific Grove, CA: Boxwood Press, 1985.

Worster, Donald. *Under Western Skies: Nature and History in the American West.* New York: Oxford University Press, 1992.

Zakin, Susan. *Coyotes and Town Dogs: Earth First! and the Environmental Movement.* New York: Penguin, 1993.

index